Women and
Self-Help Culture

Women and
Self-Help Culture:
Reading Between
the Lines

Wendy Simonds

Rutgers University Press
New Brunswick, New Jersey

LIBRARY OF CONGRESS CATALOGING-IN-PUBLICATION DATA

Simonds, Wendy, 1962–
  Women and self-help culture : reading between the lines / Wendy
Simonds.
    p.   cm.
  Includes bibliographical references and index.
  ISBN 0-8135-1833-4 (cloth) —ISBN 0-8135-1834-2 (pbk.)
  1. Women—United States—Psychology. 2. Self-help techniques—
United States. 3. Psychological literature—United States.
4. Women—Books and reading. I. Title.
HQ1206.S544   1992
306.4'88'082—dc20   91-44545
                                                           CIP

British Cataloging-in-Publication information available

FOR BARBARA KATZ ROTHMAN,
SINE QUA NON

Contents

Acknowledgments

My family has been wonderfully supportive of my reading and writing habits, from the time I first began attempting both. I want to thank my parents, Bobbie Simonds and Gordon Simonds, and my sister, Lauren Simonds, for their unceasing interest in my work; for their faith in me as a scholar; and for their nurturing love. Anne Yorra, Albert Yorra, Ruth Simonds, Danny Malamud, and Judie Malamud have also been a source of encouragement and emotional sustenance. Randy Malamud lived with this project from inception to fruition: his influence profoundly shaped my thinking and writing all along the way, and his presence in my life kept me sane and happy. Dweeb Simonds continously warmed the pages, and sweetly refrained from eating them.

Susan Farrell, Edward Farrell, Marcia Lifshitz, Yael Loewenberg, Amanda Martinsek, Dara Meyers-Kingsley, Hesch Rothman, Bobbie Simonds, and Michelle Wiggs all helped me to find participants for the reader study by circulating preliminary questionnaires; and then many of the early participants suggested others and sometimes became questionnaire distributers. The staff at Planned Parenthood in Brooklyn, New York, allowed me to give out questionnaires in their waiting room. Mary Cunnane at Norton provided me with several names of self-help editors; her name, in and of itself, seemed to open doors. I want to express my deepest gratitude to the participants and those who facilitated their participation; without their generous contributions of time and energy, this book would not exist.

This book has its origins in a rite of passage, one which is quite often agonizing, fraught with insecurity, depression, even misery; for me however, dissertation writing and defense were as close to being joyful as these activities can possibly come. My dissertation committee at the Graduate Center of the City University of New York—Barbara Katz Rothman, Gaye Tuchman, and Lillian Rubin—critiqued my work with care and offered insights that are, I hope, reflected in this final version. Barbara Katz Rothman was especially crucial to the day-to-day planning and execution of this work, discussing it with me in her kitchen, on subways, bicycles, park benches, and over the phone. Without her constant reminder, "Just write it!" I very well may not have. Along with Barbara, Gaye, and Lillian, I have other mentors to thank: Michelle Fine, Judith Lorber, Jan Radway, and Jane Tompkins have each contributed to my sense of what feminist scholarship and creative thinking are all about. My dissertation group at the Graduate Center—Susan Farrell, Marcia Lifshitz, Sharon Sherman, Jessica Bloom, and sometimes Bruce Haynes—offered valuable comments on early bits and pieces of this work, and our meetings sustained my writing. The critiques of Marlie Wasserman, associate director and editor-in-chief of Rutgers University Press, and the reader who commented on earlier drafts of this manuscript were instrumental in shaping this final version.

The labors of Kate Ellis, Stephanie Funk, Pat Mikos, and Diana Jones created time for me to work on this book; I hope they will soon be as lucky as I have been in finding great graduate assistants.

Finally, the Schlesinger Library of Radcliffe College has kindly allowed me to quote from the letters Betty Friedan received in response to *The Feminine Mystique,* which are housed in the Betty Friedan collection.

Women and

Self-Help Culture

Introduction

Self-Help Reading and the Study of Culture

BONNIE: I thought they had the answers. And I still do, in some stupid way. *Rationally*, I know these books don't have the answers; *emotionally*, I really think that if I find the right book, it will solve my problems.

CAROL: [Reading self-help books has] given me a lot of the ideas I've always had. . . . But it's given me the reassurance that I was pretty much on target with my thoughts and that I was heading in the right direction, and it's just given me the confirmation to go with my feelings and be more self-confident.

AMELIA: When I read the Bible, and I pray, I get comfort. I get comfort, I get reassurance, I get fulfilled, I get a sense of peace, you know, regardless of what is going on around me.

SARAH: See, I blurred all these books together. . . . They all seem like the same, somehow. . . . You just keep reading the same thing.

VAL: You know, all the books have different messages. . . . They're the type of book where I don't think you really forget anything you've read.

The comments of these readers evoke Rorschach tests: the very "same" inkblot construed by different people into a bat, a tree, blood, clouds. The Rorschach test was designed to affirm the notion that there are certain types of personalities that bat, tree, blood, and clouds imply. But the idea underlying inkblot interpretation, that disparate perceptions of one single—yet clearly variable—reality exist, is also a useful one for understanding the communication and reception of culture, the connections between personal perception and cultural ideology. Personality types are not written in stone (or in ink), but are written by social interaction; these women's varied responses to self-help books show how the "same" objects may become strikingly variable, even when they seem easy to read.

In broad terms, this book is about the cultural consumption and transmission of ideas about gender, selfhood, and interaction with others: women's relationship with self-help literature leads to these broader themes. I was first attracted to the genre of self-help because of the negative press it received, generally from journalists who read self-help not because they were personally looking for help, but because they were professionally interested in examining it. I was drawn in by this very dichotomy. And I saw journalists' professional displeasure with the genre as symptomatic of the general disdain usually accorded by the intellectual elite to "women's culture"—all forms of media directed to an audience of women, or media utilized (whether explicitly directed or not) primarily by women. My aim is not to debunk these detractors, with whom I *share* a professional interest in self-help (though through this work, I have come to disagree with some of the criticism issued), but to examine the phenomenon of self-help reading empirically as well as analytically, to see what it has to tell about the public and private social construction of gender and identity continually being enacted in our culture.

We cannot ever know the whole of cultural life: how culture becomes culture, and what it means, are not ever absolutely tangible or describable. Even a seemingly straightforward and simple "slice of cultural life" investigation, like this study of the self-help reading of thirty women, becomes complicated by the various ways in which meanings are made, packaged, absorbed, rejected, and reinforced. And though reading self-help books may seem to be a discrete activity—clearly distinguishable from, say, listening to the car radio, reading news magazines, or watching prime-time television—the creation of "self-help culture" cannot be seen as an isolated activity. Reading, watching, listening don't mean the same messages get "transmitted" for each reader, watcher, listener. The variable of time similarly confuses things: there is not necessarily a clear-cut linear flow between the culture of the past and that of the present, or between that of the present and that of the future. The historical, political, and economic conditions that create cultural life are, at best, messy. What studies of culture should do, I feel, is offer insight into the patterns embedded in the tangled webs of human interaction, an estimate of what happened, what happens, and why, when people make culture.

Mass-market paperbacks gained unprecedented success when Robert de Graff released Pocket Books' first list of ten books in 1939 (Davis 1984); since that time self-help books directed specifically at an audience of women have gradually gained a significant place within the trade and mass-market book publishing industries in the United States. Books offering advice about managing or improving relationships and about achieving psychologically "healthy" modes of behavior are bought by the millions today. Whole sections of bookstores are even devoted to subgenres of self-help: "recovery," "New Age," "self-realization," "codependency." This genre is both a representation of social ideology (congealed into hard- or soft-covered books) and a potential actor in the future of the American cultural landscape: the meaning we attribute to the creative and consumptive activities involved in self-help reading all depends on how we read them.

Articles in the popular press have portrayed these recently published bestsellers as evidence of a backlash against feminism (Faludi 1991); a reflection of general unhappiness on the part of women; an enormous proliferation of "drivel" designed to pacify readers (Bolotin 1987; Lawson 1986); a signal that middle-class American self-indulgence has reached new heights (Rieff 1991); indeed, an indication that "reading itself is becoming, perversely, a way out of thinking" (Kaminer 1990). Any cultural activity in which people participate enthusiastically merits the attention of students of culture; when this activity involves how women think about ourselves and our lives, it is an especially grave error simply to dismiss such a trend. In order to understand what this—or any other—act of consumption means, we must study the sociohistorical conditions that created and perpetuate it, and listen to the evaluations of the cultural consumers themselves.

As can be seen from the five brief comments at the beginning of this Introduction, women bring different expectations to our reading of self-help books: we read varied sorts of literature as self-help and come away with a range of responses. What reading is for, and what the ideal potential of reading is judged to be, are not necessarily the same thing to one woman, much less to thirty readers reading. There are, however, patterns within these women's talk of self-help, especially in terms of how they view the conditions that make the genre attractive to American women at this particular time.

Self-help books are a distinctly American phenomenon, which has grown out of seventeenth-century Puritan notions about self-improvement, Christian goodness, and otherworldly rewards (Starker 1989: 13–15). In Tocqueville's 1848 treatise on American morality and methods, he admiringly outlines the qualities which he thought coalesced to form the democratic spirit of self-help:

> The inhabitant of the United States experiences all the wants and all the desires to which a high civilization can give rise, but . . . he does not find himself part of a society expertly organized to satisfy them; consequently he often has to provide for himself the various things that education and habit have made necessary for him. . . . In his mind the idea of newness is closely linked with that of improvement. Nowhere does he see any limit placed by nature to human endeavor. (403–404)

Tocqueville might see the current success of self-help books as testimony to an enduring and distinctive American acquisitiveness fueled by a consumeristic self-reliance and encouraged by an inexpertly organized society.

Philip Rieff's more recent description of the self-indulgence of post-Freudian Western capitalism sums up the consensus of various critics of American ideology: that self-centeredness has come to define our age. Self-help, turned in on itself, becomes mired in its own insular short-sightedness and then champions this narrow worldview:

> In a society with so many inducements to self-interest, self-realization seems a noble and healthy end. The least valuable competitive position is to be self-defeating. The therapeutic cannot conceive of an action that is not self-serving, however it may be disguised or transformed. . . . The self, improved, is the ultimate concern of moral culture. (1966: 61–62)

Neither Tocqueville nor Rieff, who both concentrate on the ethos governing the behavior and thought of the quintessential American *man*, supplies reasons that can elucidate why so many American *women* would flock to bookstores, seeking prescriptive self-oriented literature. Many of the readers I interviewed agree that the self-help movement is a reflection of national selfishness, an extension of what they commonly refer to as the "me generation," despite the fact that many of these readers describe being motivated to consult self-help books by their dissatisfaction with their relationships with others.

Prior to the existence of the current wave of self-help books, which I consider as having begun in 1963 with Betty Friedan's *The Feminine Mystique,* students of culture had long been predicting and proclaiming a large-scale movement toward introverted self-involvement in the United States. This line of commentary grew more vehement as self-help books proliferated. (Bellah et al. 1985; Lasch 1979 and 1984; Riesman 1950; and Toffler 1970 are a few examples—several of these were bestsellers themselves.) Certainly, the floods of self-help books published in recent years can be interpreted as a manifestation of—or a tribute to—therapeutically induced self-interest, but do they necessarily indicate that cultural prescriptions and proscriptions regarding women's "selves" have changed? Self-help books, as a prime example of the mass communication of advice, reflect the spirit of this nation as it twists slowly away from the days when social reform aimed at modifying the effects of capitalism was more accepted—a time out of which the popular-psychological movement grew—and heads ever nearer to reactionary solutions to social problems.

Possibly all Americans, men and women alike, are becoming increasingly self-involved as we head into the twenty-first century. That the Horatio Alger spirit of the late nineteenth century enjoys a rejuvenation in the self-help books that become bestsellers today indicates that the cause-effect relationship between personal exertion (more commonly referred to as "energy" now) and personal success has remained a cornerstone of American ideology. But the "me-ness" encouraged by the authors of today's relationship-oriented advice manuals is not simply a carbon copy of the triumphant capitalist in the Horatio Alger stories or of the quintessential go-getting self-promoting Americanism that Tocqueville memorialized. The "quest for individualism" that has long been considered a nationalistic pursuit involves more than selfhood for women because selfhood itself, for women, remains bound up with others (and perhaps ought not be reduced to the word "selfhood"). Also, according to the canonized experts of psychology (like Freud, Piaget, and Erikson), women never achieved integrated or mature selfhood quite as well as men did.

My interviews show that readers approach self-help books hoping to discover how to achieve a balance between self and other, and to develop self-identity they feel they lack. What readers come away with depends on their reading of both the books and of their own situations. Psychological advice is thus, necessarily, shaped by readers to fit their interpretations of the complex web of social interaction in which they engage. Perceptions of whether or not self-help authors encourage competition or caring, isolationist or socially conscious responses to their situations, are steeped in readers' own acculturation of American ideology about how identity should (and should not) be expressed in relations with others and what selfhood should mean for women and for men.

Self-involvement, after all, cannot be the same activity for women and men in this culture. Women are caught up in a curious ideology concerning "self": we are labeled narcissistic for employing strategies (such as lavishing attention upon physical appearance) we have learned can lead to success in a society that prescribes specific versions of heterosexuality and femininity—a system in which women lack power to begin with. We are taught to nurture and connect with others, and to help carry the emotional baggage of men; and we may also learn not to expect reciprocity for our efforts. It is not surprising, within such a context, that women would look for ways to find nurturance through vehicles that encourage self-reflection. Nor is it surprising that many women would—as several readers I interviewed did—dismiss their own activities of self-nurturance or self-reflection (such as reading self-help books) as self-indulgent or narcissistic.

In this book I investigate the manner in which self-help books addressed specifically to women encourage us to develop our "selves," specifically, and diffusely—that is, in concert with our involvements with others. I explore the prescribed behavior held to be appropriate in order to attain the ideal womanly self, and how this mythical paragon of womanhood has evolved over time. The flip side of proper womanhood is, of course, improper womanhood (whether described in the form of the woman who is self-limiting, dangerous to men and children, or simply—and most recently—"dysfunctional"). Achieving a satisfying identity comes to look like a dizzying balancing act, in which toeing the line is fraught with confusion. When is lavishing attention on self-development (including, at one end of the spectrum, reading sex manuals) held as commendable, as "feminine"? When does self-attentiveness spill over into egocentrism? When is attention to others in their best interests, and when is it an example of one's own selfish desire to gain control? What evidence do self-help books give about the dissemination of feminist and antifeminist ideologies into popular culture? These are the sorts of questions I asked in conducting my own reading of the phenomenon of self-help reading—questions that are quite different from those the participants in this research brought to *their* reading of self-help books.

The readers I interviewed looked to self-help books primarily for validation of how they already felt (as Carol said, for "a lot of the ideas I've always had"), for inspiration, for comfort, for explanations of situations they could not understand. They were much more trusting readers of self-help books than I was, though they were by no means uncritical. Participants were also more inclined than I am to subscribe to a "therapeutic" analysis of behavior, which stresses individual action. But they by no means dismissed sociological explanations of social phenomena; they all had ideas about why self-help literature is published in such abundance, and about why women in particular are drawn to it, and what all of this means generally about American culture and gender relations.

Self-help books must be studied as ideologically powerful instruments of cultural commerce that are linked both with the proliferation of buyable therapy, in which assistance comes to be seen as a purchasable commodity, and with the increasing volume of the marketplace for leisure consumption. In the suburban area outside Miami where I grew up, most of the smaller lots that stood vacant in my childhood are now filled with little strips of shops, while the larger empty areas have been transformed into enormous malls. There are now four such malls within a ten-minute drive of where I lived, and three more within walking distance. I joke about where I'm from when asked: Mallville, USA. This, as William Kowinski documents in *The Malling of America* (1985), has become a common phenomenon across the country. Because of malls, chain bookstores have spread across the nation. And because of chain bookstores, it is now possible to document which books are sold in B. Dalton's and Waldenbooks stores in Peoria, Albuquerque, New York, and Kalamazoo. One need not even go to a bookstore anymore to buy books: a variety of bestsellers is available in most supermarkets and drugstores. One result of the generally increased availability of books is that bestselling self-help books *are* omnipresent in the marketplaces of the country. The history of self-help books is enmeshed with the development of consumerism and its hegemonic permeation of culture. The decision making, selection, marketing, promoting, and advertising utilized in the trade and mass-market book publishing industry to sell self-help books indicates this.

The question of influence arises repeatedly throughout any consideration of cultural consumption: how do people decide what to "buy"—in both senses of the word? Here I am concerned with how a particular commodity, self-help books, achieves success in the marketplace; with how people become convinced they need or want this cultural commodity. Women may read self-help books because we have problems that are not addressed in other ways. Alternatively, the existence of—and the reading of—self-help books may convince us that we have problems that must be addressed. Self-help books may both mirror cultural values and participate in the creation of them. Similarly, the relationship between self-help and changes in women's lives can be said to go both ways: the feminist movement, the "sexual revolution," the changing nature of families, created an atmosphere in which self-help can flourish, and, conversely, the proliferation of such books somehow enabled these developments. As self-help books have come into their own, so has the feminist movement grown, splintered, and changed alongside the genre, providing it with theory to react against, support, and water down. This study itself is a result of that movement, and of feminist developments within academia.

As I was beginning this research, a friend remarked that I should think about how *I* use books to shape my own worldview, whether the books I used were obviously self-help books or not. Though I have never been an "innocent" reader of self-help books, in the sense that I have not sought to resolve any personal quest through my reading of them (except in the sense that scholarship *is* a personal quest), feminist writings have influenced my worldview. They have shaped my reading of my life both professionally and otherwise, and have certainly shaped my understanding of what it means to do sociological research.

This book is about how generalized culture *becomes* personalized culture once the systems enabling dissemination have succeeded. How we produce ourselves as acculturated people, and how we see our involvement in this production process, must be central to cultural studies. Reading, for instance, may seem like a very personal activity, which individuals do by themselves in communion with a book, a singular act in which members of a culture participate mostly in isolation from one another. Yet it is on a deeper level, as Karl Mannheim writes, "an act of sociation": "We conceive meanings . . . not only in communicative acts, but also in solitary moments. We perform an act of sociation already in an isolated state of contemplation" (1956: 65). The sociology of knowledge, according to Mannheim, attempts to study group culture as it has been absorbed and integrated into "individual" thought and action: "the sociology of the mind is but a systematic attempt to articulate the social character of mental processes" (51). I take as my starting place the experiences and views of the readers of self-help books, whose voices helped me to shape my own construction of this unique cultural genre and its meaning for women living now in this social world.

Most works of qualitative sociology are prefaced with a quite defensive defense of the work to follow. Those who are committed to qualitative work often frame this defense as a justification, which almost reads like an apology for why what is still—regrettably—seen as the high road in sociology was not taken: complex statistical analyses coupled with highly controlled interviewing procedures. Included, usually, is a call for quantitative work within the area, often complete with a sketchy plan for what would be most useful in buttressing up the "findings" being presented: a call for the provers to move in and make it all really valid. I offer no excuses here; I do, however, want to explain how my research framework is constructed.

Validity, I believe, does not grow only out of equations, does not lie hidden in random numbers tables, does not exist any more or less if a verifiable majority does one thing or says another, in a manner that can be clearly observed and reported upon by ten or a thousand researchers trained in exactly the same way. I am far more interested in projecting possibilities than I am in paring and pinning them down.

Mannheim (1936) sees exaggerated allegiance to quantitative methodology within sociology as a product of culture, a stage of "mechanistic dehumanization and formalization" within the discipline, by which sociologists demonstrate their longing for a verifiable reality they can count on; a means of reassuring themselves that one solid and discernible truth really exists. He writes that "this reduction of everything to a measurable or inventory-like describability is significant as a serious attempt to determine what is unambiguously ascertainable and, further, to think through what becomes of our psychic and social world when it is restricted to purely externally measurable relationships" (43–44). Like Mannheim, I hope for a broadening of the discipline where the everyday life of people as they see it becomes a completely acceptable focus of scholarly attention.[1] My theoretical perspective combines elements of reader-response (or reader-oriented) theory and feminist research methodology. These frameworks share two dominant tenets: they see the participant's perceptions of her activities as valid, and question the assumptions behind traditional ways of doing scholarship (in all academic disciplines).

Reader-response theory envisions reading as a construction of the reader: s/he creates the text, in reading it, within the context of an "interpretive community"—a social world that structures her or his making of meaning (Fish 1980). Interpretive communities first referred to academically grounded reading (both a new way of considering comprehension and making scholarly interpretation), though the work of Janice Radway (1984) and Elizabeth Long (1986) examines non-professional reading activities, and researchers have begun to address the reading of television as well as print (see, e.g., Brown 1990; Ang 1990; Hobson 1990; Press 1990 and 1991).

Reader-oriented critics typically write about how *fiction* is read: how authors, readers, and books (or television) participate in making fiction signify. The genre I discuss here is considered nonfiction, but I would argue that these categories (fiction/nonfiction) are not especially relevant to a reader-oriented analysis of reading. For example, *this* conglomeration of inked-up pages is no more or less fictive in terms of *your* belief than if I were concocting a murder mystery that takes place on the Irish moors, rather than telling you a "true" story about what thirty women who read self-help books say about what they read. I would intend either of these narratives to tell a story; each could be real and each fictive, though, in terms of your perceptions. Readers' assessment of reliability, the trustworthiness of the narrative, is a separate matter from the realness or pretense of the story itself, that is, from whether it happened or not. The "reality" reader-response criticism recognizes as most significant is the reality of the activity of reading.

And though reader-oriented critics differ in our assessments of how *much* of the making of meaning occurs when a story gets told/read on paper (or in any other medium), our very work relies on the assumption that the convergence of a message and its interpretation *are* connected constructive acts. What reader-response proponents do, then, is talk about *how* reading works. Ironically, though, we rarely mention that our explication itself is part of what we're trying to explain. Reading reader-response-based scholarship encourages the notion of a neverending chain (of readers reading, and readers reading reading, and so forth); it is something like peeking into mirrors endlessly reflecting into themselves and each other. This image provides, of course, no clear answer to the question of how culture works; to say that it works endlessly, that its interweavings are inextricably interwoven is quite unsatisfying. Reader-response criticism is, then, in itself, a tautology, where the old problem of self-destructing texts that are emptied of meaning once critically decoded—as Robert Allen (1987) describes traditional literary analysis—shifts to a limitless debate over who means what and how meanings are made.

But eternal debate is not what reader-response critics are after, either. We, too, construct arguments we want understood as we mean them; we, too, offer evidence of our claims; we, too, hope our readings will be privileged as accurate. Reader-response, applied to sociology, is quite problematic in terms of sociology as "hard science." The desire to divide neatly what we study to fit into coding categories and typographies that can be distinguished with a range of distinctly different colored pens or discrete computer symbols is stymied by a theoretical standpoint that defies the definition of meaning as constant. Reader-response theory can be seen as an attempt to correct the conception of sociology as "hard" science, indeed, to question the very notions upon which ideas about science *as* hard rest: perfect capturing of truthfulness, of reality, is held to be impossible. There is no definitive, academically generated, perfect capturing of authorial or textual meaning. A reader-oriented approach better fits the study of the social world: it acknowledges that sense ultimately relies on who is doing the sensing and how, and recognizes that a full picture can never be revealed because there is no full picture waiting behind a curtain (or inside a book). Yet, again, proponents of this mode of critical inquiry (myself included) want to participate in the production of meaning which, again, we find to be, at an essential level, an unfathomable snarl of behavior.

I do not mean to say that we can't get anywhere, that reader-response-based social science is only an interpretive game. But how you read this—how you make sense of my readings (and my readings of others' readings)—is the most essential part of this process. My end is to convince you that my readings are valid, but I do not ask that you consider my readings to be the end of interpretation. In other words, your agency becomes the most essential element (and I'm not just writing this to flatter you!). Reader-response-based theory conceives of agency as central to understanding interaction, agency that is itself born of social interaction that cannot be seen separately from the hegemonic ideology—ironically, often itself denying agency—of the culture.

Sociologists forever ask one another about our findings, our conclusions; such language presumes that the patterns that emerge from research arise on their own, that results are factual deposits waiting to be mined, that real life can somehow be excerpted into truthful summaries about who we are and why we behave as we do. And yet the underlying question framing these sociological demands (tell me what you found— tell me what you concluded) clearly asks whether the respondent can convince the interrogator that what s/he has found and what s/he has concluded *makes sense* to the interrogator. Each research project, then, is an interpretive foray into the dense thicket of social life. Each investigation is itself a narrative grounded in the investigator's perceptions, through which s/he seeks to reveal a story that will persuade its readers of an apt and compelling description of something that cannot ever be captured in its fullness, cannot ever truly be caught on paper.

I do not offer these methodological caveats so that I may go on to say anything without being challenged. I do wish to call into question the conventional notion of discovery that pervades all sciences ("hard" and "soft"), the idea that there is a concrete social world out there waiting for experts to locate, to clarify, to reify. No doubt other investigators would have fashioned other narratives, made different decisions about how to conduct the research and how to interpret the material they came away with. I offer these caveats because I believe that they ought to be a necessary preface to any presentation of interpretive sociology.

I take feminist methodology to mean research that is woman-centered: an awareness of how research impacts participants and of how women's lives, specifically, are affected by gender is central to this study. Sandra Harding (Harding and Hintikka 1983) writes that existing traditional "scientific" methodologies are built upon men's experience which is generally "presumed to be gender-free." Since traditional research methods often ignore women's experience, Harding contends that they are ill-suited organizational strategies for work that does intend to study women's lives (x).

In writing on feminist methodology, what emerges most clearly is a conviction that methods ought to be grounded in research situations and a commitment against the alienation or objectification of participants (Harding and Hintikka 1983; Roberts 1981; Smith 1987). Ann Oakley (1981) nicely enumerates the formally prescribed "textbook" conditions for interviewing that are taught to students of the social sciences: the interview is conceived of as a "mechanical instrument of data-collection" that is effective only if the interviewer and interviewee confine their interaction to the asking of pre-scripted questions (by the interviewer) and the answering of these questions (by the interviewee); the best, most reliable results are obtained when the interviewer maintains a detached, impersonal, professional stance, and when the interviewee responds as s/he is cued (36–37). The imbalance of power between researcher and participants recommended by traditional methodology obscures "the goal of finding out about people" (Oakley 1981: 41) and "disrupt[s] individuals' attempts to make coherent sense of what is happening to them and around them" (Mishler 1986: 120).

I tried, throughout my interviewing, to allow the participants to shape what transpired between us as much as possible. This meant that I tried to fit the questions I wanted to ask into the women's narratives, as they developed, rather than structuring the interviews according to my "schedule." (As it happened, the questions I originally designed were broad and open-ended enough so that most discussions ended up including most of them.)

An approach has developed within qualitative interviewing in which talk is examined in a precise, codified, at times even microscopic manner (see, e.g., Mishler 1986; Riessman 1990; and Todd and Fisher 1988). The talk itself becomes data through its textuality; speech is carefully presented in its complexity, replete with symbols for long and short pauses, and the inclusion of non-lexical utterances (uh, uh-huh, mm), and then examined closely by the researcher, who pays attention to how narrative patterns shape content. This methodological practice relies on the assumption that explicitness will yield accuracy, even though practitioners do not usually include their complete interview transcripts. While I believe this methodology offers an effective way to deal with talk, it reifies the notion of meaning as extractable from a text. (In this case, the text becomes the interview translated to print.) I have not altered the words of the participants in this study, but I have altered their "texts" in that I have decided what to include and what to omit.

What I think is most useful in microconversation analysts' approach is the attention they call to the politics of talking, and the ways in which dialogues are shaped by the meaning both talkers (interviewer and interviewee) attribute to the interaction.

Interviewees, of course, though rarely trained in social scientific methodology themselves, also share traditional ideas about what constitutes an interview (because they have usually experienced other interview situations—primarily work-related). So participants and I would often fall into a pattern of questions (mine) and answers (theirs), rather than the free-flowing conversation I envisioned as ideal. I did, of course, have an agenda: these conversations may have come to seem "natural," but each was also a contrived situation, because interviews are not natural conversations.

Over the course of conducting this project, I strove to make my methods cohere with—rather than govern—the work itself. Similarly, I shaped my "readings" of the cultural phenomenon of literary advice-seeking by carefully considering the views of the people who engage in this activity, for they are the true "experts" in this situation. I tried, above all, to preserve the integrity of my participants' narratives as I made use of their words.

Participants for this research were identified through the use of a preliminary questionnaire about reading in general which colleagues and friends circulated in various work and social locales. Approximately two hundred copies of the questionnaires were distributed. Initially, twenty-five respondents indicated that they read self-help or self-improvement books and volunteered their telephone numbers. Two of the women I reached from this group did not participate in the study. Several of the remaining twenty-three women suggested other readers they knew who might participate over the course of their interviews; a total of thirty women were interviewed.

The women I spoke with provide telling commentary about their reading that can, I believe, enable us to understand better the phenomenon of self-help reading. These readers read quite a variety of books for instructive purposes: including self-help books that focus on self-image, self-esteem, assertiveness, and relationships with others (at work and at home); self-help books that are not explicitly gender-specific; books dealing with health, New Age philosophy, traditional religion; and biographies. I did not attempt to constrict or narrow any participant's description of what the genre should include. (For specific demographic data about the participants and a detailed breakdown of the types of self-help books read by the participants, see Table 1.)

The women who talked with me about their reading may be more eager proponents for self-help books than those who read them and decided not to volunteer to continue in the research. This is the case in nearly all investigations; those who feel most uncomfortable or uncertain about their own behavior or those who are uninterested in the research issues are least likely to volunteer to become involved. Those who feel the issues being studied are important or interesting are most likely to volunteer their time. Indeed, several of the participants told me how excited they were to have the opportunity to talk about their reading. Many said that they were simply interested in my topic, glad that they could be of help.

The majority (twenty-two) of the thirty readers I interviewed are white; five are black, two are Hispanic, and one woman defined herself as half white, and half American Indian. Participants ranged in age from twenty-three to fifty-nine; the mean age of women interviewed was thirty-seven, and the median age was thirty-six. Six women are Protestants (including Episcopalian, Lutheran, and Baptist); eleven are Catholic, eleven are Jewish, and two wrote "none" under religion. (Listing a religious background does not mean these women were observant.) Of the women who said they read religious self-help books, two are Protestant, and three are Jewish. (One of these Jewish women, Lauren, did not read specifically Jewish works. The four other religious readers were observant.) Five others said they read New Age literature, including astrology. The other participants said they did not connect religious or spiritual quests with their readings within the self-help genre.

Reading behavior in general is, no doubt, reflective of class status, simply in terms of the ways in which tastes are formulated and specific to class identity (Bourdieu 1984); however, within this study, class status was elusive. Income level did not "predict" reading behavior or types of self-help books read (or vice versa). Income level, obviously, is not the same thing as class. I did not ask participants to identify themselves by class; had I done so, most would have said they were middle class, I believe. Since I am not sure that even that label means anything concrete, and since it was not my aim to explore the self-definition women held regarding class, the issue of how class relates to reading will remain unexplored here.

In terms of actual income a majority of participants (eighteen) reported a household income under $45,000. Of these women, thirteen reported household incomes under $30,000; and of these, three reported incomes under $15,000. Income level was related to whether or not there were two earners in the family; married women typically reported higher incomes than women who had not been married or divorced women. (Only one woman—of nine—who reported a household income over $45,000 was generating this income alone.)

The women I spoke to are highly educated. Only one woman had not had any formal educational experience since high school; eight had attended some college or community college; six are college graduates; and fifteen have postgraduate experience. They hold, among them, master's degrees in education, social work, history, folklore, fine arts, and a doctorate in sociology. (In a nonrandom sample of this size, it would be inappropriate to surmise that advanced education is specifically linked to reading self-help books.)

All of the women interviewed for this project were employed outside the home, except for one retired teacher. Over half (eighteen) of the women I interviewed worked in areas of the paid-labor market that are dominated by women: eight did secretarial or administrative work; five were elementary or secondary school teachers (the retired teacher mentioned above is included here); two were paraprofessionals (in teaching and nursing); five did counseling (four of whom had master's degrees in social work). Of the remaining twelve, three worked in managerial positions. None of the women worked in professions typically dominated by men, such as law and medicine—though one was a college professor. None owned her own business. One was a full-time graduate student.

Eleven of the women I interviewed were married, eleven were divorced, and eight were single. Of the eight single women, three were living with men at the time of our interviews. Enhancing or understanding their relationship (or lack thereof) with men was a motivating factor for many of the readers, though not the *only* reason any of these women read self-help.

I also interviewed five editors of self-help books, to see how those who create this genre see it, both in terms of profit and nonmaterial utility. These women all worked at publishing houses in New York City. All are white.

All of the participants—the thirty readers and the five editors—were interviewed between May 1988 and February 1989. All lived in urban areas on the East Coast of the United States. Interviews with readers typically lasted one to two hours; those with editors took approximately one hour. With the exception of one, all interviews were taped.

Wendy Griswold's conception of the cultural diamond serves as an organizing guide for this book. Griswold explains the creation and longevity of cultural meaning with this diagram, the four corners of which are the "audience," the "creator," the "cultural object," and the "social world." According to Griswold, no account of a cultural phenomenon is complete without a consideration of all four corners of the diamond and of the connections between them (1986). But these categories of analysis are not easily separable from each other; for instance, the audience and the social world both work to "create" cultural objects, and the social world really incorporates all three other points of the diamond. Thinking of Griswold's cultural diamond as continually in flux will allow us to shift our view from one corner ("rounded" by motion) to another, and ultimately to gain a holistic— and perhaps frustratingly circular—consideration of self-help culture.

I begin by focusing on members of the audience for self-help books, in the first three chapters. In Chapter 1, "Reading between the Lines: How and Why Women Read Self-Help Books," I discuss the thirty interviews I conducted with readers of self-help books about their own perceptions of their reading. They speak about why they are attracted to this particular genre, and how they "read" the cultural phenomenon of self-help books. Readers discuss the genre as it compares with other types of reading, and evaluate its significance for women in general.

The women I interviewed spoke unanimously of their search for "answers" to problems both practical and sublime, and read books that ranged from traditional religious dogma to the more "mainstream" and mass-market popular-psychological manuals. An analysis of the interrelationship between religious and secular therapeutic self-help reading follows in Chapter 2, "Shrinking God: Psycho-Religious Self-Help Reading." Readers assess the therapeutic value in books ranging from the secular to the spiritual in their quest for answers. Chapter 3, "Readers Write In," focuses on letters anonymous readers wrote to self-help authors Betty Friedan and Robin Norwood, following the publication of their respective works, *The Feminine Mystique* (1963) and *Women Who Love Too Much* (1985). Readers' letters show what direct, immediate responses to self-help books can be like, and reinforce participants' assertions that reading self-help can have a strong impact on women's lives.

Next, in Chapter 4, "Making It Readable," I shift my focus to concentrate on the role of creators of self-help books, discussing interviews with editors and authors' written discussions of their motivations and goals in writing self-help books. The makers of self-help literature describe how and why they believe what they offer should be seen as a salient contribution to readers.

In Chapters 5 and 6, I explore the cultural messages offered by bestselling self-help books over the past twenty-eight years, beginning with unisex self-help and sex manuals in "Shelf Life: Bestselling Unisex Self-Help Books." In Chapter 6, "The Tangled Web: Self-Help Books about Gender," this subgenre's treatment of gender relations is examined. Authors' prescriptions for attaining success in heterosexual relationships, and for achieving a positive identity, both apart from and in concert with gendered relationships, are discussed.

Finally, in the Conclusion, "Self-Help Culture," I discuss the place of the genre of self-help literature in relation to other forms of cultural didacticism dealing with gender and identity. Here I come full circle (or "full diamond"), reading the phenomenon of self-help literature from the point of view of readers (both talking and writing about their responses); from the perspective of creators (both talking and writing about their motivations); and in terms of the books themselves, as I read them to respond to and reify ideas about self and gender in this culture. Readers', editors', and authors' assumptions about how the social world calls for, or is represented by, self-help literature infuse their discussion of it; similarly, when I interpret bestselling self-help in Chapters 5 and 6, I am invoking my sociological understanding of the social reality that structures women's quests for advice about ourselves and others. In this Conclusion, the particular activity of self-help reading is treated as an example of the diffuse prescriptiveness that pervades women's cultural experiences.

Chapter 1

Reading between the Lines:

How and Why Women Read

Self-Help Books

> What is omnipresent is imperceptible. Nothing is more commonplace than the reading experience, and yet nothing is more unknown. (Todorov 1980: 67)

It is only through an examination of the act of reading itself, which begins with the perceptions of readers themselves, that we can discover what makes women decide to read self-help books, and see what they get out of their reading. Participants' evaluations of their reading show how readers make use of self-help literature as part of the work of making sense of their own lives.

I asked the thirty participants in my study to tell me what they thought their reading means, not only for themselves, but as part of a larger phenomenon of women reading self-help literature. I asked them to describe why they thought women were finding self-help books especially appealing at this particular time, and what they thought women did in the past without a wide selection of self-help books to utilize. They compared written advice with other (past and presently available) options for receiving help and talked about the differences between the experience of reading self-help books and other types of literature.

Participants read quite a variety of books for instructive purposes: self-help books addressed to women that focus on self-image, self-esteem, assertiveness, and relationships with others (at work and at home), self-help books that are not explicitly gender-specific, books dealing with health, New Age philosophy, traditionally religious books, and biographies. Some of the books in these categories are feminist in orientation, and others are not. (For details on the types of self-help books read by each participant, see Table 1.) The women who read New Age material tended to be younger (between twenty-seven and thirty-six years old), but this was the only discernible difference in reading habits that was linked to age. All of the women who described their reading of self-help books as an activity in which they were often (as opposed to sometimes or rarely) engaged were white, except for one woman who described herself as half white and half American Indian; so, within this group of readers, white women were heavier readers of self-help books than African-American or Latina women. None of the women I interviewed said that race or class status was a topic covered in what they read; but gender often was a subject of their reading.

Learning to Read

When I pick up a book, many things can happen. I can merge into another world, the time and space in which I physically exist seemingly suspended. I can look for answers to specific questions and feel an excited satisfaction when I find them (and frustration when I don't). I can become bored, agitated. My focus can blur. I can fall asleep. For a long time, I thought of the disparate possibilities for reading experiences as residing solely in the books themselves. (This one was great! That one was tedious.) A book could envelop me, instruct me, bore me. But I always thought of the book as the actor and of myself as the object upon which its action occurred.

Exposure to ideas about the meaning to be found in written material begins when we first start reading and expands as we are formally schooled in reading strategies. Part of becoming literate is learning to ask certain questions, to develop certain expectations of different reading experiences. Of course, in the process of internalizing reading strategies there are many demands we do not learn to make, many ways of reading we do not consider. And as we learn evaluative strategies to apply to fiction, we learn other—often *opposing*—methods for digesting nonfiction. Most of our critical techniques filter down to us from academic experts, who thus have significant control over aesthetic and symbolic interpretations, and how they are made. Since fiction, with its potential status as art, has been the primary mode of writing evaluated, most of the academic experts on whom we rely for critical strategies are English professors.

The theoretical implications of reading have become a respectable topic of inquiry within the realm of literary theory only in the past fifteen years (reader-oriented work includes, notably, Armstrong 1990; Eagleton 1983; Fish 1980; Graubard 1983; Iser 1978; Jauss 1982; Rabinowitz 1987; Radway 1984; Smith 1983; Suleiman and Crosman 1980; Tompkins 1980 and 1985). Before reactive trends like reader-response, postmodern, feminist, and deconstructive literary studies, critics attempted to extract universal or author-intended meanings from canonized texts. Readers were considered passive spectators to the literary process, lucky if they could skillfully pick apart the meat of the text and understand its symbolic implications and stylistic nuances as "New Critics" taught them to do. New Critics exhaustively pontificated on the intricacy, the correctness, the brilliance of motifs, images, words, assuming a priori that these motifs, images, words, were inherently laden with value, ensconced as they were in the solidity of the Canon of Great Western Books. According to Robert Crosman (1980), the movement of New Criticism within literary theory was a well-grounded product of Western cultures: "Because we have all been taught to believe in the [Western idea of] Imperial Truth, we have imagined the process of writing as antithetical to the process of reading: the writer, in contact with the wordless realm of Truth, somehow embodies his ineffable vision of reality in words and sends it to the reader, who (if all goes well) removes the 'meaning' from its verbal envelope" (163).

Within the frameworks of these relatively new movements against New Criticism, aesthetic value—and consequently overall meaning—have come to be evaluated differently. Feminist scholars, for example, have attributed importance to cultural works that have never been considered aesthetic successes—or "art"—by literary authorities. These writers see the masculinist organization of the field of literary studies as responsible for relegating women's work to literary obscurity, and attempt to reclaim it as a subject of historically grounded literary criticism (see, e.g., Baym 1978; Ferguson 1985; Fetterley 1978; Gilbert and Gubar 1979; Miner 1984; Russ 1983; Spacks 1972; and Tompkins 1985). Popularity among groups other than academics or literary critics has become a recognized indication of significance. "The way in which a literary work, at the historical moment of its appearance, satisfies, surpasses, disappoints, or refutes the expectations of its first audience obviously provides a criterion for the determination of its aesthetic value" (Jauss 1982: 25). Even so, debates over the exact qualities of authorial intent and reader reception persist (see, e.g., Armstrong 1990; Rabinowitz 1987).

Studying Reading

A number of studies have been conducted to measure and compare readers' comprehension of fiction in order to chart various lines of literal understanding (e.g., Holland 1975), but little research has focused on literature's impact on—or relationship to—readers' life experiences (exceptions include Radway 1984; and Long 1986).

A movement parallel to that of New Criticism, which aimed to make the work of sociologists "scientific," has held sway since the mid-twentieth century in the United States. Drawing on the intentions of Emile Durkheim, functionalists sought to make sociology scientifically respectable, using the natural sciences as a model, and borrowing the notion of the uninvolved, objective scientific observer and methodology as verifiable through reproducibility. As in literature and "hard" science, questions of agency and empowerment (in making culture as well as in making theory and methods) were ignored by sociologists practicing a social construction of reality that which aimed to strip away subjectivity entirely.

To date, sociological studies concerning reader behavior have been primarily quantitative projects undertaken to determine who was reading, what they were reading, and where they got it (Berelson 1949; Yankelovich et al. 1978), but not *why* they were reading or what they got out of it. In early cultural studies, sociologists attempted to trace the line—then considered to be an arrow pointing in one direction only, like a hypodermic needle—between cultural creators and recipients. Marxist and production-of-culture theorists offer a twist on the injection model, tying production and reception of cultural messages to the workings of hegemonic institutions (Becker 1982; Gitlin 1983; Griswold, 1986; Powell 1985; Williams 1958; and Wolff 1981), but the agency of the cultural consumers is subordinate to the authority and power of the cultural creators within these frameworks. Of late, feminist cultural scholars have begun to take into account the influence exerted—in terms of both collusion and resistance—by users of culture objects.

Janice Radway's book on romance reading (1984) and Elizabeth Long's study of women's reading groups in Texas (1986) center on how readers construct meaning as they read. In the collection *Television and Women's Culture: The Politics of the Popular,* several authors write about how women create meaning out of the television shows they watch (Brown, Ang, Hobson, and Press [all 1990]), and in her own volume on the subject, Andrea Press (1991) compares middle-class and working-class women's views of television and emphasizes age-based responses to the medium. The focus here, as in much of the cultural studies work coming out of the Birmingham school (in Birmingham, England), is on participation *as* resistance, or as "discourse" made relevant by viewers to their everyday lives (authors who discuss resistance include Ang, Brown, Fiske, Lewis [all 1990]; Fiske 1989; and Press 1991). Resistance, as conceived by the Birmingham school, means interpretation of content to suit users' needs—usually working-class subversive appropriation of middle-class cultural forms to mean something other than what their creators intended (as scholars read creators' intent).

Quantitative analysis has also been applied to the study of cultural reception. Several studies of self-help reading have been designed, rather like market research, to measure its prevalence and utility (vs. "live" therapy). In a random-sampled telephone survey of one thousand people in Portland, Oregon, Steven Starker (1989) found that women were more frequent readers of self-help books than men and were more likely to say they found their reading helpful (152). Starker does not provide exact figures on this data, however. According to a 1988 Gallup telephone survey, women were more likely than men ever to have bought a self-help book; 36 percent of women said they had, as compared with 30 percent of men polled (Wood 1988: 33). In the Gallup poll, when self-help is broken down into topic areas, women are more likely to buy books dealing with "love and relationships," "stress and anxiety," and "weight loss." Men are more likely to buy self-help books dealing with "self-improvement" and with "motivation" (Wood 1988: 33).

While this survey shows that women are, in general, more likely than men ever to have read a self-help book, the 6 percent gap between men and women readers is not especially large. Survey responses don't tell about the general or repeated use of self-help books by women and men, and don't show why people consulted books or what they felt was meaningful about their reading experiences. Also, the categories within which self-help books were grouped were rather vaguely defined, were not mutually exclusive, and may well have confused respondents.[1] The categories themselves were poorly conceived; for example, 12 percent of respondents—the third largest category group—said they read books about "other" topics.

Though vague in many ways, the Gallup survey does show some interesting differences in reading behavior depending on the five most reported subtopic areas within self-help (not counting "other"). People between the ages of eighteen and thirty-four were more likely to read books on relationships than those thirty-five and older; people with incomes under $30,000 were more likely than those with higher incomes to read books on motivation; and people who had been to college were also more likely to read books on motivation. Women who were working outside the home ("employed") were more likely than those who were not ("not employed") to read books about "self-improvement," "motivation," and "love and relationships"—whereas women who were not working outside the home were more likely to read books on "weight loss" (Wood 1988: 33).

Unlike the Gallup poll, Starker's survey had participants discuss the quantity and quality of their reading:

> The Portland sample reported reading an average of 2.82 self-help books per year. Asked if they had ever read a really helpful self-help work, 64.7 percent responded affirmatively. When asked for their overall evaluation of self-help books on a 5-point scale from "harmful" to "often helpful," not a single respondent considered them to be "harmful," only 2.2 percent judged them to be "unhelpful," and 14.4 percent found them "rarely helpful." The largest group of responses indicated self-help works to be "sometimes helpful" (50 percent), the remainder found them "often helpful" (33.3 percent), creating a pooled positive evaluation group of 83.3 percent. (1989: 151)

As a clinical psychologist, Starker understandably focuses on issues concerning the clinical effectiveness of self-help books. He also polled "experts"—psychologists, psychiatrists, and interns in the Seattle area. Psychologists judged self-help books most favorably: 88.6 percent said they "personally prescribed self-help books to supplement their treatment," and 93.2 percent judged that they were either "sometimes helpful" or "often helpful" to clients who read them. Psychiatrists were less likely than psychologists to recommend self-help books—though a majority did—or to deem them helpful (153–155). Practitioners, especially psychiatrists, were quick to point out that reading could not substitute for therapy, and several felt (unlike psychologists) that reading self-help was either useless or harmful (155).

A *New York Times* article on July 6, 1989, reports that Forrest Scogin, a psychologist, "has combined the results of more than forty studies that compared using self-help books with actual psychotherapy. 'By and large, the books worked well,' he said. 'Psychotherapy had an advantage, but only a slight one'" (Goleman 1989: B6). Starker's surveys, and those Scogin discusses, focus on perceived utility rather than specific usage, and since the researchers themselves are psychologists, concepts of effectiveness of treatment are taken for granted to be measurable in various psychological scales (although no Rorschach tests!). Scogin's own work shows that "bibliotherapy" can be as efficient as face-to-face therapy "for mildly and moderately depressed older adults" (Scogin et al. 1989: 403). In response to work on bibliotherapy and complaints against it within the profession of psychology, Michael J. Mahoney points out that measurement of effectiveness in comparison with live therapy is problematic since "the success rates of professional counseling and psychotherapy are themselves nothing to brag about" (1988: 598).

None of the quantitative studies of self-help reading focuses on the act of reading itself and what the reader sees that act as accomplishing for herself or himself. Nor have researchers asked participants to talk about *how* their reading—helpful or not—fits into their lives.

In "Theory of the Text," Roland Barthes (1980) holds that reading experience is inextricably connected with social life and that it cuts deeply through our collective intellectual history: "The notion of the text is historically linked to a whole world of institutions: the law, the Church, literature, education. The text is a moral object. . . . It subjects us, and demands that we observe and respect it, but in return it marks language with an inestimable attribute which it does not possess in its essence: security" (32). I have gradually come to see that persuasive power resides in books, not because, as Barthes asserts, they "subject" or make demands on readers, but because readers *allow* books persuasive power. Readers give authority to texts; yet this authority is always constructed and mediated by societal institutions and practices because the act of learning to read and all the reading that follows are "sociated acts" (Mannheim 1956: 65).

Perhaps it is because we rarely attempt to examine the act of reading—or the social construction of that act—that we rarely recognize it as an activity at all. Since we don't move, physically, while we are reading, and since reading is largely a solitary involvement, it doesn't seem to fit into the same category with other *acts* we commit. And since we have been schooled to think of books as authorities to which we submit our open minds, we often ignore our participation in the reading process. But, as Robert Crosman writes, "Once we decide that readers can make meaning, and ought to be doing so, we begin to see it happening all around us—that is what reading is, after all" (1980: 164).

Talking about Reading

Lauren, one of the women I interviewed, describes the power books have simply because they are books:

> Books are amazing things. They're old things too. . . . At least in the history of Christianity . . . the book had this holy quality, because the things that were written down—at least in elite culture—were always the most important things. You wouldn't put things into writing that weren't sacred. . . . When the book first started, it must be something so moving that has happened, a revelation that has happened, that [the book] . . . holds it still, like a photograph. . . .
>
> One has the feeling with a book that one is in the presence of something important. Not with all books, but with these kinds of books, there's the feeling that the books have a key. And I've felt some kind of mythic feeling, a lot of times, about . . . a book.

In speaking of the power of the written word to hold something "still, like a photograph," Lauren echoes Barthes's declaration that the text provides language with "security." The readers I interviewed were unanimous in their recognition that self-help books were repetitive, and thus secure. Reading could be a ritual of self-reassurance where repetition was *desired*. Bonnie, who had been reading books to help her deal with grief after the recent death of her mother, told me that her father and brother had both read one "grief book" each, while she had read several. Her primary interest was not in finding the newness or nuance in each author's strategy for coping with grief, but rather in gaining the reassurance the activity of reading offered her. Reading this group of "grief books" enabled her to see what she was going through *in print* over and over again:

> The grief books, interestingly enough, most of them say the same things, but I get a lot of *comfort* from seeing it in print. . . . It gives me a kind of comfort. . . . Like the grief books will tell you: "A lot of other people are going through this too. It's normal to feel anger." Now, somehow, seeing that in print is more comforting than having other people tell it to me verbally. It seems more real. Also, I can go back to it. . . . Whereas, it's harder to recall a person saying it, and getting the same kind of comfort.

Many other readers spoke about their respect for the printed word; during our conversation, Emily described the difference she sees between reading a book and talking to a friend when in search of a solution to a problem:

> You can get very wrong advice from a friend, wherein if it's a professional, you know, book that you're reading . . . you would tend to kind of agree with [what's written] because you figure that the person who wrote the book might be a professional, or know a little more than some of your friends do.
> W. S.: A book is authoritative?
> EMILY: I would say yes. . . . You know there's no wrong information in it. . . .
> W. S.: How do you know that?
> EMILY: Well, it doesn't necessarily have to be wrong information, just something that you don't agree with.

Even when challenged, Emily refused to alter her description of books as loci of "right information." Most of the readers I interviewed tend to respect what comes to them in the form of a book, often seeing the book as having been written in direct response to its audience's needs. In *Women's Ways of Knowing* (1986), Mary Field Belenky et al. describe women's tendency to look to authorities, such as books, for "truth." They call such thinkers "received knowers." They cite one such received knower's explanation: "Things you look up in a book, you normally get the right answer," and assert that this woman, "as typical of received knowers . . . did not realize that authorities have the capacity for constructing knowledge" (39). Like this woman, several of the readers I interviewed discussed the information found in books as though it were disembodied, unconnected with any creator—as, indeed, it *appears* to be when it arrives in book form. Unlike Belenky et al., I don't think this makes them immature "knowers"; believing in authority in some circumstances doesn't make one necessarily uncritical across the board.[2]

Though respectful, most participants did *not* refrain wholly from criticizing books: they did not believe everything they read. However, not one of the women who offered negative caveats about self-help books told me women should abandon such reading, though many journalists investigating the genre have made such assertions. Books were often viewed as suspect when they appeared sensational to readers, which generally meant that participants saw publication as motivated by authors' desire to make a lot of money. Rena, for example, describes how she decides whether or not to place trust in an author:

> Well, firstly, if the book is sensational I dismiss it. . . . You know, if it's obviously an appeal to you know, glamour, current thinking, trying to—I can almost tell when a book is trying to make money, and that's the key thing. And when it's definitely just the expression of an ordinary person, I normally dismiss it, because I could write that book too. I'm looking for someone . . . who has some background, who knows something about what he's writing. . . . And also if they go overboard on a particular thing and don't seem to have any other respect for an alternate opinion, then I dismiss it too.

A self-help book strikes Rena as authoritative if its author demonstrates credentialed expertise, not if "he" shows himself to be a person to whom she can relate on a personal level. She prefers authors who are moderate in their views, and will put down a book in which the author "goes overboard." She doesn't like glitzy media-propelled successes and believes that she can sense whether a book offers substantive information or superficial chatter. Other readers like being able to relate to an author and do not demand the professional distance between author and reader that Rena prefers.

Readers' respect for a well-liked author can crumble. Evelyn told me about her immediate identification with Nancy Friday's *My Mother/My Self,* and how her opinion of Nancy Friday as respectable expert deteriorated when she read a subsequent book, *Men in Love:*

> I don't remember [*My Mother/My Self*] clearly, but I remember— because it was a long time ago—that it was very intensely personal to me. I don't remember how, but I know I felt . . . that it changed my life. It really made me feel differently. And then I read her other book . . . *Men in Love,* and I almost threw up. I thought it was horrible. . . . What happened was that a great deal of it was sexually—and I'm very sexually liberal, and you know—I thought it was horrible, horrible. . . . Kinky stuff. . . . It just nauseated me.[3]

The readers I interviewed clearly distinguished between books they liked and the rest—books that they either disliked or that had no impact on them at all. While several women remembered, like Evelyn, books that had angered or upset them in some way, the majority of the participants said that if they were reading a book they didn't like, they would simply stop reading it. Liz described reading a book entitled *Don't Say Yes When You Want to Say No* and getting angry because the book never fulfilled the cover promise: "I couldn't even get to their square one. . . . It was like, 'Analyze: Why are you saying yes when you want to say no?' And I was like, 'That's why I'm reading this book! . . . . If I knew that already, I wouldn't *need* this book!'" Respondents all tended to voice dissatisfaction with books they perceived as facile (these evaluations varied considerably among the group). Participants were also on guard against books they considered intrusively instructive. For instance, Allison said that she didn't like books that "would tell a person to be manipulative." And though several women said they felt badly about stopping in the middle of a book, all the respondents said that when a book got repetitive, they would either begin to skim or put the book down altogether (unless they were experiencing the repetition as comforting, as Bonnie described earlier).

Reminiscing about Reading

Many of the participants said that before our interviews, they worried that they would not be able to remember anything—or enough—about their reading. Many apologized when our conversations came to an end, saying they wished they had been able to remember more. A few told me they had looked through their books the night before, in preparation. One woman had stacks of books out on the table when I arrived. Their expectations regarding our interview made sense: someone calls you to ask if she can talk to you about your reading, and you apply your past experience in talking about reading. You want to do a good job for this academic stranger. You, no doubt, envision a string of oral book reports.

I *did* ask questions about specific books, so, in a sense, I did not disappoint these women's expectations. Participants showed satisfaction when they were able to describe the main ideas in books and seemed annoyed with themselves when they could not.

Talking to readers made me reevaluate the underlying assumptions of my questions: what do you remember about such-and-such a book, and how would you say it helped or influenced you? Originally, I felt that a text's "ability" to leave a lasting impression on a reader's mind must mean it did something for that person—at least in comparison with books that were not remembered. Looking back, I see that when I began this research, I assumed that the amount remembered was an indication of a reader's effective usage of a book, and that I could measure, in some way, the causal relationships between readers, their books, and their actions. Participants did tell me about acts that were inspired by reading, such as carrying on conversations differently with specific people, or trying to alter their thinking about a certain relationship or set of relations according to techniques they had read about. They gave me plenty of examples of "successful" utilizations of self-help books. For example, Janet explained how self-help books helped her to monitor and professionalize her behavior at work: "Well, I have learned one thing in particular, which is, I am somebody who has absolutely no patience, and when you're gonna be working with somebody [inexperienced], you have to realize that you have to have some sort of patience and time. . . . [Reading] has taught me to give people a fair chance. . . . And give them opportunities, listen to what people have to say, you know, and not taking sides in an office, which is very important."

Participants also insisted on a book's temporal, immediate importance. For instance, Pat said, "When I don't need it, why do I want to
remember it? When I don't need it, I don't care. So I really use it when I
need it. I don't know anything about them when I don't need them."
Abby describes her "use" of Erich Fromm's *The Art of Loving*, and Lauren
her involvement with the spiritual *Course in Miracles* similarly:

ABBY: I remember it affected me a lot at the time I read it. . . . It
was helpful. . . . I remember talking about it, and talking about
relationships with friends in college, so it probably changed my
thinking in some ways. It's hard to say exactly *how* did it change my
thinking.

LAUREN: I was just thinking the other day that it must not have
done anything at all. It's funny, when you get out of working with a
tool like that . . . it feels you maybe never even really did it. It's very
hard to measure how things change, and to be perfectly honest, I
really can't see clear evidence of it, since I'm not working with it
consciously. But at the same time, I'm really sure that it did
something.

Self-help books, unlike other types of books read by the women I
interviewed, were often discussed as items to be used, as "tools" for
accomplishing specific goals. In retrospect, many women find it difficult
to articulate exactly how useful a certain book has been in resolving the
situation for which it was originally enlisted. The question arises, do
readers claim a significance for their reading because they don't want to
look back and see their reading as a waste of time? I think not. Most of
the women I interviewed spoke freely about books they considered a
waste of time. But, as Lauren said, "it's very hard to measure how things
change"; perhaps, indeed, it is impossible for a reader to put her finger
on how, exactly, she has allowed a book to influence her, if she can see
no strong indications of continued influence in the present.

One woman (Sandy) came to question the importance of her reading
over the course of our interview:

Talking about this is really making me see why they never really—
you know, I don't remember them. Because I was wondering why
that was, and I was getting all nervous about this because I don't

remember them, and there's a reason I don't remember them!
. . . . I haven't really learned anything. It's funny. I didn't realize
that. I thought there'd been some great effect on my life. . . . [I
remind her that, prior to this point in our conversation, she has
said many good things about self-help books, and she says, frus-
tratedly:] I think I do feel both ways about a lot of things.

I came to recognize that it was unrealistic to think I would be able to
measure the influence of self-help books, and I came to accept readers'
ambiguous replies not as testimony against the notion of lasting effects
of reading, but as evidence of the complexity of their reading pasts. Most
of the women who described ambivalence about their self-help reading
attributed this ambivalence to the "fact" that there were good books and
bad ones; the good ones made them conclude their reading was worthwhile, while the bad ones led them to see reading as a waste of time.

Reading self-help books can be a momentary means of alleviating the
pressure of a certain problem and offering hope for a less stressful
future, and may then be forgotten altogether—as several readers said,
used as a "quick fix." Bonnie's comments elucidate this most clearly:
"I'm sure—there's something, when I see the book, and I touch it, it
excites me . . . because I'm sure, that within that book—even though I've
read five other books on the same subject—it's gonna have the answer. . . . You see, the self-help books give me a sense of total possibility.
I'll make the right choices, I'll find a man, I'll do everything." Bonnie
compared her self-help habit to drug use; she said she imagined that
going from one book to another was like going from one high to
another. Self-help reading was, for her, a fleeting sensation which she
looked forward to. She would save books up like treats.

Reading self-help books, then, can be a means of obtaining instant
gratification, with no special concern for content. Cindy said that she
found reading self-help literature (and she included biographies as
some of her favorite self-help books) to be like hearing a pep talk. She
described reading as one of many creative outlets she would turn to
which would help her to feel strong: "I use it almost I guess as a mirror
. . . to look at myself and say, 'Don't give in.' You know, 'fight it. You can
do it. . . . You *will* do it.'" Reading can also—as I found with readers of
religious books and feminist books—be used as a way of continually
bolstering a reader's desired conception of the world.

Reading as Gendered

Recently, scholars have discussed the ways in which the perception of meaning is a gendered activity. One well-known example, Matina Horner's incomplete anecdote of successful men and women medical students, is often cited for its contribution to psychology because of the seeming oddity of women's responses. Students were asked to complete the sentence: "after first term finals, Anne [or John] finds herself [himself] at the top of her [his] medical school class," (Gilligan 1982:15). Women often assigned a tragic future to Anne, but not to John. This has been most commonly interpreted as an indication of women's "fear of success." Carol Gilligan has since asserted that what women fear is a break in their web of relations with other people, and that traditionally masculine success for women does pose such a threat. Clearly, gender contributes to the interpretation of the story: women bring their direct and indirect experience of success and its ramifications to the task of enlarging the Anne/John anecdote.

In a similar experiment, Gilligan, borrowing a "dilemma" from Lawrence Kohlberg's tests of moral development, asked eleven-year-old girls and boys to project a moral ending to the story of a man whose wife's death could be prevented by his obtaining an expensive drug. The druggist will not lower the price of the drug, and the man cannot afford to buy it. Children are asked, "Should [the man] steal the drug?" (Gilligan: 26). Again, it is not relevant whether the act, itself, of reading varies, nor are the answers given reliant on issues of basic comprehension. Gilligan argues that the situation is perceived differently by boys and girls because, generally speaking, boys and girls learn to make moral judgments using alternative (and often opposing) value structures. Boys are more likely to stick to the rules of a game, to pay attention to issues of legality, whereas girls are more likely to step outside the constraints of a problem to ensure that what they hold as moral imperatives (in this case, that life should not end because of a lack of money) are not compromised.

Certainly, if women and men gain access to and practice different strategies for structuring meaning, this will affect our lives as readers. This is not to deny the influence wielded by the "masculinist" reading strategies we all learn in school (as discussed earlier), but rather to assert that differences in taste and reading experience may persist despite formal education. From birth, women and men are bombarded with cultural messages about gender, with which we construct the hazy line between male and female realms of appropriate behavior. Gender becomes messy: women are often taught to aspire up to the male realm, and away from the least-valued areas within the female realm, while also receiving the traditional line on what femininity should be. Reading is one of those experiences so deeply embedded in gender issues, and yet so taken for granted in itself, that it is nearly impossible to point to clear-cut differences in reading behavior between men and women, outside of counting who buys what and who doesn't.

Self-help literature is a genre that participants recognize as existing specifically for women. This is true even for self-help books that are not overtly marketed toward a female audience (books that do not have the word "women" in their titles and that do not have obviously "feminine" covers). Participants see women either as uniquely equipped with positive abilities that enable us to use this kind of book, or as uniquely disadvantaged or incompetent in a society that discriminates against women, and thus induces us to turn to self-help books as a crutch for guidance. Within academic and popular feminism (including many self-help books), these conflicting ideas about women's socially constructed assets and liabilities reverberate. Feminist scholars both attempt to enumerate the various ways in which women have been oppressed; the ways in which women have resisted oppression; and the ways in which women have adapted to, accepted, and advanced the conditions of patriarchal hegemony.

I asked the readers I interviewed to explain why they, themselves, were drawn to self-help books, and why they think this genre appeals to women. In describing their personal use of self-help books, participants would describe certain concrete problems, or areas about which they sought information for personal reasons, but their generalized explanations for women's reading were much more firmly linked to social conditions.

Twelve participants described their reading as primarily focused on themselves; they read to find information that would help them work on certain characteristics that they believed needed amending (such as becoming more assertive or more organized), or they read hoping to attain self-understanding, or simply to gain edifying information on psychological matters in general. Often this self-work was connected to problems with other people; assertiveness, for instance, is a way of resisting the manipulations of others. Shelley said that reading books on assertiveness training helped her to dissect the problem—lack of assertiveness—as it operated for her: "I think that reading those sorts of books helps you to, first of all, identify what the issues are: that the behavior has certain sources, and that there are reasons—look at the underpinnings of the behavior. And once you begin to examine your own behavior, then through experience, and hopefully, positive reinforcement in those experiences, you're more willing to take those kinds of risks." As a child, Shelley felt she was taught to be afraid to ask for what she wanted and to feel like a victim. She first recognized a problem when she was placed in a supervisory position at work and "wasn't able to handle it." Reading self-help books helped her to gain this insight and to feel "much more assertive."

Liz read Dale Carnegie's *How to Win Friends and Influence People* (1936) to help her deal with a tense work situation, where she was having trouble with someone she supervised:

> The woman who's the secretary for our office constantly ran away. You know, she would say . . . "There's something to pick up somewhere," and she'd disappear for an hour. . . . And I . . . would just say, "Donna, you can't do that!" And Donna would just go. . . . And *my* boss was getting upset at me for not keeping up with Donna, and so I said, "You know, this isn't working." My friend Bill had just read this book . . . and he said, "You know, maybe some of this would help out in your situation."

Reading the book did help, Liz said, because "it made me examine how I was going about trying to solve a problem. And what I was doing was trying to express myself without ever really listening to [Donna's] underlying message." Carnegie's analysis convinced Liz that Donna was bored in her job, and that she absented herself to demonstrate this—perhaps unconsciously—to the rest of the office staff. "And what I did was, instead of telling Donna what *I* wanted her to do . . . I listened to why she ran away . . . and why she didn't want to be in the office. And we reexamined the tasks to which she was assigned, so that she had more to do in the office, and she could feel useful there." In this instance, Liz was motivated by a relational problem, but she conceived of the situation as self-oriented; her own behavior, she felt, was crucial to a satisfactory resolution of the problem.

A majority (eighteen) of the participants in my study read books concerning relationships with men because they were dissatisfied with the ones they had; because they wanted to understand something problematic in a specific relationship; or because a relationship had recently ended and they didn't understand why. Women in both categories (self-centered or other-directed readers) said that feelings of depression or dissatisfaction would often impel them to turn to self-help books. Women who read self-help because of their problems in relationships ranged from those who were very dissatisfied with this aspect of their lives, to those who thought there was always room for improvement or introspective examination.

Evelyn, at one extreme, felt that her relationships with men were completely and inexplicably terrible, and through self-help reading, she sought reasons for why this pattern persisted:

> If I understand things, I feel a little bit better about them; I don't feel so overwhelmed and so helpless. Because I've been very, very hurt, and very confused and very despairing in my relationships with men. I've been hurt in my relationships with women, and with others—meaning [my] children—too, you know, but nothing like—it's not the same. It's the depth, the intensity, the confusion, the craziness. I could always kind of figure out what's happening with myself and women friends, children—but not with men. I've always felt very victimized . . . and this has been helpful, so that maybe I could explain it to myself a little bit.

Ultimately, Evelyn said, reading was unsatisfactory because it did not offer analyses that she felt were complex enough; thus, the proposed solutions were superficial. "At the end," she said, "they just tell you the same thing anyway: 'Don't do it! Stop!'" Evelyn continued to read self-help books despite her feelings that they were overgeneralizing and simplistic because she found them soothing, because they made her feel less alone, and because she continued to hope that she *would* one day find a book that would offer a revelation, an answer.

Sarah said that when she broke up with her boyfriend, she turned to self-help books—checking about ten books out of the library at once—because: "I felt totally unable to deal with it myself." Like Evelyn, Sarah

said, "I was trying to put meaning to: why did Gary and I break up? . . .
'cause, you figure if you see it in black and white, it's like, 'Oh, good, I
feel better.'" And also like Evelyn, Sarah did not really expect the books
to provide her with an answer, but rather to make her feel less depressed
while she was reading. "I think [they] try to sort of simplify things that
are really, like, complex, and I don't end up getting too much help from
them. But I do get certain ideas," she said. Sarah said she did use
simplistic strategies offered by self-help authors from time to time, and
that they had been effective. "Like in the *How to Fall Out of Love with
Someone*, it had something like: If you can't get the person out of your
mind . . . you can go to the extent of like, smelling rotten eggs when you
think of the person." Sarah had done this, and laughed when she said it
did help a little.

Another participant, Sandy, said that reading self-help books helped
her to become more tolerant of "differences" between her husband and
herself, and that it encouraged her willingness to compromise with him.
She said:

> In my marriage, we come from two different ideologies, I think,
> and you have to find a middle ground. . . . He's very willing to . . .
> compromise, to see things other people see . . . . He's come a long
> way . . . from doing all the bills, and doing everything for me, to
> being more of a partner. And I think that's learned behavior for a
> lot of men—it was learned behavior for him. . . . I'm not sure what
> the direct effect would be, but reading someone who says—like
> [Leo] Buscaglia says—"You have to be very accepting of another
> person but not let that modify your behavior," I guess, [helped me]
> just be more accepting of the way [my husband] is. Because I was
> very judgmental about what he does. . . . [Reading has made me
> more] accepting that *he* has a choice to make. It's not *my* choice to
> make.

Through her reading, Sandy has come to conceive of her husband's and
her own behavior as much more separate; she feels less of a need to try
to influence him, as long as he remains willing to "compromise," and she
feels stronger in her unwillingness to adapt to his expectations, if they
are not in keeping with her (feminist) beliefs. Reading self-help books,
then, can be seen as a means of *not* changing, a way of defending the
integrity of one's views by aligning them with one's actions.

Nell described an instance of how a self-help book helped her to tackle a very concrete problem in her marriage. She said that she began reading *Intimate Partners* by Maggie Scarf (1987) because she was newly married and just generally interested in the topic of marriage. She found, as she read, that Scarf's analysis was applicable to the resentment she felt at her mother-in-law's constant attentions to her husband. She said, "It gave me, I think, a bit more insight into what was really going on there." She felt that reading *Intimate Partners* enabled her to understand her own anger at her mother-in-law's overbearing behavior (she felt invaded, and felt a judgment was being made against her as a wife) and helped her to understand the reasons behind her mother-in-law's behavior (her mother-in-law felt lonely and was trying to keep herself necessary in her newly married son's life). Nell said she also discussed her feelings about her new reading of the situation with her husband, and that together, they had talked about ways of resolving the problem. So for Nell, this particular self-help book enhanced communication in her relationship, which, she said, was "basically a very good marriage" in the first place.

Three of these (eighteen) women whose reading centered on relationships said that they first sought out self-help advice after they were divorced, and a fourth said her divorce intensified her reading. Carol explained that after her divorce, "I had a lot of free time, and just wanted to explore my feelings, and started reading them. And a lot of the ones [I read] at that particular point in time were dealing with . . . oh, self-confidence, self-image, and things of that nature, and positive attitude." So, for Carol, the breakup of her marriage led her to become more introspective.

Whether their reading was self- or other-oriented—or both—participants recognized that the problems they perceived as leading them to consult self-help books were often issues with which women, in particular, were likely to be concerned. In their more general explanations for why the genre attracts women readers, participants ranged in their valuation of self-help reading.

Val, Carol, and Lauren see women's use of self-help books as part of a skill women have in dealing with the emotional realm of life. Men, in contrast, are seen as emotionally inept.

VAL: I think we're emotionally more secure than a man could even begin to want, need, or desire [to be]. . . . Emotionally we're able to deal with every situation, whereas men have trouble just emotionally, with a lot of things that come across. That's what I think. And I don't think any self-help book is going to change that for a man. You know, they just don't have the same makeup women do. Emotionally, we're just totally opposite.

CAROL: I think women are more open to . . . be in touch with their feelings, and find things to make changes, where men avoid issues. And they don't, you know, they don't want to be confronted with a problem. They want to avoid it. And women will confront it. Women are the ones to take the initiative, and make the changes, and make all the effort and find out what can be done.

LAUREN: I think women tend to have more of an active world acting *in* and thinking about things, and reinterpreting things, and experiencing emotions, and experiencing maybe reactions to the outer world. . . . I think there's really a live inner space, which I don't think is any less real than what the outer world is, and I don't share this kind of contempt for it that some feminists do [where] it's just like a mushy, emotional, ridiculous, housewife, unreal space that isn't valid. . . . I think there's more tendency for women to work with that space, and imagination, and changing attitudes . . . resolving inner conflict and the inner conflict of others, being mediators for people, being emotional centers for people.

Val, Carol, and Lauren describe their own reading as providing a source of strength and growth. They tend to attribute this quality to the reading of women in general, as well. In their continuum of thinking behavior, Belenky et al. (1986) put what they call "connected knowing" at the apex. Connected knowers, they write in *Women's Ways of Knowing,*

> want to embrace all the pieces of the self in some ultimate sense of the whole—daughter, friend, mother, lover, nurturer, thinker, artist, advocate. They want to avoid what they perceive to be a shortcoming in many men—the tendency to compartmentalize thought and feeling, home and work, self and other. In women, there is an impetus to try to deal with life, internal and external, in all its complexity. And they want to develop a voice of their own to

communicate to others their understanding of life's complexity.
(137)

Connected knowers combine what Belenky et al. see as the best of what
has stereotypically been defined as masculine rationality and female
intuitive knowledge. They are holistic in their approaches to their lives
and to the world around them.

By describing their reading as an example of "emotional security,"
"confronting problems," and enhancing a "live inner space," Val, Carol,
and Lauren attest to reading's integrative capacity. These women, like
the "connected knowers" discussed by Belenky et al., describe their
reading as part of an effort to unify their life, to confront even painful
facets of their selves, in a way that they feel men are incapable of doing.
They also echo Gilligan's assertions that women are nurturers (for
whatever reasons), and that this "ethic of care" (as Gilligan names it)
motivates us to read books that can be applied to our relationships with
others.

Other readers' responses to my question "Why do you think women
are so much more likely to read self-help books than men are?" high-
lighted the same themes over and over again: women are more emotional, and men find the emotional world alien. Women are more
comfortable seeking help for problems we perceive in our lives, and are
more willing to recognize that problems exist than men are. In Bonnie's
words: "Men would rather go bowling, or go to a ballgame or drink three
beers. A man could be in enormous pain, and someone would say, 'How
are you?' 'Oh, fine'—even to a friend." Since women are more inclined
to express ourselves verbally than men are, according to Bonnie, we are
more apt to read about our problems since "a book is almost like talking
to someone, so it's kind of verbal." Bonnie saw her own reading experiences as interactive, "like a dialogue," and as a skill she had learned well
as part of her socialization as a woman in this culture. Despite the
increased valuation of an interdependence based on heightened communication within heterosexual relationships (Cancian 1987), these
readers do not perceive men as the able participants in self-knowledge
and expressiveness that women are.

Occasionally, readers would see women's self-help reading as evidence
of women's emotional deficiencies, as compared with men. Sarah,
Nancy, and Mona described women's predilection to read self-help as a

step taken out of weakness or unhappiness, and as part of women's general overindulgence in things emotional:

> SARAH: [Reading self-help books is] a passive kind of thing; it's not an active kind of thing. You just kind of sit back and the book tells you what to do. . . . I think men would tend more to, like, go out and do something and not tend to just sit and be passive and have somebody feeding them stuff.

> NANCY: They say it's a man's world out there, right? And women let themselves be manipulated all the time—and I'm not saying *all* women, but a certain type—I don't know. It just comes, I guess, from centuries, you know, where women always . . . were manipulated by them. And some men feel so superior. Women have a tendency to love too much, and they go by their emotions, and they let everything get carried away.

> MONA: Some women feel they have more to deal with than men, more emotional problems to deal with than men, because what you would take seriously, most men might just, oh, they'll brush it off and say, "that's not important." . . . Like, some women feel they're stuck in a rut. They're not working. They're housewives. . . . They just do the same thing over and over and they get so tired of themselves. They're looking for an escape, something else to do. So they figure, "Where am I going from here? What can I do to heal myself?" In that way, they may just look for a self-help book or something like that.

Sarah, focusing on women's passivity, seemed rather contemptuous of her own reading. Sarah had a master's degree in social work and viewed her reading of these popular-psychological books as both an extension of *and* a deviation from her professional interests. She knew that she turned to self-help books in times of bewilderment or trouble (e.g., when she and her boyfriend broke up), and thought that they fell far short of prescribing solutions that would answer her questions or solve her problems. At times in our discussion, she sounded resentful of her use of self-help books. Both Nancy and Mona, however, were only occasional readers of self-help and spoke as if they were distinguishing themselves from needier women users in their descriptions and criticisms of women readers in general. Neither had found self-help reading to be an especially empowering experience.

Other readers attributed women's reading to more specific factors that currently isolate women and create a need for comfort, of a sort. As Sandy, a twenty-six-year-old self-defined feminist, said:

> I think it's harder to be a woman. . . . I think that our roles right now are very complex. . . . It's kind of embarrassing almost, to talk about it. Especially, I have a hard time because all of the women I work with are much older than I am, and their experiences are different. I mean, they even had a harder time being women. And yet, they had an easier time, because the women that are older than thirty-five, they came at the height of the women's movement, where it was good to be feminist, and we're kind of at the tail end . . . where it's, "what are you bellyaching about? Everything's wonderful now." . . . I just think that there's no place to go for advice. You certainly don't go to your clergy, because they'll yell at you. . . . The impression I get is that there aren't as many women's groups as there used to be. . . . My impression of the sixties and early seventies is that it was much easier to network. And now, because we're supposed to be assimilated already, I think it's much harder.

Sandy sees self-help reading as filling in gaps—or providing outlets for discouragement—which were once satisfied by organized religion or feminist groups. Historically, American women within specific class and race-based groups have had more close-knit personal networks than American men, through which support and advice were offered pertaining to all realms of private life, and out of which protest often grew (see, e.g.: Collins 1990; Cott 1977; Echols 1989; Jones 1985; Smith-Rosenberg 1985).

It is possible that the emphasis placed on friendship in women's lives has diminished as we have entered the paid labor market in greater and greater numbers, as the division of labor has become more specialized, and as families have become smaller and more isolated. All these trends may have helped to professionalize the giving and receiving of advice, at least among the rich and middle class. Conversely, the professionalization of advice giving may have made obsolete certain therapeutic exchanges formerly taken care of as a matter of course in ordinary friend-ship. Women's reliance on distanced professionals (therapists as well as therapeutic authors) can be seen as another example of the increasing institutionalization and packaging of areas of women's experience—once considered to be simply a part of everyday life—into services that can be mass-produced for purchase.

Reading self-help books allows women to feel a part of an invisible, and thus somewhat illusory, community of other women readers who have the same concerns and problems. Most of the women I interviewed said that they talked to other people—at least, occasionally—about the books they read. Many said that they would recommend books they liked to their relatives or friends. So, books can enable women to make this illusive community real, to a certain extent. Sometimes readers find sharing self-help books with others beneficial, and sometimes not.

Several participants mentioned that they no longer recommend books because they had done so in the past, and their friends or relatives (most often, husbands) did not read the books. Carol and Val both said that they talked about the self-help books they read only with each other. Carol said she would recommend a book to Val if she "found that it's been inspirational and helpful to me, and if I know that she's either dealing with a similar situation, or the potential could arise." Carol and Val read many of the same books and think that this type of reading separates them in a positive way from their friends who don't read self-help. Carol said about Val: "She's about the only person that is—I'm not sure if this would be the appropriate word, but—*intense* enough to either have a discussion of this nature with, or that would enjoy these type of books." Joan said that she often discussed self-help books with her friends, and that, in the past, she had done this in an organized setting: "Three of us had formed a little C-R [consciousness-raising] group way back. . . . And we tend to, when we get together, always talk about what we've read, because I think we're still in that kind of trying to help each other kind of thing." Self-help, for Joan and her friends, became a group effort.

Most of the women I interviewed did not habitually discuss their self-help reading with others. Most women said that if it "came up" in conversation they would discuss their reading, or that if they read a book that they thought was particularly applicable to a friend's life, they would recommend it. Liz said:

I do [recommend books], if [my friends] seem to be in this kind of state where they would be, you know, at all interested. . . . Sometimes I do it if they like, want to dump this huge load of things that are related, you know. Like I kept on hearing about this woman's arguments with her boyfriend. And I was like, you know, "you do the same thing all the time, so . . . why don't you read this, and see if you can get out of the rut of it?" But mostly, you know, unless I hear it twice, I don't recommend books, because I figure that they're fairly, you know, kind of personal, and . . . I guess I basically feel that a lot of people don't read them, and would be insulted if I suggested it.

Readers were well aware that many people view self-help books as trashy or wasteful reading. Bonnie told me that upon finding out that she read self-help books, a friend of hers said, "You're so intelligent; I can't believe you read that crap!" Knowledge of disapproval or condescension impelled many of the women I interviewed to keep their reading to themselves. Indeed, many participants said that they would not read certain self-help books in public, especially at work. Carrying a book like *Smart Women, Foolish Choices* around, Bonnie said, is "really making a statement" that she would prefer not to make. She said—and many other readers concurred—that she would prefer to read self-help books "in the privacy of [her] own home." Just as these women read to feel less alien, they don't want other people deciding that they are maladjusted or stupid for reading these books.

Reading the Genre

Throughout my interviews, I asked women about the differences between reading self-help books and reading other kinds of books. Their interpretations of reading varied. Some women indicated that they distinguished self-help from fiction in terms of art: fiction, seen as art, could generate sensations in readers that nonfiction could not. Originality—in style or plot—was to be found there. Though identification with characters is also a part of reading fiction, participants rarely read novels for didactic purposes; rather, this identification was valued as an end in itself. Fiction was seen by some readers as having a more profound effect than self-help books could; and thus it was considered to provide a reading experience that was ultimately more valuable (than that provided by self-help reading). But fiction was also described as a provider of "escapes" from everyday life, whereas self-help reading made real life all the more inescapable by highlighting its most painful aspects. Many readers voiced *both* views: that fiction was a more sophisticated type of reading than self-help reading, and that it was a more escapist (and, consequently, useless) way to spend time. Certain kinds of fiction were seen as more admirable reading than others: Janet complained about women reading romances (which she said she had read avidly as a girl, herself): "I feel that all the women—grown women—who are . . . involved in a career should try to keep away from reading too many of those Danielle Steele and Harlequin romances . . . which I totally object to because I think it's very silly reading. Because it creates no knowledge for you. All it does is entertain you for a couple of hours." Self-help reading, in contrast, was seen by readers like Janet as more practical and applicable—definitely not entertaining.

Other readers also valued self-help more than other sorts of reading because it dealt with "reality" as opposed to the "make-believe" worlds offered by novelists. Rena said:

> When I go to the library I look at the nonfiction, I'm not very interested in fiction unless somebody has recommended something that they really have found good. . . . I don't like love stories. I don't like mysteries. I did read them when I was a kid, but I sort of feel I know them already. I mean, there are just so many plots to novels, and there are just so many mysteries that there can be. . . . But I think the other is really always fresh because . . . you're reading about something that pertains to you and your life.

Self-help makes stronger demands on readers than fiction does, participants believe. Self-help becomes difficult when it forces a confrontation with painful problems. (It can do so only if the reader allows it this power, and readers all have veto power.) Though reading can be painful, it can also lead to a strengthened self-conception. Molly explained that "those books helped me to identify the fact that I was not a victim." She contradicted the popular notion I heard when many nonreaders reacted to this research: that self-help books encourage self-blame and lead readers to shoulder responsibility for the consequences of deeply entrenched societal institutions (for example, patriarchy, which provides a plentiful supply of abusive men) over which readers can wield no real control.

When I asked another reader, Lucy, to explain what she gained from her reading, she said, "I keep thinking that word, individuation; I think that's what I get. You know, trying to find out where my center is, being an individual, appreciating myself. You know, celebrating myself, 'cause I'm a unique person." Many readers discuss self-help reading as a way to gain control over certain aspects of their lives, a way to bolster their self-confidence and to make them feel good about themselves, but they do not see these books as a force that will "change the world." Nor do readers expect self-help books to offer an all-encompassing plan to live by. (Readers of religious self-help books are an exception and will be discussed in the next chapter.)

The romance readers Radway (1984) interviewed often described their reading as a fulfilling "escape" from everyday life; she writes:

> These women believe romance reading enables them to relieve tensions, to diffuse resentment, and to indulge in fantasy that provides them with good feelings that seem to endure after they return to their roles as wives and mothers. Romance fiction, as they experience it, is, therefore, compensatory literature. It supplies them with an important emotional release that is proscribed in daily life because the social role with which they identify themselves leaves little room for guiltless, self-interested pursuit of individual pleasure. (95–96)

Self-help readers are less likely (than the romance readers Radway interviewed) to describe their reading as pleasurable—that is, as escape—though it does provide them with good feelings and with a different sort of emotional release or compensation. Bonnie, for instance, described her excitement to see and hold new books, and her obsessiveness in simply shopping for them: "The shopping for the books is very ritualized. It's like an aneurectic [anorexic] with food. I have to go to B. Dalton, I have to look at the whole rack, take them out, touch them." She laughed at her own behavior but assured me that what she said was true.

Frequent readers would describe looking forward to new self-help books, even hoarding them. Several said they knew which one they would turn to the next time they felt a need. The reading itself, however comforting, was not seen as diverting, like reading fiction. As Bonnie explains, "[With] the novel, you can forget yourself a little bit, it's like watching a movie. Even though you see similarities, or things that touch you, it's different. It's outside of you. The self-help book is piercing right into you. . . . You're always—you're reading the book—but you're looking at the book separately and objectively, saying, 'How does this impact on me?' The novel, you enter the world of the characters." And Cindy, who said that she considered biographies to be self-help books because they enabled her to reflect on her own life and because they gave her ideas about her own artistic development, valued these books for their reality; she said: "I like biographies 'cause I can relate to the person, see their actual face in my mind. . . . But when you're reading fiction, you know it's a story. It could have very strong possible truisms in it, but it's still a story. And you can separate yourself from it." Cindy sees biographies as *true* stories; and she believes the truth has the power to educate the reader in a way that fiction (untruth) cannot.

Readers see the activity of reading self-help books as a serious and self-reflective activity in which they seek a deep connection with the material they read, hoping, indeed, to read themselves. Despite the plenitude of case-study "characters" served up by self-help authors with whom readers can (and do) identify, this identification does not result in a detachment from reality the way it can in fiction. And though these women may find themselves *at times* in the characters of a work of fiction, this accomplishment is the whole point of their reading of self-help books.

When reading self-help, participants said they are more likely to subvert the physical authority of the text than they would in fiction: they skip around, read halfway through and abandon the book, read only the chapters they think will pertain to them or their particular situation, or even use a book by reading the back cover and quickly skimming through it in the bookstore. These methods do not mean that these women necessarily consider this a more casual or less demanding type of reading. At one point when she was reading self-help heavily, Carol kept a notebook which helped her to organize and encapsulize her reading: "[A] lot of times, during the particularly stressful period in my life, I even kept like a little journal of certain paragraphs or things that had specific impact on my life at the time, where I would just write them down and keep them handy so that I wouldn't have to go back and thumb through the whole book to locate that particular comment."

Just like the "connected knowers" discussed by Belenky et al. (1986), self-help readers "establish a communion with what they are trying to understand. They use the language of intimacy to describe the relationship between the knower and the known" (143). Self-help readers often spoke of their books as "friends," acknowledging that such a statement sounded "sappy" or "silly," but emphasizing how comforting an activity their reading could be. The women I interviewed described finding both nurturance and support through bad times by reading self-help books.

Self-help reading may be seen as a feminist activity in that readers come away feeling they have been addressed *as* women; but the sort of feminist inclinations that are affirmed for these readers are liberal ones. This may very well be because most of these women are already feminist in the liberal sense. Individualism and rational personal action are advanced by most of these women in their discussion of what they believe to be relevant strategies within the feminist agenda, as they see it. Women and men should be "equal" in a way that would not entail rebuilding institutions and revolutionizing the current constraints that structure intimate relationships. Most participants would balk at radical feminist—or Marxist feminist—interpretations of the depth of gender-related pathology in our culture, and these theoretical frameworks' assessment of the changes necessary to correct our problems. It is precisely for these reasons that I see self-help reading as falling short in terms of feminist practice. Though self-help readers do feel a sense of commonality with other women through their reading, the genre fails them in that it encourages individually oriented and adaptive endeavors to achieve personal change. So even though this reading does not necessarily lead to any radical change in women's lives, it does provide its readers with, at the very least, a momentary respite, a chance to be self-reflective and evaluative. These are opportunities that women, who are often cast as providers of such nurturance and counsel for men and children, have difficulty finding and receiving from other people. In this sense, like romance reading, self-help reading can be said to enable women to express dissatisfactions with gendered interactions, while it also represses a definitive challenge to the ways in which the social construction of gender works against women. This will become clearer as we examine the therapeutic assumptions with which women approach self-help books.

Chapter 2

Shrinking God: Psycho-Religious

Self-Help Reading

Her little Bible was extremely precious now; Ellen had never gone to it with a deeper sense of need; and never did she find more comfort in being able to disburden her heart in prayer of its load of cares and wishes. Never more than now had she felt the preciousness of that Friend who draws closer to his children the closer they draw to him. . . . [I]t was a joy to think that He who hears prayer is equally present with all his people, and that though thousands of miles lie between the petitioner and the petitioned for, the breath of prayer may span the distance and pour blessings on the far-off head. (Warner 1892 [1987 rpt.]: 540)

What was in [women's magazines] was promise. They dealt in transformations; they suggested an endless series of possibilities, extending like the reflections in two mirrors set facing one another, stretching on, replica after replica, to the vanishing point. They suggested one adventure after another, one man after another. They suggested rejuvenation, pain overcome and transcended, endless love. The real promise in them was immortality. (Atwood 1985: 201)

In *The Wide Wide World*, Susan Warner's bestselling novel of the late nineteenth century from which the first of the above epigraphs is taken, the protagonist is orphaned and mistreated. She finds hope and reassurance through the active practice of Christianity. Daily Bible reading makes her miseries bearable; being a Christian enables her to make sense of her life. In Margaret Atwood's *The Handmaid's Tale* (the source of the second epigraph), the title character finds a momentary respite from an overwhelmingly oppressive life in a future predicated on the current beliefs of the fundamentalist right. Religion, for the handmaid, structures her prison. Her clandestine perusal of a woman's magazine of the seventies in a society where reading is forbidden for women allows her a reverie similar to the spiritual release described by Warner.

Participants repeatedly said that their reading was prompted by a "search for answers" to overarching questions, on the one hand (e.g., "Why are we here?" and "What happens after death?") and less ethereal and more pragmatic questions, on the other ("How can I get along with so-and-so at work?" and "How do you exist in a world where you have to be appealing to men, but you also want to do something for yourself?") Readers differed in their opinions about whether or not answers to the "biggies" could be found through reading, and about which types of self-help books (religious or psychological or New Age) could best facilitate such a search. What these readers shared, regardless of the magnitude of their questions, was a quest for order and for sense. And though many readers articulated their search in specific terms—telling about reading to eradicate procrastination, or to deal with depression brought on by a severe case of asthma—most also described their reading as part of a struggle to define themselves in terms of everything else, a struggle to gain a coherent worldview.

Recent self-help books are most often associated with the field of psychology and may seem, on the surface, to comprise a secular genre. But several of the readers I interviewed spoke about their spiritual "growth" and religious convictions. Five women (of thirty) had read books that they described as religious self-help, and five others had read New Age books (including one reader of astrology). Odd though it may seem, a belief in supreme powers outside the self (which forms the foundation of religious belief) has developed strong ties with a genre that offers guidance toward gaining supreme faith in the self, itself, and that is predicated upon the principles of psychology-made-simple. In this chapter, I explore the links between religious and secular quests, between mainstream self-improvement, traditionally religious works, and New Age readings.

Assessing the Psycho-Religious Landscape

Perhaps the only thing one can safely say about the spiritual state of American society today is that a smorgasbord of possibilities exists for those who are looking for a place to put their faith. In the nineties, we hear less about est and more about the New Age; less about acupuncture and more about crystals with healing power; less about being reborn and more about achieving "recovery." "Deprogramming" sounds as if it might have more to do with evangelical cable shows going off the air than with parents retrieving their children from the Moonies. New Age, like the mellow music associated with it, does not pose the same kind of spiritual threat that fringe religious movements once did; we are not worried, as we were in the seventies, about strange cults snatching away our children, but more about hard-core traditional religious groups calling them "back."

We hear less now, too, of new kinds of therapies than we did in the seventies, when people were walking on coals and primally screaming. Encounter and consciousness-raising groups, if any, are seen as remnants of a more touchy-feely time. Instead of "getting in touch with their feelings," people try to figure out what their priorities are—a pragmatic eighties touch that contrasts with, even contradicts, the mushiness of the sixties and seventies pushing self-indulgence aside to let in efficiency. Yoga has yielded to Jane Fonda, who strips exercise of spirituality and drowns out the possibility of meditation with rock music. And endless therapy has shifted to programs that promise "recovery" in twelve steps. But now, more than ever before, our language is saturated with the dramatic, self-oriented vocabulary first popularized by the human potential movement; we discuss "having our needs fulfilled," "working at our relationships," "growing emotionally" through various involvements. The New Age contributions to this language straddle the line between practical and mushy: "channeling," an occult practice, sounds decidedly directed, while "getting in touch with one's inner child" smacks of California.

Religion can offer a worldview through which believers may understand their lives in relation to eternity; religion can be a way of fixing one's gaze and putting an end to disturbing questions. It can be a way of making sense out of nonsense, resigning oneself to the seemingly unalterable in life, or, as Marx described it, an "opium of the people" (1844 [1963 rpt.]: 44).

Psychology can do all the same things: in all the ways religion can be seen as liberating, or limiting and reactionary, so can psychology. Many recent self-help books are based upon an amalgam of both religious and psychological thinking. We have reached a point at which it is increasingly difficult to tell where one starts and the other begins.

Many scholars have attempted to define the current American spiritual and psychological climate, and to explain how it reached this point. Most see the American collective conscience as religiously fractured, fragmented, and pluralistic, infused instead with a therapeutic approach to living that seriously limits the social consciousness of its adherents by encouraging them to focus their energies selfishly inward (Bellah 1976; Bellah et al. 1985; Conway and Siegelman 1978; Glock 1976; Johnson 1981; Rieff 1966; Robbins and Anthony 1981; Rosen 1975; Tipton 1982a and 1982b; and Yankelovich 1981). But among these writers, there is less agreement about the precise nature of the convergence between the religious and psychological roots of what is happening now; about what the present state of affairs means in terms of today's social world; and about where it will lead us culturally. And none attempts to reveal how women's and men's experience of psycho-religion differs. I cannot offer a solution to these debates; but I believe highlighting them can help unravel—or perhaps reknit would be a more appropriate word—the fabric of psychological and spiritual practice in everyday life.

The dominance of the therapeutic worldview is seen as the result of a combination of factors: a highly fragmented division of labor within a competitive profit-oriented system (alienated labor); the breakdown of trust in traditional institutions (namely, the family, government, and the church); and modern antiauthoritarian developments in psychology (and popular-psychology) since Freud. Lack of direction, lack of commitment, and lack of community prevail, instigating introspection and self-involvement on a grand scale (Bellah 1976; Bellah et al. 1985; Conway and Siegelman 1978; Glock 1976; Mannheim 1956; Tipton 1982b; and Yankelovich 1981).

This interpretation, whether applied to Germans in the 1930s (Mannheim) or to the youth of San Francisco in the 1970s (Glock and Bellah), makes sense: social complexity leads to complications, contradictions, and conflict. The idea that modernization (industrialization, technological "advancement," urbanization) chips away at strong faith is certainly not new. In 1893, Durkheim described the declining salience of religion and rise in "individual variations" that accompany increasing division of labor (290).

The spiritual cohesiveness of the past to which many dismayed contemporary writers allude may be no more than idealistic yearning, for, according to Mary Douglas: "there is no good evidence that a high level of spirituality has generally been reached by the mass of mankind in past times, and none at all that their emotional and intellectual lives were necessarily well-integrated by religion" (1982: 29). She argues that secularization cannot be proven to be an effect of modernity.

In his essay "America's Voluntary Establishment: Mainline Religion in Transition," Wade Clark Roof writes: "The era of countercultural protest and institutional alienation has passed, yet the themes of personal freedom and individual fulfillment are very much alive" (1982: 142). Such values need not be taken as an indication that religious energy in America has been fading away, but simply that it has become more varied, and more self-oriented with recent developments. God may not be "far from things and men" (or women) as Durkheim wrote (290), just differently interpreted and applied to modern life. Roof argues that individualized religious beliefs are fostered through allegiance to "mystical" groups—or New Age groups, now—along with a regrowth in adherence to extremist factions of traditional religions. At the same time, "mainline" (politically liberal, or middle-of-the-road) religious movements are suffering a loss of membership. He writes: "Believing without belonging is an increasingly popular form of religious expression" (142). We have become secularized, but we have not lost religion altogether.

Central to scholarly evaluation of the modern self-absorbed religious spirit is the issue of whether or not a therapeutic approach means that we will become so self-consumed that we will not be able to interpret events in our lives using a sociological frame or a sense of social responsibility. Do psychologically oriented books encourage a narrow view—a laissez-faire conception of social interaction and of success (whether it be financial, romantic, or emotional)?

Richard Rosen (1975), who derides the recent popular-psychology phenomenon as "psychobabble," asserts that a single-minded focus on the individual results in an egocentric worldview, in which people are erroneously encouraged to feel that we can control every aspect of our destinies. He criticizes pop-psychology not for its ignorance of sociology, but for its glossing of *pure* clinical psychology, which he respects, but does not define clearly. In an essay on the prevalence of the codependency theme in current self-help literature, David Rieff sees links between the atomistic thinking of "inner child seekers" and the liberal or radical academicians he derides as "militants" whose "facetious cant of deconstructionism and Third World apologetics" has "hijacked" academic practice (1991: 50). The core of both movements, Rieff proclaims, is "the politics of victimhood": "In P.C. [politically correct] circles, this idea is inherently self-limiting in the sense that if the concept of oppression is to make any kind of sense, the situation of the various groups of victims—be they blacks, Hispanics, women, or gays—must be opposed to that of an oppressor group—these days, straight white males (50–51). Rieff does not follow through with his linking of academics with propounders of therapeutic "recovery," though he does go on to criticize self-help books for their inability to describe realistically social problems (which seems to be what he thinks is wrong with progressive politics in academia). Selfhood *as* a social problem, Rieff explains, is pure and simple self-indulgence.

Robert Bellah (like Rosen) traces the roots of overwhelming self-involvement to the sixties, which he describes as a time that caused "the erosion of the legitimacy of the American way of life." Bellah attributes more critical capabilities to those involved in the destruction than Rosen does, but the results are no more attractive. "Out of the shattered hopes of the sixties there has emerged a cynical privatism, a narrowing of sympathy and concern to the smallest possible circle, that is truly frightening," he writes (1976: 341–342). Though we may possess the faculties necessary to communicate, we are too apathetic to bother.

Daniel Yankelovich (1981), Flo Conway and Jim Siegelman (1978), and Steven Tipton (1982a and 1982b) concur with Bellah's indictment of the past as a morass of events and trends that have boggled the collective mind-set of the United States. They add fuel to Rosen's depiction of the sixties' creation of a language so full of meaningless jargon that it can't be applied successfully toward genuine expression, and that it limits its users' abilities to take stock adequately of the world around them. Yankelovich describes a conversation with one of the people he interviewed: "An excessive use of 'need' language, borrowed from self-psychology, makes it hard for her to think clearly. She can't arrive at lucid judgments about her life in these terms. She can't understand her true choices—within the private world she has created for herself as well as within the larger world she shares with others" (1981: 54). So first, therapeutic culture provides the illusion of unlimited choice, and then it makes people so inarticulate (when mired in its jargon) that we can't conceive of what our "true choices" are.

The therapeutic approach *has* become part of the way we think—or describe our thoughts through language—and presumably has become part of the way we behave also, as notions about satisfaction, self-determination, and obligations have altered. New religious movements (such as New Age philosophy) are considered a product of a solipsistic popular-psychology born of a solipsistic decade and, like both, are labeled antisocial twists on the theme of frustrated lack of connections.

Women are uniquely situated amid the psycho-religious confusion produced by and since the 1960s because research has so long neglected or trivialized our experience, and because women's interactions with both psychological and religious institutions have always been different from men's. American women have long used religion as a means of reassurance that a better world existed, creating woman-centered, comforting, and empowering religious communities (Cott 1977; Douglas 1977; Simonds and Rothman 1992; Tompkins 1985). What does religious reading do for women, then, and how do its effects compare with psychological self-help reading?

Many of the women I interviewed see their reading as a result of the increasingly weakening influence of institutional forces (most often mentioned were religion and family). These changes are viewed as having been sparked by the political activities of the sixties. Social critics are wrong, I think, to hold the sixties responsible for the political or social apathy of today, and to ridicule sixties politicos for their unfocused radicalism, or the unrealized goals of such a political agenda. For women, especially, the political developments of the sixties should be seen, rather, as an inspiration worth reclaiming in these reactionary times. The sixties mood, whatever it was exactly, was not the creator of the present mess, however it might be defined, but a potential revolutionary force that has been silenced.

Ehrenreich, Hess, and Jacobs (1986) argue that for women, the sixties was a time of political and sexual awakening. They chart changes in ideas about sexuality through an examination of sex manuals that draw on popular-psychology. These books are even antireligious in their adherence to self-centeredness and sensual fulfillment. Can adherence to psychological principles offer a valuation of the self that would not be possible within traditional Judeo-Christian pre- and proscriptions for what womanhood should mean? The answer is not so clear, according to Ehrenreich et al. They demonstrate the complexity of advice offered to women by including a chapter about the influx of popular-psychological notions about sexuality into fundamentalist Christian prescriptive literature for women. However bizarre the result of this mix (and it is bizarre), the very existence of such a merger indicates that it may be impossible to try to separate the psychological from the religious components of belief as they swirl together into cultural expression. Indeed, the religious participants—none of whom are completely fundamentalist in their views—reveal the odd, yet entrenched, union of psychology and religion in their words. There are, however, distinct differences between the two realms, which resist combination.

Psychological Reading

Many psychologically-oriented self-help authors want to deemphasize women's connections with others. Even some self-defined feminist authors conclude that women's problems could be solved if we would only strive to be more like men: more aggressive, more detached, more rational. Beginning with Betty Friedan's *The Feminine Mystique* (1963), women are told that our "overinvestment" in others (men and children) can become pathological: we are told we are damaging them and ourselves. Friedan recommends that (middle-class) women abdicate control of the homefront (presumably by hiring poorer women to do the work) and pursue satisfaction by becoming educated enough to gain access to fulfilling work in the paid labor market.

Ironically, at the same time that Friedan issued her appeal, middle-class men were bemoaning the alienation involved in conforming to company standards in the work world (Ehrenreich 1983). Germaine Greer (1970), Nancy Friday (1977), Colette Dowling (1981), and others follow in Friedan's footsteps; all offer versions of this interpretation of women's dangerous socialization (*as* women and *of* children). Connections themselves come to be seen as dangerous when women, especially, forge them—as the bestselling *Women Who Love Too Much* by Robin Norwood (1985) indicates so clearly by its title. The culprit, according to these books, is not women's biologically based masochism à la Freud, but a cultural disease passed down to us by our mothers, who were sometimes abetted by our fathers, which we have mistakenly clutched in desperation and unhappiness. Still, in all these books, authors focus not on the context so much as the results of the problem (now, invariably, with a name), and women appear to be the cause.

For women traveling through a world landscaped by popular-psychology, "identity" seems a very fragile, intangible construction, one which is very easily misplaced. Friedan writes, for instance, "It is my thesis that the core of the problem for women today is . . . a problem of identity—a stunting or evasion of growth that is perpetuated by the feminine mystique" (77). Authors' focus on questions of identity exaggerates women's contributions to our own obscurity: How do you know when you have identity? How can you stop it from trickling away, or becoming eclipsed, or merely reflected, by the radiance of a man?[1]

In *The Social Construction of Reality*, Peter Berger and Thomas Luckmann (1966) describe therapy as a means of social control, in which "a body of knowledge that includes a theory of deviance, a diagnostic apparatus, and a conceptual system for the 'cure of souls'" is required (104). The books, as I read them, do convey the message that women's actions are deviant; however, they are, at the same time, *not* deviant, because (the books explain) so many women are acting this way.

The meaning of therapy varies considerably among the women I interviewed, but most were therapeutically oriented in that they saw the goal of therapy as a meaningful one: to forge a positive identity both apart from and in connection with others. (To me, this sounds a lot like Berger and Luckmann's notion of a "system for the 'cure of souls.'") Several participants described entering therapy as a pragmatic line of action: one has a problem, one admits it, one pays someone to help with it, and ideally, through these actions, one eradicates the problem. More often, therapy was described as a lengthy process that could help one deal with a whole conglomeration of problems that extended back to childhood. Or one might not even have any specific namable problems—who wouldn't benefit from the opportunity to unload emotional baggage on a weekly basis? Therapy was thus described as a productive unburdening of everyday problems that could be helpful to anyone.

Reading therapeutic self-help books was different, the women I interviewed agreed, from entering into therapy itself. The power dynamics

were different; the cost was significantly different; the processes themselves (of reading and therapy) were different; and the outcomes would
often—but not always—be different.

Therapy was often described as an unaffordable luxury (or if not a
luxury, most women mentioned that therapy may be prohibitive in cost).
Many participants described self-help books as the cheaper end of a
therapeutic continuum, where therapy was seen as the most desirable,
but least attainable, end. As Val said: "I would love to be able to afford to
go to a therapist, but unfortunately that's not in the budget, and I don't
really have that many close friends that I could really say how I really felt
about a situation. So it's sort of a process of elimination, really."

Though therapy can be socially stigmatized, it can also help to establish status, as Lauren described her first experience with a therapist in
tenth grade: "All my friends were doing it, and it was a social thing. . . .
It was something that we did . . . but I didn't think I really had a
problem."

Most readers in my study recognized therapy as a legitimate and
fruitful endeavor, but part of what made them decide to read therapeutic literature rather than seek face-to-face therapeutic intervention was
their distrust of professionals in this area. They were suspicious of
therapists both because they were being paid to help as long as treatment continued (so why should they ever "cure" you?) and because
professional training alone was not necessarily respected. Readers did
not respect psychology the way they might chemistry; it was not seen as
completely reliable and "scientific." Many readers suggested that therapists could have the same problems they did. As Lucy said, in formal
therapy "you have the chance of running into a real asshole of a
therapist."

Why, then, should a psychologically trained author be treated as an
authority? Doing therapy is not necessarily thought of as applying a set
of skills that take years to master, but rather as something that people
can (and should) undertake themselves. One reader, Janet, who read
mainly work-related self-help books, voiced one of the same objections
about psychological self-help books that other readers raised about
therapy: "I hate to read something and I'm pinned down. I hate to read
a book and the book is telling me too much, 'you must do this, and you
must do that.' I want the book to give me examples, take me into an
experience . . . and I will feel a little bit more comfortable. Once I am
reading a book, and this book is telling me 'well, you should do this, and

you should do that,' I put it down right away because it's too demanding on me."

Janet said that she reads self-help articles in women's magazines, but would rarely purchase and read an entire book, because of her belief that it would be overly prescriptive and repetitive. For most readers I interviewed, however, authority is questioned less in book form than in person; it's almost as if the actual physical personhood of the author of the book melts away, and all that is left is the book itself, and the reader's self applying the therapy. (Participants also tend to respect what comes to them in the form of print because it is in print, as I discussed earlier.) Several participants voiced the belief that if something were not well-researched, genuine, or expertly presented, it would not have been selected for publication.

Emily raises the issues that resonate throughout these women's descriptions of the differences between solitary and face-to-face therapeutic action:

> Well, reading . . . let's say, you're in a quiet room . . . and you can more or less weigh the situation for yourself, but with a therapist, don't forget, that's time, money, and I would question sometimes. . . . Maybe this person has the same problems I do. Where does this person seek help from? Or who is this person being guided by? Or whatever. Maybe the books don't have all the answers, but it would give you . . . something to direct you on the right path. . . . With someone that you're going to see once a week, or twice a week, maybe you don't feel comfortable enough to open up to this person all your inner thoughts and your ideas. . . . [But] as you're reading, you can kind of be your own therapist, more or less . . . kind of get it together yourself.

Emily does short-term counseling in a health clinic where most of her clients are women. She holds therapy in lower esteem than the other women in social-work professions who participated in this research, all of whom were involved in providing more extensive, long-term therapeutic services to their clients. Reading, as Emily describes it, is an activity over which the reader has ultimate control: there is no one else shaping the situation or intruding upon her privacy. Ironically, it is almost as if the author—who Emily thinks is likely to be more reliable than a run-of-the-mill therapist performing *in person*—does not exist.

Emily's discussion of the potential mistrust one would have to overcome to "open up" to a stranger, and thus make of a stranger an
intimate, recurs in many of the women's explanations of how therapy
differs from reading. Several women focus on the intrusiveness they see
as inherent to a relationship with a psychological professional: "opening
up" is seen not as a therapeutic accomplishment, but as a potential lapse
in judgment or at least as an unreasonable expectation on the part of
therapeutic workers. As Mona commented:

> Okay, a therapist might say it's confidential, but . . . you're not
> going to open up 100 percent unless you're under drugs or you're
> hypnotized. Because I know I won't. . . . Because there's deep dark
> secrets that we keep that you wouldn't want anyone else to
> know. . . . When you go to someone, you're going to talk, but
> you're not going to tell them everything. When you read a book,
> certain chapters, or certain things are going to . . . relate to your
> specific problem. You can relate to that, and maybe analyze your-
> self through what they're saying. Whereas, with a therapist, or
> whoever, they're going to do all the analyzing for you after they
> hear all your secrets—if you tell them all of it, which I know you
> won't, because I can't see anyone revealing their inner soul to no
> one.

Most women were not as suspicious of therapy as Mona (who had never
been in therapy). But most did touch on the possibility of getting bad or
inappropriate therapy. Entering into therapy entails a risk because there
is no way of knowing in advance what you will get. With a self-help book,
readers decide what to take. Self-help reading and therapy are potential
sources of authority offering validation, but readers actively evaluate
whether or not to accept such authority. So, though they respect and
accept authority at times, they do not look to experts to supply a value
system (cf. Adorno et al. 1950 for a treatment of people as much less
active participants in shaping personal ideology).

Readers differed in their expectations about what a good therapist
should do, but most agreed (therapists included) that s/he should not
be too authoritative. They recognized that therapists walk a fine line
between offering opinions and helping clients to uncover their own,
between telling clients what to do and helping them to discover by
themselves what their course of action should be. Though books were

often perceived as more overtly directive, this did not necessarily mean they were better, but simply less subtle than a real, live therapist might be. As Lauren said:

> Reading is like going to a lecture; you're kind of anonymous. You don't necessarily have to ask questions or really apply it to yourself or really think. You just kind of listen. And sometimes the writing is very strong, and will say, "this is you!" . . . But [authors] reach you in a different way from someone in therapy would, who . . . begins in a totally different direction of *you* starting with *you*. . . . when you're reading a book there's a line, it's like a book is being written for a reason, it's to address like one issue, or something. Even the spiritual books that are addressing the issue of the human condition—it's one issue. . . . And you know it's them, and their shtick, and you kind of do it. But in therapy it's not as clear that that person has a shtick. . . . I mean, obviously they have something they're trying to do, but they're not as open about it. . . . At least with the book, they can't manipulate you as directly.

There is some confusion in Lauren's description of the authority or point of view of the therapist versus that of an author of a self-help book. She describes face-to-face therapy as a situation in which interpretation of the expert can be more difficult than it would in reading ("it's not as clear that [the therapist] has a shtick"). But she also asserts that in therapy one has less power to resist the views offered by the expert than one does with a book (which you can reject without risking hurting anyone's feelings or confronting any troublesome power dynamics in the therapist-client relationship). So Lauren portrays face-to-face therapy as requiring more interpretive power, and possibly more resistance ("At least with the book they can't manipulate you as directly").

Participants, especially those who had experiences with one-on-one therapy, viewed therapy as much more diffuse than therapeutic reading, an experience which was valued for the process itself. Sarah explained that, "at this point, the therapist I have right now wouldn't [recommend or discuss self-help books] at all. She's more like analytic, and into dreams and that kind of stuff." Therapy is, thus, much less practical or pragmatic than the self-help books that derive from its tenets, and some readers (therapists, especially) valued it more for its abstractions. One of the social workers I interviewed said that she would recommend self-help books to her clients because she thought they were an effective, albeit overly simplistic, adjunct to face-to-face therapy.

A recent article in the *New York Times* reports that many psychologists do recommend self-help books to their clients, while others study the difference that results from reading. Self-help books can be effective, researchers report; Forrest Scogin, a psychologist at the University of Alabama, has compiled the results of over forty studies that compare reading self-help books with entering therapy, and concludes that "psychotherapy had an advantage, but only a slight one" (Goleman 1989).[2] Of course, Scogin's—and other trained therapists'—views of what makes different activities therapeutically effective may differ from the evaluations of the users of these methods.

Comments made by Lucy and Bonnie illuminate the differences many of the women I interviewed raised in comparing therapy with reading self-help books:

> LUCY: Well, I figure a therapist is there, you have one hour, you know. And a lot of those hours—I wouldn't say wasted, but—they are like a lead-up point to maybe a lightbulb or a revelation. Where a book sometimes you can get that a lot quicker.

> BONNIE: I know how it's different. An official therapist does not say: "Now here are three things you're gonna do to meet a man." Now the self-help book will promise me that if I do five things—the promise is either stated or implied. . . . Therapy is more like real life. The self-help book is this artificial world, fantasyland.

Although therapy may be more effective in the long run, self-help books enable readers to accomplish goals faster, or at least—as Bonnie implies when she calls a self-help book an "artificial world, fantasyland"—may provide the illusion of a solution faster. Some readers, like Bonnie, were explicit in their assertions that this "illusion" was what they sought, what they found comforting in times of stress or pain. Face-to-face therapy was generally seen as freer of illusion, and certainly freer of false promises than self-help books.

Several participants stated that reading was easier in that it meant they did not have to go to the trouble of negotiating a relationship with a professional therapist. The "clinical situation," as Carol calls it, can be intimidating and can work against gaining "information."

> I think the books actually have been as much of a benefit as the therapist. I think they've—in a lot of cases—given me a lot more information because when you're in a clinical situation, a lot of times, you're nervous and everything is happening so fast, and you know you're restricted because you only have an hour or something like that, where things, you know, escape you. And you don't remember what actually was said or what you were actually told to do, where with the book, you have an instant recall. You can always go back and reread the chapter, or you know, take your time reading it, highlighting specific information. And I've found that the books are very, very helpful.

Carol framed both therapy and therapeutic reading as quests for information, practical exercises where one could reveal emotions through the intervention of a therapeutic instrument (the live or paper expert) and eventually overcome the problems these emotions cause.

However much the reading process may be controlled by the reader, therapy in book form is seen by most participants as much less specifically geared to their needs, because these books are written with the explicit goal of appealing to a mass market. An author of a book can offer insights, but not personalized insights in the same way a therapist might. People with whom you have an ongoing interaction have the ability to show you parts of yourself you might not be able to see, and might not be able to tap into while reading. Sarah (who said earlier that her therapist would not recommend or discuss self-help books because they were facile compared to her [the therapist's] psychoanalytic methods) also stressed her personal connection with her therapist as a factor that made face-to-face therapy more effective than self-help reading:

> I think therapy really gets into things, really gets into issues, and really helps me change. Because I think the whole root of it is really changing certain behaviors or thoughts, or whatever. And also that [therapy] helps me really see myself more clearly, and a book normally, a book doesn't do that for me, because a lot of

times, it's hard to see yourself. So it's nice to have a person sort of telling you what they see, or telling you what they hear you saying kind of thing. That just can't happen in a book.

Good therapy, according to Sarah, works like a mirror held by someone else, because "a lot of times, it's hard to see yourself" by yourself. A therapist who knows you can help solidify a sense of ever-elusive identity.

But, Sarah goes on to explain, live therapy is not always available, nor are friends. Books can be used to fill a gap created by propriety. There is a point when you feel you are imposing on friendships; books, in other words, can be your friends, can be your therapists, in time of need. She explained: "When I'm feeling very needy, I think just for me, it's hard to like keep calling friends, or you know, you can't keep going for therapy, and so there's the book, it's right there, so you could just open it up . . . so it's like reassurance to just open a book and read a line . . . and feel like maybe that's something a friend would have said, actually. . . . It might not really help, but it is like a reassurance."

Hiring a therapist or buying a self-help book is like buying a friend. In a time when most women are working full-time outside the home it becomes increasingly difficult for friendships to remain central to women's lives, so friends become providers of leisure-time diversion rather than of an intimate, everyday connection. Women still have what participants consider to be much deeper friendships than men do, but friendships do not necessarily involve the day-to-day intimate knowledge of one another's lives that they seemed to in the past. And since services like therapy *can* be purchased, providing therapy in friendship may seem less appropriate or necessary than it once did.

In talking about the conditions that have led to the current success of the self-help genre, Lucy said: "Women were home thirty years ago. Women talked on the phone. Women talked, you know, in their daily life. We don't have time now. We're so busy. We're so pressured. I don't always have time to talk to a friend. I'm not going to call a friend at 11:30. But I'm gonna read a self-help book." Purchasing self-help books to fill in the gaps that come from becoming work-oriented seems easier, and often more practical, than buying a professional's time.

Ironically, privacy and independence are much more highly valued in a therapeutic culture than communalism and interreliance, and the encouragement of these very characteristics may lead to the anomic conditions that create a "need" for professional therapy—in live or book form. Though many participants implicitly stated they felt the need for therapeutic connections with others, only Lauren expressed her desire explicitly and objected to the idea of paying for a service that should be considered a regular part of human interaction, something "offered by the world."

Participants who did therapy for a living were much more likely than nontherapists (unsurprisingly) to talk about self-help books as possibly the first step in a therapeutic process in which therapy itself was seen as the ultimate, crucial, and most promising means toward change. They saw reading as a much simpler step to take, not only because it didn't involve the same social stigma as therapy might, but because it didn't require the sense of commitment which they viewed as necessary to ongoing therapy. Anna said: "I think for some people . . . if therapy or counseling or whatever is too threatening, or even, like, even self-help groups like AA, which isn't really run by a professional. . . . if that's too threatening, I think people are more prone to pick up a book." She went on to say that reading, though "one step removed" from actual therapy, could allow its participants to opt out of actively working to solve their problems: "If you're in a situation that's painful or . . . that's something that you want to change, you don't have to confront it directly by talking about yourself." She felt that a good therapist would be more effective at treating deeply rooted problems and criticized the books for providing what she saw as only a surface level of treatment.

Anna and Hillary (also a therapist) both discussed the possible danger in reading self-help books, if readers were to treat them as a cure-all or as a substitute for therapy in the face of complex problems. This, they felt, would be a shortcut that would lead readers only in the wrong direction.

Religious Reading

A traditional religious interpretation of the "feminine mystique" opposes the psychologically based, identity-focused thinking: women have become selfish—or, if not selfish, misdirected—in their energies. Ideally, women should be home, ministering to their husbands, children, and home. Traditional religious women who participated in my study sometimes had trouble reconciling their conservative, religious-based views with economic reality and with the egalitarian rhetoric that has become taken for granted by many people in the eighties. I asked Marianne, a self-defined Christian who thinks the Bible is the best, most complete self-help book available, to discuss her beliefs about the differences between men and women, as they have been influenced by her religious reading. She explained that though "men and women are equal," gender-based differences in power made sense to her:

> I think inside we're equal; we just have different bodies. . . . But in a marriage relationship, to me, the husband is the head . . . of the wife and the head of the home, but it doesn't mean they're not equal, it's just, *somebody* has to be in charge. I think as far as decision making, it's equal, but if there's a disagreement, I think the husband has, like, the final say. . . . And I, personally, think that mothers should be home with their kids. And I don't have any qualms about—like, my sister works, you know, and I know a lot of people—a lot of women—do, and I have no problem with that. But it if was me, I would—if I had children—I would try and stay home, because I think a mother should be with 'em, you know, 'til they get in school, at least.

The tension between patriarchally based religious prescriptions and proscriptions regarding women and a popular-psychological framework—shaped, in part, by the women's movement—results in similar, but more self-conscious, equivocations on the part of the other religious readers I interviewed. Shelley, who considers herself both a feminist and an Orthodox Jew, said, "I won't tell you that there's not a lot of sexism in [Judaism], but that's the trade-off that I've made." Achieving the sense of community and wholeness of life she desired led Shelley to strike a bargain of sorts, in which she would deemphasize some of her feminist beliefs.

Involvement in traditional worship tends to include membership in a religious community, whereas therapy is commonly thought of as a simple one-on-one exchange (designed for the benefit of the client and the profit of the professional). I interviewed two women who had become practicing Orthodox Jews during their adulthood (of whom Shelley was one); both explained that the community and the sense of belonging they hoped to gain were a large part of what motivated them to embrace religion:

DIANE: I think this was appealing to me because this is who I am. These are my roots. I am a Jew, and I think on a spiritual level or a soul level or a very internal level, I am connected to Torah because I am a Jew. It's just a matter of sticking in the plug, you know, to get plugged into the source where you come from.

SHELLEY: I decided that there had to be a better way of life. . . . When I was . . . twenty-six, I was living on the East Side, and I was teaching at a small girls' college . . . spent the summer in a house full of singles. . . . And I was living in the middle of this, you know, enormously anomic situation. . . . People weren't connected to each other. And I met somebody . . . I really had the sense that he was part of a community. . . . There was something very appealing to me about this sense of community that I saw this fellow talking about.

Both Diane and Shelley describe their adult involvement with Judaism as a return. Reading helped both to reinforce and to expand their newfound sense of community and religiousness. Diane said she had been led away—and astray—from the values of Judaism by a decadent suburban life-style which led to a divorce, which led to an even more decadent urban life-style. Shelley said she had had a Jewish upbringing, and that "my parents had always told me that if I married a non-Jew, they would sit *shivah* for me," so a rebirth of Judaism in her life eliminated potential family problems.

Amelia, a devout Christian, tells of a similar return to the religious structure of her youth: "We were really brought up in a Christian home. . . . My mother would make sure we prayed in the morning and prayed at night. You know, when you become a teen, you start partying . . . these [religious] things are not important anymore. And as you get older, you realize that it *is* important. It's helped you through your life. . . . And then you go back." Each of these three women describe their religious revivals as natural developments. This belief that belief itself is fated adds to each one's sense of security, and her sense of the rightness of her return.

Amelia read both psychologically oriented and religious self-help books, but had difficulty finding words to describe the differences between these two types:

A religious self-help book gives me what I need in—spiritually. Sometimes you can put both together, and come out with the results that you want, but I prefer to read spiritual self-help books, because I feel that, like, professional self-help books, I know where I'm heading, but I'm also trying to get there. . . . I want to be a good Christian. . . . I want to be a good person, that I am able to really help someone . . . and be unselfish. This is the big word, being unselfish.

Religious reading, for Amelia, offers necessary affirmation of the sort of person she has chosen to be, like positive reinforcement. She believes that religious self-help reading is more important than "professional" self-help because it helps to maintain qualities she sees as residing on a deeper or "spiritual" level. Amelia does not consider psychological and spiritual advice incompatible; she does not see the unselfishness to which she aspires to be negated by psychological prescriptions.

Psycho-Religious Reading

One might expect that women who lead lives structured by Orthodox religious dogma—Jewish or Christian—extol the values of self-sacrifice, of giving, perhaps even of self-abnegation for the sake of their families. As Marianne's exhortations about staying home with her children and Amelia's descriptions of "a good Christian" indicate, they do cling to these traditional values. But they also don't. Conventional "feminine" qualities were not the central components of the belief systems of any of the four religious women I interviewed. Though a belief in the importance of serving others for the sake of a better world was certainly part of their faith, each explained what religion did *for* her, and how it had attracted her to it with its promises of a better life.

Diane, for instance, insists that the basis of Judaism is that "God made this planet and made us . . . to enjoy the planet. . . . We're here to be happy." The human part of the bargain involves following "simple rules for living." Amelia said, "If I come in [to work] and I feel very heavy, I have a problem, and I sit and I read the Bible . . . I feel better. . . . Since I started reading my Bible and reading books like that, I have felt much better as a person."

The main difference between religious and psychological orientations is that in a religious quest, the searching is far more likely to come to an end that satisfies the searcher. In a sense, once the commitment to believe has been made, the hardest work has been done, and major doubts are overcome. You have your answers ("blueprint," as Diane calls it, and all that's needed is daily maintenance. You don't have the anxiety of not knowing—or not knowing the most important material—or wondering if your belief will change. With belief comes a reason to live, and only believers (believers believe) are provided with an uncomplicated program to carry out. As Max Weber wrote: "Religion claims to offer an ultimate stand toward the world by virtue of a direct grasp of the world's meaning" (1915 [1946 rpt.]: 352). As these women experience it, religion involves a therapeutic sense of entitlement and a feeling of certainty about how the world works.

Therapy, on the other hand, can go on endlessly; the search for the elusive self you want to know intimately may never end. The psychological search is built upon repeated reexamination of one's particular past, but the religious quest need not concern itself with this at all. (Perhaps this is why there has been a recent surge of interest in Orthodox religious movements, as Roof contends.) So, though it can cohere with psychologically-based self-exploration, religious searching may also be seen as a rejection of therapeutic self-centered values.

Though predicated upon different values, religious and psychological searches may yield the same general ends. The narratives of Diane and Molly show how two self-proclaimed searchers achieved a contented tolerance about aspects of their lives that had once made them unhappy. Diane explains that within an Orthodox Jewish framework, she has learned to accept what happens to her as "God's will":

> Everything God does to us is for the good, even though we might not perceive it as good. . . . I've looked back over my life, at things that I was angry about and couldn't handle, and [things] I was heartbroken [about]. . . . I realize that everything that was denied me, in this life, here—*thank God* it was denied me. I mean, I would have been miserable in each situation had it gone the way I thought it should go at that point. . . . So anything that happens to me, whether I like it or not, at this point, somewhere down the road, I'll be able to look back and say, "I understand." . . . I can deal with anything that happens to me now.

Diane tells about being jilted by the man who originally "brought her back to Judaism." Heartache was still heartache, but it was heartache that made sense to her, because it was part of God's plan. Diane sees mainstream self-help books about relationships as overly analytical: "If you run across a 'man who can't love,' you go on to another man. You don't bother analyzing: 'What if I do this? What if I do this?' It gets me crazy." Women don't need self-help books to understand their relationships with men, because, according to Diane, "Now, when you date a guy, you really know deep down in your gut what the story is. You don't want to believe it, perhaps, or . . . want to say, 'no, I can change it.' "

Diane asserts that women suffer in relationships precisely when we attempt to dissect them psychologically: "I think that we've gotten so wrapped up in overanalyzing everything that we've forgotten to trust our instincts." For Diane, Judaism incorporates definitions of women and men as instinctual beings designed to love one another in a specific, prescribed manner, and meddling with this can lead only to problems.

Though this may sound like a sort of "blind" faith that might be experienced only by the deeply religious, I would argue that it is not completely blind, nor is it simply religious. Diane has clearly chosen this route. Though it may result in a decided lack of critical analysis, *she* has decided that such critical analysis never accomplished anything for her, and her faith in the omniscience and omnipotence of God makes it meaningless. Prior to becoming a religious Jew, Diane said she had "investigated" Hinduism, Buddhism, and Christianity. "I was always searching, searching to make all the pieces of the puzzles fit—in my life, and in society. . . . I was spiritually searching because I felt I needed something to tie my life together." And Judaism clearly satisfies Diane's desire for order and structure. When something about the system she has chosen doesn't make sense to her, she waits. "In Judaism, if you believe, you take a lot of things on faith, without understanding. Then, eventually, the understanding comes to you, and *invariably*, it makes sense." Diane uses religion *in a therapeutic manner* to make sense of her life.

Like Diane, Molly talked about having changed her expectations about her life—especially about her involvements with men—but as a result of psychological reading: a self-imposed behavior modification exercise that has taught her to expect less in the long run. She said: "I've made like a deliberate attempt to be less demanding and less intense, and I've tried to think more, well . . . 'what are their [men's] feelings?'

instead of just always being oriented toward what I was feeling. Try to feel them out and be more tolerant."

The question arises: can't both the religious and therapeutic routes to the same end be seen as methods of adapting to the inadequacies of heterosexual relationships? Both Molly and Diane have accepted the notion that involvements founded upon socially enforced divergent gender behaviors for men and women—where men's behavior stays the way it is, and women adapt—are appropriate. They have both found ways of accepting that the love they want, need, even crave isn't going to come. (Molly described being "almost frantic" without a romantic prospect in her life before her therapeutic revelation.) Diane would object to this analysis, saying that she didn't become an Orthodox Jew because she was having trouble in her relationships with men. Judaism, for her, now, is an all-encompassing solution to the problems of life in general (not just romantic ones). She did not come to Judaism "in pain," she said, but rather because she was looking for a better way to live. And Molly might object as well, saying that her behavior before reading self-help books was truly detrimental to her own well-being, that now—as less demanding, less concerned, more "manlike"—she is better off.

I asked Molly whether she thought that self-help books encouraged self-blame and obscured a recognition of larger, even uncontrollable social factors, and she replied: "I just think that anything that's gonna help you as an individual realize, like, why you're acting the way you do, like, even though . . . there may be broader things that are gonna prevent you from changing it, it's got to help you in some way, just to even be able to recognize it in the first place." Psychologically oriented self-help books promote an image of the individual as the unit of society, so even when a problem is societal, the unit of change can only be the individual.[3]

Molly continued her explanation of how books don't blame readers by saying, "If you can't recognize it [whatever the problem is], then you certainly can't . . . make a change." When I put similar questions of blame to other therapeutic readers, they responded similarly: maybe the books encourage readers to focus on their own behavior as the problem, but "you can't change anybody else, anyway, can you?" The unit for analysis, before reading even began, was always considered to be the self.

Religious reading done by orthodox believers, on the other hand, is part and parcel of their group experience—they do not read together as a group, but their reading is a result of membership in the group, as well as a method of strengthening their allegiance to the group: learning how to be a good member. There are psychological groups that have arisen also, such as groups based on Robin Norwood's *Women Who Love Too Much* (1985), that confirm a looser sort of membership but also draw on religious tactics for binding members together. These groups are neither purely religious nor purely psychological, but grow out of the marriage of the two. Neither sort of group challenges the status quo of gendered arrangements, except in helping women to adapt to how things are. But the group experience itself may foster a social awareness of what is wrong with how things work; this seems more likely in a psychologically oriented group that sees its goal as change, albeit on the individual level.

Where the Twain Do Meet:
New Age Reading

Traditional religious advice is, for most self-help readers, not a valid possibility for answers to present-day questions. Mainstream religion, which most people had some sort of brush with as children, seems out of date, out of sync with current moral views, especially regarding sexuality. Celia describes how New Age books appealed to her, as compared with the formal religious prescriptions she had been taught growing up, and which she had come to resent as an adult:

> When I was younger, I was a devout Catholic. And . . . unfortunately, through education, and just different experiences, I'm not as devout as I once was. And I used to get a great high just out of going to church, and what I believed in. And I still get it, but for different reasons. I don't readily accept the standing of the Church's teachings at the present moment, and I cannot pretend I do, and go along with it. . . . So that's why I read. . . .
>
> Catholicism: you can only do it if you follow their doctrine. This [New Age philosophy] is not so rigid. It's not like you have to not eat meat on Friday. And I can be married twenty times, and it's not to say I'm a bad person. . . . I'm looking for something more than [the Church]. I'm looking for something that's not based on money. . . . I'm looking for something that's going to accept me

and all my flaws. . . . I'm looking for a way to find peace with myself and nature in general.

So, for some self-help readers, psychological religion—New Age, astrology—steps in to fulfill the same functions that religion does, or that psychology does.

The New Age movement is a strong manifestation of the psychologification of religion, offering an odd mix of commericalism and spirituality. The New Age movement's most visible congregation points are its bookstores, where buyers browse in solitude to monotonous music. There are little shrines in which one can meditate (sans shoes) in some bookstores. The shops are often staffed by people in the know— whose role falls somewhere between Waldenbooks clerks and clergy— people who can recommend holistic healers or hook readers up with New Age organizations.

New Age has many precedents. Drawing on data collected by the General Social Surveys of the National Opinion Research Center from 1972 to 1976, which provides "information . . . [about] approximately 7,500 representative Americans," Roof writes that for young people, "traditional theistic beliefs and values have lost much of their plausibility and are being partly replaced by more mystical, personally oriented approaches to life. . . . Many have turned away from visible group loyalties as a basis for self-identification. Consequently, many youths in the seventies have been weaned away from the established faiths and now seek their identity in either secular or countercultural settings" (1981: 90).

The New Age movement attracts young people today in the same way that Eastern religious practices or cultish therapies began attracting young people in the sixties. Certain aspects of sixties-era experimentalism—such as the ideal of self-actualization—remain, but the movement fueling the dissemination of radical values has all but disappeared, making New Age religion a sort of yuppification of hippie spirituality. (I should point out that proponents of New Age philosophy and promoters of New Age literature object to charges that New Age is appealing only to yuppies [Jones 1989b].)

Many of the participants who said they did not read any New Age or religious self-help books looked at these books with suspicion. A few readers dabbled in books that combined spirituality with self-help, reading, most notably, the bestselling and very visible *Dianetics*. Gloria, one of these "mainstream" self-help readers, talked about her inability to gain anything from her reading of *Dianetics:* "My son brought the book into the house, and he was reading it, you know. . . . And so I took it. I took it for about a month. I started reading it . . . . And I kept on reading it, and reading it, and reading it. And I was like, 'Wait a minute. Am I getting anything out of this book?' I didn't like it. Now, I didn't finish it; I must have read like half of the book. . . . I didn't get it. I kept on reading it to see if I could get it." Emily also was disappointed with *Dianetics.* She said, "Usually when I finish reading a book, I display them nicely. . . . This particular book is just thrown down . . . like it's going to be discarded." Unfulfilling reading experiences such as Gloria's and Emily's could lead to a rejection of all books that readers group with the ones that disappointed them.

I asked the women who said they read New Age books with some regularity to define "New Age" and to tell me how this type of reading compared with "mainstream" self-help and with "straight" religious self-help. Sarah describes New Age as having "a spiritual kind of thing to it—not any religion in particular, but a spiritual, meditative kind of thing to it." She went on to say that New Age books "tell you how to be," explaining that "they'll talk about just being mindful and, you know, awareness . . . so [you're] walking around being more quote unquote conscious." Abby said: "The backbone of [New Age] is sort of accepting reincarnation." When I asked her how New Age religion was different from mainstream religion, she said:

It's not all that different. It's just, I sort of don't identify with any of the religions, so I guess it's working on my spirituality—not really religion. But there's a lot of similarity. That's one of the things that I got from it. Because I was kind of not sure—you know, I was brought up Jewish . . . but not very Jewish, and not really following stuff. My boyfriend's Catholic, and you know, it just, it hasn't been something that I identified with. So I kind of fell into hearing about New Age stuff. . . . Just the basic idea of . . . trying to make gains in this life . . . sometimes to make up for . . . things that might not have gone so well before. . . . Sometimes when hardships happen, I think a lot of that might have to do with things that happened in other lives. I mean, it's not a punishment, but . . . it's a chance to try to . . . make it come out a little bit better.

Perhaps the only thing that readers agreed upon was that New Age philosophy was different from—even antithetical to—mainstream religion in key ways, and that it offered experiences on another (somehow supernatural) plane. Mystical experiences of salvation or transcendence, of course, have long been part and parcel of major world religions (Weber 1922 [1963 rpt.]), though not included in these women's experiences of what Roof terms "mainline religion," by which he means long established varieties of Judaism and Christianity. As with readers, publishers do not agree on a definition of "New Age," but most talk about individual transformation that has the capacity to affect society as a whole (Jones 1989a and 1989b).

Fergus M. Bordewich (1988) was quite disturbed by the New Age cults he investigated in New Mexico. He sardonically describes the search for spiritual enlightenment that is the core of New Age philosophy: "What virtually all participants in New Age movements have in common is the belief in a cosmic destiny for mankind, which individuals pursue mainly through mystical examination of the self; and in a 'new age' of existence that will be peopled by superior beings who have undergone a process of inner 'transformation'" (38).

Of course, how odd to look for a "cosmic destiny for mankind" through "mystical examination of the self." This is the point at which popular-psychology blends into religious practice. It doesn't make sense, Bordewich would have us think. And yet, it makes perfect sense in a world called "postmodern," where religion collides with science in the guise of popular-psychology, where the "self, improved, is the ultimate concern of [our] culture" (Rieff 1966: 62).

The effects of such a merger are contested. Does New Age combine the worst of the psychological and the religious, producing fanatical and self-centered believers? Bordewich would say so; he writes:

By validating mystical and magical experience, [New Age thinking] sows corresponding doubt about the trustworthiness of rational thought. By denying the importance of the past as a basis for action, it has the capacity to separate the individual from both his own and society's history. New Age thinking encourages the belief that what "feels right" is the best—perhaps the only—measure of human behavior. . . . New Age philosophy mimics liberalism with its idiom of globalism, cooperation, tolerance and truth through self-understanding; it rejects as mere "reformism," however, liberal-ism's traditional concern with social issues like racial justice and equal opportunity. Indeed, New Age thinking generally regards such problems as mere states of mind. (44)

New Age, to Bordewich, means an unhealthy collapsing of judgment, a postmodern relativism that does away with morality in its focus on self as omnipotent. Marx wrote that "religion is only the illusory sun about which man revolves so long as he does not revolve about himself" (1844 [1964 rpt.]: 44). Now, by utilizing New Age philosophy, man—or woman—can sort of do both: revolve about him- or herself through a religious practice that centers on self-realization. Bordewich draws upon the same argument that has been leveled against psychology in lam-basting the New Age movement: introversion is unhealthy.

Unlike their soul-searching predecessors of the sixties, New Age ad-herents do not have to examine society to "find themselves." New Age, like self-centered psychology, holds that reality comes from within, or as one of the New Aged women Bordewich spoke to said: "You work on yourself because there is nothing else. . . . Everything outside is cor-rupted" (44). Bordewich takes the reification of apathy in which New Agers engage as an absence of critical thinking, a complacent dismissal of real world events in whose place are substituted platitudes about universal oneness.

Robert Wuthnow (1981) and Donald Stone (1981) were both in-volved in a San Francisco Bay area study conducted by the Survey Research Center at Berkeley, in which one thousand randomly selected people were polled about their religious involvement. Stone writes that of those questioned, 17.3 percent said they "had taken part in an encounter group, similar kind of training such as sensory awareness, sensitivity training, a 'T' group or growth group" (217). It seems that researchers expected to find that membership in pre-New Age spiritual groups would rely on or encourage exaggerated self-involvement. Wuthnow writes: "It was not anticipated in our research design that there would be a positive relation between mysticism and political ac-tion. Accordingly, no attempt was made to build into the design a means for exploring this relation" (235). What the research did reveal was that people involved in "mystical" spiritual movements were *not* more politi-cally apathetic than those not involved.

Though these groups (and their New Age progeny) may encourage self-involvement, it is not a self-involvement that necessarily encourages disinterest in everyone else. Stone writes: "In all, the survey and interview evidence does not indicate that awareness group participants are any less sensitive to social forces, less interested in improving the lot of disadvantaged people, or less individualistic than other people from similar backgrounds" (224–225).

Wuthnow asserts that people involved in groups such as Zen, Hare Krishna, Scientology, and Synanon—but not in neo-Christian groups—"tend to be more committed," more socially conscious, than those who are not (1981: 233). But mystical movements do not seem to provoke a radical social conscience. Wuthnow posits that the success of such movements in the seventies may be attributed, in part, to their adaptability to capitalist ideology; "For young people who have found themselves suddenly incorporated into the mainstream of modern American culture, mysticism may have become a quick and relatively painless means of developing a new identity at the personal level that squares with the larger values to which they are exposed through education and the marketplace" (240).

Like these preceding psycho-religious movements, New Age philosophy does not challenge the ideology of capitalism. It does not require a worldview that is contradictory to the world of work where believers earn their money. Like a mild dosage of valium, New Age allows people to get on with their lives, free—if only temporarily—of anxiety.

The women I interviewed were not deeply involved in the New Age movement, as were the people Bordewich reported on. Participants who read New Age literature were merely looking around, browsing for a spiritual fit. Psychological reading led, for some readers, straight into New Age. None of the participants who read New Age literature seemed to view New Age thinking as the first step into a quicksand of dangerous reality-avoidance as Bordewich believes it to be; rather, they saw it as a tool toward greater—though mystical—interpretive power.

The Gains of Psycho-Religious Reading

Blueprint. Comfort. Reassurance. These are words that women themselves have applied to the religious, psychological, and psycho-religious self-help they read. The similarity of participants' descriptions of the books, regardless of classification, is striking:

MARIANNE (about Christian self-help books): Well, most of 'em, I would say the majority of 'em, will lift your spirits. To me, they'll make you feel better about yourself.

ANNA (about astrology): I guess [the point of reading about astrology] is to get more understanding of yourself, and probably ultimately to change yourself. To point out, you know, what your strengths are, what your weaknesses are.

VAL (about psychological self-help books): Even though they're generalized . . . there's always something in there that seems to hit home, which is nice.

Self-help books, wherever they fall on the spectrum that runs from secular to religious, are like a camera, pointed by the reader at herself. She may wish to discover what's there, focus on it, freeze frame, and keep that single photograph as her evidence, her faith. Or she may wish to shoot from many difficult angles, varying the shutter speed, hoping to arrive at some genuinely representative composite. Perhaps a bit of both. She may wish to use these prints to make alterations, but, more often, her primary focus is on "understanding" herself: her motivations, her actions, her childhood, how she fits in. Accepting the self-help authors' views may mean altering herself to fit into existing, unchangeable, conditions. So, in a sense, self-help reading can serve to buttress the status quo; as we have seen, it can, and often does, reinforce patriarchally created forms of interaction. But, however misguided or insular her attempts to know herself may seem, her search is about hope for immortality, about change, about redirection.

Chapter 3

Readers Write In: Letters to Betty Friedan and Robin Norwood

Reading your book was like finding water in the desert.
(Letter from a reader to Betty Friedan, 1963)

Before I read your book I thought I was going crazy.
(Letter from a reader to Robin Norwood, 1988)

Participants in my study described their reading as an interaction in which they hope to gain insight into their lives and their problems through the words of experts, even though authors don't know anything about them in particular. What happens when readers attempt to realize the connections they feel for writers? Letters to Betty Friedan and Robin Norwood, in which readers have written about their specific reactions to *The Feminine Mystique* (1963) and *Women Who Love Too Much* (1985), confirm participants' observations about the nature of the reading experience and expand upon their valuations of the effectiveness of reading to gain introspective knowledge, insight, and advice.

In the preface to *The Feminine Mystique* (1963), Friedan writes that her inspiration for the book came out of her own life, which is where she first noticed that "something is very wrong with the way American women are trying to lead their lives today." Friedan sought the answer to what she calls "a personal question mark"; she "wondered if other women faced this schizophrenic split" she had begun to notice dominating her own life (9). The whole point of *The Feminine Mystique,* Friedan felt, was to forge a connection, to enable other women to experience awakenings similar to hers in our own lives, to help women who suffered as she had suffered. She writes: "There would be no sense in my writing this book at all if I did not believe that women can affect society . . . that, in the end, a woman . . . has the power to choose, and to make her own heaven or hell" (12).

A quarter century later, Robin Norwood begins *Letters from Women Who Love Too Much* (1988) by explaining how her connection with—and concern for—other women had led her to publish this book, a sequel to her bestselling *Women Who Love Too Much* (1985). She writes: "the seeds from which this book [*Letters*] would grow were sown with the first letter I received in response to WWL2M [her abbreviation for *Women Who Love Too Much*]" (xi). This letter was from a woman whom Norwood calls Beth B. (Norwood gives all of the letter writers in this book a first name and last initial—reminiscent of grade school, or perhaps confession magazines. She also prints all the letters in italics, to contrast with the portions of the book where she responds to the letters. I have dropped the italics throughout.) Beth B. wrote:

> Never in my life have I been so moved by a book to put pen to paper to write the author. . . . I must say your work affected me so profoundly that I am certain it was the key in fostering an entire positive direction out of so many years of ceaseless pain and confusion. There were times when I felt this book was written just for me alone. . . . I remember one night sitting on my kitchen floor poring over each page; at times I had to close it and put it by my side until my weeping lessened. (xi–xii)

Beth B.'s letter provided Norwood with a sense of déjà vu, she writes in *Letters from Women Who Love Too Much*, a memory of "that experience of sitting on the floor sobbing with pain and relief and gratitude because another woman had honestly described her struggle—a struggle so like my own" (xiii). Norwood never tells what it was that she read which had her sobbing on the floor herself "with pain and relief," only that "that experience had come after reading a magazine article in the early 1970s in which the author described how it felt to be a woman in this culture."[1] Like her own readers, and like participants in my study, Norwood had a reading experience that made her feel less lonely: "When I read that author's words, I knew, with almost a shock, that I wasn't alone anymore" (xiii).

Presumably, then, Beth B.'s missive sparked a new idea for a helpful tool for women. After receiving "what seemed like an avalanche of responses" to *Women Who Love Too Much* which "spread beyond [her] desk to nearly every flat surface in the house" (xiv), Norwood decided that she would publish her readers' letters, allowing readers, in a sense, to communicate with each other: "Now, hopefully through the vehicle of this book, you will be sharing with each other" (xvi).

Reading the Mail

Both Norwood and Friedan received a slew of letters in which readers thanked them, above all, for doing away with their (readers') sense of loneliness. This mail attests to the power of the activity of reading in women's lives. Both *The Feminine Mystique* and *Women Who Love Too Much* were immediate bestsellers—thus, in both cases, the authors' definition of the situation was perceived by their audiences as compelling. The quantity and enthusiasm of the letters indicate that the authors' arguments were perceived as deeply meaningful. In their letters, readers tell of the various ways in which they construct meaning out of these books. Considered as a group, however, the letters give hints about how readers enact (or attempt to enact or, at the very least, think about) social change in their own lives. One might expect that books written twenty-two years apart would elicit very different responses, but the groups of letters received by Friedan and Norwood are remarkably alike.

These sets of letters—the unpublished ones Friedan received during the sixties and seventies and selected to be maintained as part of the Betty Friedan collection (at the Schlesinger Library of Radcliffe College), and those Robin Norwood chose for publication, received between 1985 and 1987—may or may not be representative of the "average" tenor of letters received by these authors, or by other self-help writers. Obviously, people do not write neutral letters to authors; they write when they have been particularly affected by what they have read. Many write because they feel alone; what they have read makes them feel a sense of connection with other women, but especially with the writer, and they want to maintain this sense of connection. Many write to complain. It could be argued that if Friedan and Norwood were selecting which letters would be preserved or printed, they would be most apt to dispose of letters that were either negative in tone or inarticulate in style, and they may have done so. But in both cases, critical letters were included as part of the final collection. (Also in both sets of letters, complaints are far outnumbered by letters of praise.) What is most pertinent to my study is that the letters provide the opportunity to compare the forms of expression that two different groups of readers—divided by many variables, most notably by time—share in describing their responses to two self-help books.

Of course, part of the similarity over time may be explained by the form that a fan letter—or a critical letter—to an author takes; there is not a lot of variation within this structure. But it is not only formal qualities that the letter sets share; the nature of the effects of reading described was strikingly similar in both cases. What an examination of these letters offers that my discussion of interviews with readers does not is a sense of the immediacy of readers' reactions to books. Also, readers writing to authors are fundamentally different from my participants in that they did not express themselves knowing that what they wrote would become the object of sociological inquiry. (So if the activity of research itself taints what it touches, these letters at least originated purely!)

My reading of these letter sets has strengthened my belief that the content of an inspiring book is less important than its author's style and what can be called the "service" the author offers the reader: the sense that the reader has a guide, or even a friend in the author, who, though not with the reader physically, knows what her life is like and would like to help improve it through writing. The letter-writing reader perceives that *she* has been understood: she writes to realize this understanding, this connection her reading has enabled her to feel with the author.

When Friedan wrote *The Feminine Mystique,* it was unique. There were not stacks of books claiming to define and address women's problems as there are now; there were no bestselling feminist works at all. By the time of Norwood's writing, *The Feminine Mystique* had paved the way for the burgeoning genre of self-help geared for women. At first glance, the books seem very different: Friedan's is far more politically and socially grounded than Norwood's. She writes sarcastically, vehemently, forcefully, because she wants to incite her audience to action: these women had been sitting idle for far too long.

Norwood's tone, on the other hand, is calmer; she soothes her readers, encourages them to take their time, move slowly, and urges them not to bite off more than they can chew. Nonetheless, *The Feminine Mystique* and *Women Who Love Too Much* are thematically similar.

Both Friedan and Norwood attack a problem they believe to be paramount in women's lives during their particular "today." Their respective definitions and evaluations of the problem are different, but the way each author sees the problem acting on women's lives is quite similar. Upon close examination, Friedan's "problem that has no name" bears a strong resemblance to Norwood's "man-addiction." The women Norwood addresses may well have followed the advice given by Friedan; they may be daughters of the middle-class women who read and reacted to *The Feminine Mystique*. They may have received a top-notch education as Friedan suggested they should do. And they may have escaped the life of drudgery and overinvolvement with their children which Friedan rails against. Norwood's readers presumably are not mostly housewives, and yet they are still suffering because their reliance on men has remained central to their lives. They are still emotionally unhealthy, according to Norwood, because their focus on heterosexual involvements has not weakened as they have gained independence in the forms suggested by Friedan. Thus, in *Women Who Love Too Much*, the feminine mystique is alive and well, and causing all sorts of physical and emotional trauma.

Though Friedan and Norwood advocate seemingly different solutions, they both seek to remedy this generalized dissatisfaction of women they perceive. Friedan tells her readers to get educations, to seek rewarding and remunerative careers, to spend less time at home and with their children: to emulate upwardly mobile men. Norwood encourages her readers to treat problems as they would a disease: to seek out therapy, especially in groups with other similarly afflicted women, to place faith in a higher power, to reevaluate and perhaps end their relationships with the men with whom they are involved. She suggests that women readers should apply disinterested and pragmatic strategies at home, as they would at work.

One of the prime differences between the evaluations of Friedan and Norwood is that men fare much better with Friedan. True, she sees them as part of an omnipresent and overarching system that has worked to keep women down, but, she assures her readers, men would really prefer it if women would liberate themselves and, in so doing, become more like men. Women would become more intellectually stimulating companions, Friedan asserts, rather than drab housewives all-consumed with the drudgery of housework and child care.

Many of the men Norwood describes, however, are brutes. They range from insensitive to violently abusive; they are sexually aggressive and emotionally repressed. They are schizophrenic in their attempts to cement and sabotage their relationships with women. Norwood's women, like Friedan's, are implicated in maintaining men's psychological failings as well as in maintaining their own. Readers, in both cases, have accepted these readings of the inherent problematic nature of heterosexual relationships; in fact, many write that they have found them immensely appealing. Friedan received letters from women who told how glad they were that they could improve themselves for their husbands' benefit, and Norwood's readers sent in tales of men's horrendous, reprehensible behavior toward them.

Earth-Shattering Revelations

Women who wrote to thank both Friedan and Norwood word their descriptions of their reading experiences in strikingly similar ways. For instance, a woman writes of reading *The Feminine Mystique:* "It's like a bombshell has exploded inside me, shattering old images of a women [*sic*] and throwing light on the woman of today. . . . Now it is a comfort to realize that I'm a normal women [*sic*] entangled in the world of today." More than twenty years after Friedan received this letter, a woman Norwood calls Moira D. writes: "The thoughts that I write to you are thoughts that have rattled around inside of me for so many years that I've thought that I would explode. I've always felt that no one else would really understand what I was feeling until I read *WWL2M*" (27). Both these readers describe the effects of their reading as earth-shattering. Their reading has helped them to understand that the alienation they felt was not unique; and it is almost as if reading the books makes a community of other similarly miserable and alienated women a reality. As participants in my study agreed, the act of finding oneself in one's reading can dissipate loneliness. Knowing others are suffering in identical ways can help, even if one does not know these others personally.

A reassured reader writes to tell Friedan: "I rushed upon [your book] like a drowning person, because, at length, I had found the problems spoken about, explained and solved, problems of which I had always believed only myself on earth to think in the same way." Reading can provide answers to long-felt problems; these answers are perceived as monumental by letter-writing readers. A Friedan reader writes that *The Feminine Mystique* "is the answer to my inner struggle," and, likewise, Moira D. informs Norwood that "reading *WWL2M* gave [her] the strength to end the [destructive] relationship" she had been having for a

year with a married man (19). These readers, much more than participants in my study, found revelations through their reading.

Women writing to both Friedan and Norwood are vehement about the
degree to which they identified with what these authors had to say. One
woman writes to Friedan, "I'm the gal in your first chapter! Remember
me?" Another writes, "I felt as if you had sat in my house and in my
neighborhood and in my bridge club and spied on me and my friends."
Similarly, a woman whom Norwood calls Gina R. writes to tell her, "I fit
the prototype in your book quite exactly, and if I had known about you, I
would have been quite upset that you wrote about me and spread my
intimate thoughts and feelings on the pages of your book for the world
to see" (328). Readers who "find themselves" within the pages of a book
are quite delighted and surprised. Gina R. goes on to tell Norwood: "The
knowledge I've gained . . . has enabled me to have strength in this
ongoing struggle" (330). As the women I interviewed explained, and
letter writers confirm, the possibility of self-discovery leads them to self-
help books; fiction is held to be less capable of sparking this type of
awareness.

Readers' letters attest to women's feelings of reassurance gained
through reading. Where before they had felt self-doubt, after reading
they often feel electrified, exalted. Reading about emotions or experiences they had suffered through made women realize that they were not
abnormal and not alone. One woman writes to Friedan: "For the first
time in my life—I have the feeling that I'm not an 'odd-ball'—and that
the guilty feelings I have had for the past ten years are not warranted. I
cannot express in words what your book as [sic] meant to me." And
Catherine N. writes that Norwood's book has helped her to stop doubt-
ing her sanity (118). Readers are heady with the relief they feel the
reading experience has given them. Another letter to Friedan reads: "It
is hard for me to convey exactly how released and at peace I feel now."
And in a letter from Willow D. to Norwood, one finds a nearly identical
expression of relief: "I don't know what will happen in the future for me,
but for now, I am more at peace with myself than I have ever been
before. I like myself. I'm okay" (40). Identification with self-help reading, as participants in my study have stressed, can be experienced as an
enormous relief. Just having her own dilemma there in print, simply
having a label to fit on the problems she was experiencing, felt empowering, could make formerly insurmountable problems seem less formida-
ble to a reader.

Readers writing to both Friedan and Norwood indicate that prior to their reading, they had been looking, unfruitfully—and perhaps desperately—for meaningful help, for "answers." As several of the readers I interviewed said, self-help books could provide revelations where other methods of searching failed. One woman writes to Friedan, "There were times when I wondered whether I needed a minister, a doctor, a marriage counselor, or a psychologist. I find I needed your moral support for my convictions." Several others write to tell Friedan that upon their illuminating reading of *The Feminine Mystique,* they realized that the long hours they had spent in therapy were wasted. Norwood's writing readers were more likely than Friedan's to place value in therapy, especially group therapy, as she did (and as she wrote about extensively in *Women Who Love Too Much*); but they write also of finding revelatory answers *only* in her book. For example, Leslie S. elaborates: "I have spent the better part of thirty years actively trying to find out what this life of mine was all about and why it was always such a mess. My library consists mainly of self-help books. My courses in college were almost all in sociology or psychology. I have been involved with various kinds of groups and have had a lot of individual therapy, but nothing has ever really hit the nail on the head or explained me to myself [until *WWL2M*]" (51).

Many women write to Friedan and Norwood simply to thank them for "hitting the nail on the head," for describing situations in which they had been involved—but situations in which the power dynamics had gone unexamined—until their reading. Reading is thus experienced as eye-opening and liberatory. One woman writes to Friedan:

> I have always felt that I had the potential to do *something* significant with my life but when I got married last June I began to fall victim to the mystique you so adequately describe and analyze. . . . I was beginning to feel more and more that I would end up living more and more through my husband. . . . I am extremely grateful to you personally and to your book for having helped me to reject the above plans. . . . It's much easier to reject the right to choose than it is to choose; but it is more satisfying to choose.

After reading *The Feminine Mystique,* this woman writes to say that she has accepted Friedan's line on the then-current "Woman Question." She came to believe that women were responsible for the "mystique" that made them live "through" their husbands, and that, thus, only women could take action toward achieving change. Readers are elated to see what they feel is the "truth," even if it does not reflect well upon them or validate the way they have been living their lives. One woman writes joyously to Friedan, "We are all sick, and most of us don't know it. And even if we know it, we can't quite figure out *why*. Your extraordinary book gets straight to the heart of the matter."

The accusing finger Friedan pointed at housewives across the country had an exhilarating effect on many other readers. For instance, one woman writes to Friedan describing how the newly recognized self-inflicted nature of her problems is freeing: "I have gone through many periods of depression, not knowing why . . . and blaming my husband. . . . I was mad at the world. . . . Now I know I had no one to blame but myself. . . . It has taken me five years of marriage and being trapped, and your book to make me realize that the one at fault is me. Thank you again for giving me a start in the right direction." Readers' responses to *The Feminine Mystique* are rife with expressions of self-deprecation: "At last I have something worthwhile to say [to my husband]"; of suddenly recognized, though long-harbored, feelings of inertia and worthlessness: "Thank God, I now have the courage and determination to start living again." The legitimacy of such feelings was reinforced by Friedan's analysis of the problem, and her recommendations for resolving women's dilemma challenged these particular readers to attempt a new start.

Finding one's life on paper can also be a painful experience, as participants in my study have also indicated. Fans writing to both Norwood and Friedan discuss the pain they felt while reading, as well as various procrastinating strategies they used to avoid it—such as reading only a few pages each day or putting the book in another room, so as not to have to look at it and be reminded of the "truth" it held waiting for them.

Acting on Reading

Readers who believe the books they read describe situations that resonate with their own experiences do not see internalizing the problem and single-handedly fighting to solve it as unreasonable tasks. Rather, once they have seen the light, self-amendment becomes their goal. As the readers I interviewed proclaimed, you can't change anyone else, but you *can* change yourself. The tendency to see problems as internally located (and thus solvable by focusing on the self) runs rampant in the genre of self-help, and these two books are no exception. Even though Friedan and Norwood deliver social criticism in their works, the unit they recommend altering for social change is each individual woman's psyche. And, in both analyses, a woman's psyche begins its oft-warped journey when she is born. Friedan and Norwood both describe how social forces conspire to maintain the unfortunate status quo; but both emphatically declare that women can cure ourselves—and in so doing, cure others as well.

In a letter to Norwood, Terri D. writes about how she has continued an addictive legacy handed down to her by her mother, which fits perfectly into Norwood's description of how women's problems can be the results of maternal malpractice: "I was determined not to trap myself the way [my mother] had trapped herself. Nevertheless, she taught me to be a woman who loves too much and to use alcohol as a coping mechanism. I developed a different life-style from hers but we still ended up with the same addictions" (135–136).[2] Writing readers like this woman have striven to break familial chains, encouraged by Norwood's tales of the success of her clients. Readers thus share Norwood's conclusion that addictive behaviors are personal problems first, though they may translate into social ills as well, if enough women suffer in the same manner.

Many of the letters Friedan received were from women whose reading of her work had somehow spurred a sense of initiative; several women write specifically of the actions their reading of *The Feminine Mystique* has led them to take. Some are not explicit about what they will do but assert that they will, indeed, do something; for example: "After having lived with your book for a week now I must admit to an inner state of controlled chaos. . . . [*The Feminine Mystique*] will serve to move me to do that 'thing' which has been nagging at me for a long long time . . . to pull together these talents + abilities of mine into some definite pursuit."

The most common step writing readers said they would take was to return to the classroom (usually college); Friedan emphatically recommended this throughout her book. Young women write that they are not going to allow themselves to fall into the traps that ensnared their mothers. A woman who enclosed a poem she had written informs Friedan, "For the first time in two years I am writing seriously, goaded by your beautifully written book." Another woman exclaimed dramatically,

"Thank God, I now have the courage and determination to start living again." And another describes in detail how Friedan's influence drove her into a frenzy of activity, writing: "Half an hour ago I finished reading *The Feminine Mystique*. Since then I have been added to the list of substitute teachers in my community, obtained an on-call babysitter for my two year old son, made an appointment at a nearby college to take brush up courses & am truly looking forward to my husband's return from work."

It is possible that the excitement and ambition expressed in letters such as these dissipated after the intensity of the reading experience faded. As one participant in my study, Bonnie, explained, when she was actually reading, she would feel that anything was possible. Eventually, however, she would be forced to confront the "real world," where problems appeared far more difficult to tackle. But to Bonnie, and to Friedan's enthusiastic correspondents, these purposeful feelings and the elating sense of identification which reading provides are valuable in and of themselves. As one Friedan fan writes, "I can't say my struggle has ended, but . . . *at least I know now what it is I'm struggling against*" (emphasis in original).

Norwood's writing readers had much more specific step-by-step advice to follow than Friedan's did, and many of her readers undertook her recommendations with the same avidity Friedan's readers describe. One such reader details her course of action by including a litany of the "new" answers to the problems of women: Wendy D. writes a letter that is strongly evocative of the list of reading-propelled activities provided by the woman writing to Friedan (cited above):

I hated *Women Who Love Too Much*.
I hated it so much that it took me months to read it. . . .
I hated the women you wrote about. I hated the stories. . . .
And then I finished the book.
And then:
—I went to my first Overeaters Anonymous meeting.
—I found Al-Anon.
—I joined ACOA. . . .
—I got into group therapy.
—I found VOICES and for the first time in my life talked about having been sexually abused.
—I stopped binge-eating.

—I got a new job.
—I made a budget for the first time (I'm thirty-three).
—I have begun a new life. . . .
I thank you. (3–4)

The responses to reading described by Friedan fans seem less self-oriented than those Norwood fans describe, but this may be because Norwood's recommendations are far more therapeutically oriented than Friedan's. One of the primary differences between Norwood's and Friedan's approach to women's problematic lives is that Norwood borrows the therapeutic and spiritual program utilized in Alcoholics Anonymous and other "Twelve Steps" programs, and applies it to curing "man-addictions." While traditional Christians object to Friedan's rejection of conservative values, such women need not be put off by Norwood's underlying liberal feminism, because it is subtly interwoven with traditional religious prescriptions, New Age spiritual practices (like chanting affirmations), and various psychological exercises (like role-playing). Fay K. writes to Norwood to thank her for the book's "middle ground" between feminism and traditional religiousness:

I have been attending an excellent program for battered women . . . and yet I hear so much "Leave the bastard," "Screw him" . . . "File for divorce," etc. that it seemed to be the only line of thought, and quite frankly disturbed me. The other extreme, which I am exposed to through church, a women's Bible study and most Christian friends is that you stay in the marriage NO MATTER WHAT. . . . So many people seem to be running from God these days that I was almost shocked to find Him even mentioned in a book that I did not buy in a religious bookstore. (93–94)

It is unclear from Fay K.'s letter whether she has found a way to integrate the two conflicting approaches to the problems she has encountered in her involvement in the battered women's group and in religious activities. But her reading of *Women Who Love Too Much* has clearly led Fay K. to feel that a compromise exists that can be appropriated in the name of self-examination. A focus on the self can draw on bits and pieces of various disciplines; in creating a fitting merger for themselves, readers can deemphasize whatever seems strident, distasteful, or inappropriately political to them. Norwood's approach encourages readers to make their own combination grab-bag of strategies and theories. And while it may leave them without a grounded or clearly articulated worldview, readers did not write of feeling uncomfortable or confused in their applications of Norwood's combination-dinner approach to problem-solving. As one of my participants responded when I asked her to talk about which kinds of self-help books she thought were most effective in addressing women's problems today: "Whatever floats your boat." This sense of limitless and unique personal choice as the cornerstone of individuality is characteristic of New Age expression, which has increasingly become integrated into mass-market and large-scale trade publishing.

Reading and Relationships

Many readers' letters provide examples of how women's excitement over these authors' books made them want to spread the word. In a letter to Norwood, in which Rhonda D. says that she had been involved in a destructive relationship since June, she explains that she came to read *Women Who Love Too Much* after several friends recommended it to her: "By August, I was once more almost incapacitated by stress. Within four days, three people in three different locations told me to read your book. . . . I figured (Alcoholics Anonymous person that I am) that God must be trying to tell me something so I bought your book and read it" (177–78).

Many readers write to complain about the price of Friedan's book, because it made their task of spreading the word more difficult. (Hardcover prices today make these objections seem laughable.) One woman describes her proselytizing activities among family members: "My only complaint is that $5.95 is too much for a book which should be required reading for just about everyone! When will it be in paper-back? I have given copies to my daughters-in-law, sister—and have kept my own marked copy and have another which I lend."

Readers write of group discussions with other women readers that have been spurred by their enthusiasm over *The Feminine Mystique*. Norwood concludes her first book by offering suggestions on how to form a "Women Who Love Too Much" group which is clearly a descendant of the consciousness-raising group of the seventies spurred by *The Feminine Mystique*. Ramona A. writes to tell Norwood how founding such a group has helped her to improve her life in many ways:

I felt my only hope of recovering was to start my own group for women like myself: addicted to men. I was already in therapy but I felt I needed more. . . . I can't begin to tell you how my life has changed since then, how the doors have opened for me, how my self-esteem has grown, how my faith has grown, or how I have grown. . . . Since I formed the women's group, besides working at my regular job, I've started working part-time at a halfway house for recovering addicts and alcoholics. . . . I no longer sit and cry, or isolate myself, or pray to die. Nor am I constantly depressed. Nor do I feel I need a man in my life to be happy or to take care of me. (286–287)

Women write to Friedan also about trying unsuccessfully to get their husbands to read *The Feminine Mystique,* or of husbands who read and discredited the appeal of Friedan's argument. One woman writes, "I only hope enough husbands will take the time to read your articles. . . . Mine wouldn't. He doesn't believe in trying to live by books." Another Friedan fan, whose reading experience was "almost like reading my own diary in places," writes that she gave it to her husband to read, and that "he says he 'can't get any sense out of it.'" Though reading may result in a desire to share the excitement and intensity of the reading material with others, this desire may be thwarted. Sharing Friedan's book with their husbands may have led some readers to feel the effects of "the feminine mystique" even more strongly than before. Writing readers, like the readers I interviewed, feel that men are unlikely readers of self-help books because of their cultural conditioning, which allows them to evade the examination of problems that affect their lives, or to feel that women are the ones who should carry out introspective tasks.

Critical Mail

Not all letters were full of praise for Friedan's or Norwood's definition of the situation or the remedies they offered. Both Friedan and Norwood received letters that criticized their books for the narrowness of their arguments in terms of race, class, and sexual identity. The following letter points out the classist assumptions embodied in Friedan's suggestions that the tedium of housework and child rearing could be relieved by hiring others to do it:

The book seems only to apply to fairly well-off women. At the beginning you stated that women suffering great poverty did not have the boredom problem. . . . Perhaps your aim in writing was to liberate the more well-off women, and not these. You say one should get an outside job, and in some cases have hired help to do the housework. Yet somebody still has to do this work, and it's still a woman, so these women are still in bondage. I should like your opinion in this.

Whether or not Friedan ever sent her opinion was unclear from the files housed at the Schlesinger Library. Occasional responses from Friedan dotted the files of letters I studied; these were form letters that thanked recipients for their letters and closed with the inspirational line "Good luck to you on your road." There was no indication from the files as to who among her fans and critics received responses.

Norwood, on the other hand, provides detailed, very personalized, and sometimes very long answers to her mail in *Letters from Women Who Love Too Much*. It may be that Norwood had more time on her hands, that she is a more concerned person, that she hired a secretary, or that early on, she anticipated a second book composed of the letters she had received coupled with her own conscientious responses. It is also possible that Friedan, too, wrote detailed responses and did not store them with the letters to which they corresponded, or simply didn't save her responses. In any case, Norwood has responded to the criticism offered by writing readers, while Friedan apparently has not.

Norwood includes fewer letters that criticize her analysis in *Letters* than Friedan maintains in her files at the Schlesinger Library. One of the handful of critical letters about *Women Who Love Too Much* is from a women who states that Norwood had the problem backward. Marcie K. writes: "When will you . . . write a book on the subject of 'men who love too little'? After reading these women's recollections of their fathers and ex-lovers, I wondered to myself, 'Where in the hell did these men learn to be such rotten fathers, lovers and husbands?'" (314). Marcie K. urges Norwood to reformulate the dysfunctional behavior in heterosexual relationships as originating from men's lack of concern, rather than from women's overinvestment. She also asks, "do you work only with white women? I seem to be reading only about them" (314). Here Norwood snips in her reply: "I no longer 'work with' anybody, white or otherwise. It has become very important to me at this point in my life simply to continue to pursue my own recovery in a support group of peers. I do not have a private practice any longer." She then goes on to explain that when she was writing *Women Who Love Too Much,* she saw primarily white women clients, the implication being that she could thus write authoritatively only about them (315).

Phyllis R. writes to tell Norwood that she feels excluded from her (Norwood's) discussion of her clients—though she believes Norwood's analysis certainly applies to her habits in relationships—because she is a lesbian. She asks Norwood to bear this in mind in the future: "If the book is reprinted, which I'm sure it will be, I was wondering if you could add a clause to your introduction to include me and others like me. . . . The feeling I had of being invisible to you was difficult to get past. Your book is very helpful and I ask that somewhere in it you acknowledge my existence" (335). In a similar vein, Friedan is criticized for mishandling homosexuality. She received several letters from readers who are outraged at her implications that homosexuality is an aberration created by smothering mothers.

In more general reactions to *The Feminine Mystique,* readers write that Friedan overstates her case. Readers direct their attacks against Friedan personally, calling her a man hater, and including various other insults along this line. For example, one letter reads (in its entirety): "I can't tell you how nuts you are—I bet—*you're* not happy at home and I'll bet your children suffer because you don't know the joys of being a real woman." Critics range in tone from bitter and attacking (as in the preceding letter) to polite yet provocative.[3] Many men write to tell Friedan that she clearly does not understand what women want. Many women indicate that they see *The Feminine Mystique* as an unjust attack upon housewives like themselves, who, they assert, are happy doing what they are doing; are fulfilling God's will or Nature's plan; and are lucky to be doing it. Readers perceive many of the points that make up Friedan's overall call for doing away with housewifery as personally insulting and enraging.

One woman writes: "I'm mad, I'm sick, I'm *tired* of being told by every article in every magazine that because I'm 'just a housewife' my husband finds me a dull companion, my children are not self-reliant, and my time and talents are being wasted on 'trivial unimportant matters.'" Another reader writes that she agrees "most emphatically" with Friedan, but feels that Friedan has "pass[ed] too lightly over the rewards of motherhood." She reminds Friedan that there are realistic barriers that serve to prevent women from finding "satisfying job[s]," and making housewifery "the one area remaining to women where there is any satisfaction of achievement." A (possibly man) reader writes more angrily: "A harried mother preoccupied with a career or extra curricular activities is neglecting her duties as much as if she spent the day in a saloon."

So, while there were, indeed, many readers who accepted Friedan's assertion that women were leading meaningless lives as housewives and mothers, there were also readers who vehemently rejected this assertion or who rejected Friedan's implication that women should shoulder the blame for a situation that was, in many ways, so deeply institutionalized that it was beyond women's control.

Letters from angry, even hostile readers do not indicate that Friedan's or Norwood's arguments were wasted on such readers; these readers, too, were deeply affected by her book, in that it made them think about their own lives, offended their sensibilities, and conflicted with their conservative—or more leftist—views. These angry letters to Friedan show what readers may do when they find what they read objectionable, and when it hits close to home.

The women I interviewed said that if they disagreed with a book, or it made them angry, they would be unlikely to finish it. They might throw it away: this would be the ultimate rejection. But participants said they were most likely to get angry at books in which authors provide facile theories or recommendations; that they would not be likely to read a book in the first place that they thought might be ideologically offensive to them. Most were rather unperturbed by substantive differences between their own beliefs and those presented by the author—as long as they perceived that there was something of substance there to read. Also, participants in my study were reading books that might include feminist content at a time when such ideas were not new or unusual to them—as they would have been to many of Friedan's readers. (Many participants said they would define themselves as feminists; and those who would not said they believed in "equality" between men and women in the workplace.) Readers' critical—or outright nasty—responses show that challenging or deeply disturbing reading experiences may also result in attempts to make these reactions known to the author.

Letters as Evidence

Readers' letters, like conversations with readers, testify to the importance of the reading experience. Since they are more immediate evidence of the effects of reading, letters show an intensity of reaction that readers, in the interviews I conducted, rarely expressed. (They might tell me about books they loved, but they often had difficulty detailing exactly what made those books so exemplary, in retrospect.) Letters offer an intriguing entrée into readers' thoughts, when seen as attempts to forge a relationship with a distant "authority," a woman who has, in many cases, helped to effect changes in unhappy lives, and, in many cases, somehow upset the balance of such lives. Many writing readers held out the offer of friendship to these authors (especially to Friedan). So, while several of the readers I interviewed spoke about feeling a connection with the authors whose work they found influential on their thinking, the letter writers went one step farther by attempting to make this figurative link real.

These letters may have served as a part of the self-help process for the readers who wrote them: writing itself can be therapeutic, as both Friedan and Norwood indicate. Writing about what they read allows readers to act creatively, to put their situations down in words on paper, in an emulative gesture of self-affirmation. If reading is experienced as an act of unburdening, writing confirms and reifies the intensity of this experience.

In their letters to Friedan and Norwood, readers confirm many of the thoughts about the self-help genre that participants aired in the interviews, but, most important, they confirm that the activity of reading self-help books is constructive (in both senses of the word) in the eyes of those who engage in it. Whether or not readers then act upon what they have read, and whether or not the sense of control authors encourage them to build is a realistic response to their problems, they have felt—however briefly—that their lives can be different.

How might reading enable women's lives to really become different? Certainly, this was the aim of both Friedan and Norwood, as they describe it. Encouraging action may very well be the first step to enabling it, as enthusiastic fans have attested. But as long as readers and authors conceive of social action as women's atomistically individual attainment of what certain men have through self-edification, social change is problematic. Insofar as changing how people think can be said to precipitate social change, readers' letters—especially to Friedan—show that socially based conceptions of women's oppression can be facilitated or reinforced through reading.

Chapter 4

Making It Readable: Editors
---
and Authors of Self-Help Books

There is an audience out there . . . hungry for alternatives. It is an audience that consists of anyone who has a problem for which the old answers won't work. (Cheryl Woodruff, senior editor at Ballantine, cited in Jones 1989b: 16)

All books that make it in the marketplace are reassuring. (Roiphe 1986: 22)

It can get pretty wacky. (Unnamed editor cited in Jones 1990: 20)

Sociologists have long sought an heuristic strategy that would enable us to understand the creation of culture, to describe the acts and contributions of producers, users, and the social world of cultural commerce. So far, I have focused on the activities undertaken by readers in absorbing, reaffirming, and rejecting the cultural messages found in self-help books. In this chapter, I shift my examination to the creators of self-help books—namely editors and authors, and the publishing industry in which their activities take place.

Wendy Griswold (1986) defines a "cultural object" as the ever-varying product of social activity, "an artifact constructed from previously used cultural elements, current conventions, contemporary aesthetic and social interests, the individual vision and expertise of the artist, the demands of the audience mediated through an existing institutional structure, and sometimes a dollop of unpredictability which heirs to Romanticism labeled genius" (187). Authors are usually seen as sole creators of their works, but the production of all cultural commodities is structured by institutional requirements and practices and, thus, should be seen as a creation of a multivaried interaction between those who make and use them (Becker 1982).

Editors occupy a unique position in the process of generating self-help books because they negotiate both with authors and with higher-ups in the bureaucracies that structure their work, and among the community of workers who make an author's work into a book, they are central. Editors' activities are most crucial in determining what will and won't be published. I conducted interviews with editors working at five different publishing houses in New York City, all of whom have been—or were at the time of the interviews—involved in the production of self-help books. (All of the editors I spoke with are women.) I first discuss the participating editors' perceptions of their work, their descriptions of the institutional requirements and constraints upon the production of self-help literature, and their views about the genre itself. Next, I examine authors' statements about their motivations and goals in writing self-help books.

Profit or Perish

The history and usage of self-help literature for women is tied to the history of book publishing and distribution as well as to the social, political, and economic changes that affect women's lives. A brief discussion of the development of the publishing industry serves as a necessary backdrop to editors' and authors' views of the genre and their positions as cultural gatekeepers and producers of self-help books.

In June 1939, Robert de Graff founded Pocket Books and began an experimental plan to market a list of ten books—ten thousand copies of each, at twenty-five cents a book—in New York City (Davis 1984: 12–13). Before Pocket Books appeared on the scene, hardcover books were quite difficult to find and expensive to own, and earlier schemes to market paperbacks had never been successful on a large scale (Davis 1984: 16–19). Bookbuyers had limited access to books, as there were only about four thousand businesses that sold books, and among these, approximately five hundred "legitimate" bookstores. "In two-thirds of America's counties, there were no bookstores at all. Thus only half of the books produced by American book publishers sold more than twenty-five hundred copies" (Davis 1984: 16). Successful paperbacking, begun by Pocket Books, transformed the distribution system publishers utilized and "democratized reading in America" (Davis 1984: xii).

Technological innovations in publishing, changing conceptions about authors and audiences, and the past success of magazine and newspaper subscription novels—all predating de Graff's debut of paperbacks by up to one hundred years—enabled the large-scale manufacture, sale, and success of his company's books (Radway 1984: 19–29). Janice Radway describes how the traditional view of the book "as a unique configuration of ideas conceived with a unique hypothetical audience in mind" was challenged in the early 1800s by "an alternative view which held that certain series of books could be sold successfully and continuously to a huge, heterogeneous, preconstituted public" (21). The editors I spoke with in 1988 demonstrated that they rely on both the traditional and objectified conceptions of reading material, often differentiating between books that they believe fall into the first category (those with inherent literary merit) and books that fall into the second (appealing—though not necessarily artistically remarkable—commodities).

Usually, a book is published in hardcover (or "cloth") first, and if it sells, or sells reasonably well, a paperback edition will follow. On occasion, when publishers and editors believe a market can be created for both types, books are published simultaneously in cloth and paper editions. The hardcover publisher usually owns the paperback rights, but this is not always the case. Authors may negotiate cloth and paper sales separately, or increasingly, since many publishing companies produce both types of books, make a joint hardcover and paperback deal with the same conglomerate. The difference between trade and mass-market paperbacks is often fuzzy, but basically, mass-market books are printed in larger quantities, are smaller in size, generally cost less, and are more widely distributed than trade books, owing largely to their sale both in and outside of bookstores (e.g., drugstores, newsstands, and supermarkets). Self-help books are published most often in mass-market rather than in trade form.

The majority of books lead very short lives. "The average books is dead in days or weeks; 90 percent are dead, in their original editions, within a year" (Shatzkin 1982: 3). Mass-market books are destroyed when returned by retailers, whereas hardcover and trade-paperback books are warehoused, remaindered (purchased in bulk by booksellers and sold at a discount), and/or backlisted (advertised along with newer titles). Part of the reason for the early demise of so many titles can be attributed to the distribution system. Sales representatives from publishing companies negotiate deals directly with bookstores—or chain offices—twice yearly. This process is time consuming and often not completed before books go to press, so the supply of books printed (the press run) does not necessarily correspond with the demand from booksellers. Roughly one-fourth of new books are never sold on the retail market (Shatzkin 1982: 12–13).

One editor of trade books, who had previously worked as an editor of mass-market books, explained why mass-market paperbacks were less likely to "live" as long as trade books in bookstores: "A mass-market book is a disposable commodity. When a mass-market book doesn't sell, they cut off the cover, they destroy the book, and the cover comes back to the publisher for credit. . . . [In trade books] in order to get credit, you have to return the book, so . . . the retailer tends to keep the book around a lot longer, and these books have a longer life, and do backlist [and sell well after their initial printing]."

Editors describe the publishing business as a series of steps where selling books successfully marks the end of the process. There are obstacles to be tackled at each successive level, and various gatekeepers monitoring progress along the way. First there are the agents, who winnow down the plethora of written material that will be submitted to editors. Each editor I spoke with said that it was entirely possible for a work to be bought without an agent's representation, but they agreed that projects bought in this manner ("over the transom") were rarities. Editors said that a very low percentage of the total projects they saw (with and without representation) would become books; one estimated that "we usually see somewhere between 20 and 50 books before we buy one of them. We spend a lot of time turning stuff down, because you don't see how to market it effectively, or you simply don't like it." Projects may visit many publishing houses, of course, before finding a home or being discarded altogether.

Next, editors determine whether the projects given to them by agents are worth pursuing. When a project is highly desired—usually when the author is well-known—publishing houses take part in an "auction" where they call their bids in over the phone to the author's agent. In order to deal with the quantities of manuscripts that pass through their offices, editors will often "farm out" reading to their assistants, who make up another step in the process of weeding out the "good" from the "bad." Editorial assistants are almost always the readers of unrepresented (agentless) manuscripts, or "slush." The editors I interviewed said that they would always read a project themselves before going forward with it, and saw assistants as time savers, whose labor they were grateful for.

Once an editor has decided in favor of a project, s/he must present it at a group meeting. The participants and format of editorial meetings vary from house to house, but the editor's goal is always successfully to sell the project to the editorial board, which often has veto power. Whether or not the board has explicit veto power, its support is always seen as desirable. In some cases, an executive editor or publisher will have ultimate discretion over the final approval of projects.

Picking and Choosing

I was particularly interested in uncovering the strategies editors use to determine that a book is worth buying, and that it is, thus, potentially salesworthy. That is, I wanted to find out what their professional reading processes were like. Editors' views of self-help books often echoed those of the readers I interviewed. Each of the editors I interviewed stressed the many unknown factors that affect book publishing. First and foremost was the fact that books that don't sell can be returned (and, as discussed above, often literally destroyed). Awareness of the transient nature of their product makes editors' decisions to buy and produce books weightier than such decisions in other businesses, they feel. Indeed, the option to return was developed beginning in the thirties and forties to induce retailers to buy books under conditions in which the risk of incurring great financial loss was eliminated for them (Shatzkin 1982: 97).

Most important, and evident from each editor's comments, was the belief that unpredictability enhanced the work involved in editorial decision making. Guesswork, gutwork, and serendipity were all seen by the editors I interviewed as motivating and exciting parts of their jobs. Uncertainty is a dominant backdrop to all aspects of editors' work. One editor said:

> There's a lot of psychology involved because . . . you're taking this pile of papers, and you're asking someone to pay you for it. And there are so many steps in between. I've got to sell it here. My people have to sell it to the sales force. The sales force has to sell it

to the bookstore, and the bookstore has to believe, and have an expectation—based on all the support we say we're going to give it—to sell that book to someone else. And how fraught with danger it is. Especially if you're saying, "I've got to get her on 'Donahue,'" or, "I've got to get Michiko Kakutani at the [*New York*] *Times* to review it."

Each editor took pleasure in describing the unpredictable nature of her work, and the "educated guesswork," "hunches," or "instinct" upon which she relied in her attempts to make profitable decisions. Editors were reluctant to quantify their success rates in prediction making; they saw profitable choices as arising from a delicate balance between certain abilities they possessed as astute cultural observers and sheer luck. One editor describes the nuances of her own decision-making process:

> You think. You work a lot on gut. . . . An old boss of mine used to say that . . . if an editor buys ten books, seven of them are going to fail, two of them are going to succeed, and one of them is going to be a blockbuster, and you're not going to know the reason why for any of it. And you give it your best shot, but a lot of the times you just have no idea. You know, you do a lot of educated guesswork . . . based on your experience, and very often the track record of the particular subject or genre, and the track record of the particular author. Or you just see a need. . . . This is an extraordinarily subjective business. Every editor has stories about the book they turned down that went on to sell two million copies. But every editor has a set of criteria that a book must meet if it is something that they want to take on and champion and sponsor.

Editors, like readers, had difficulty articulating what this set of criteria is—what, exactly, makes a book appeal (or not appeal) to them. All five editors did acknowledge several loosely defined qualities they seek in determining whether or not a project is worth an investment of time and money. Self-help books must be "well written" by authors who, in the editors' judgment, sound *appropriately* authoritative. Self-help books must offer something "new" or "different." They must be "timely."

One editor said that self-help books "written with a particular passion" or "a sincere impulse" will do better than ones written cynically, glibly, or condescendingly. When I asked how she tells if a book is well written, she said, at first, "the same way you do." Then, when pressed to elaborate, she said, "it's subjective." The editors I interviewed wavered between the belief that "goodness" is measurable and clearly discernible to a well-trained reader, and the feeling that quality, itself, is elusive and can be determined only by each individual reader. Thus, editors expressed beliefs in both the universality of appeal (of particular books) and the individuality of the reading experience.

When I expressed amazement at the fact that the publishing industry relied on a small circle of editors in New York predicting the tastes of people all over the country—and that this process *worked*—one editor reminded me that "we're all members of the same culture." Things may happen faster or slower in certain places, she said, but eventually the same things transpire all over the country. And we are, she insisted, culturally alike enough to read similarly enough for editors like her to be able to predict reading tastes fairly well. In order to be a good editor, all five agreed, one must know "what's going on." Editors said they try to stay attuned to the pulse of the nation by reading a lot—newspapers and magazines, especially—by talking to friends and relatives, and by watching television. But, ultimately, their decision making would always bring them back to their own personal experiences and impressions. One editor described the social construction of "instinct" which she felt guided her decisions:

> If you can't trust your own instincts, then you can't be in publishing. Obviously [instinct is] a product of experience. You get better as time passes. I can sort of track my books through my own life experience, and it really reflects where you are at a given time. And I don't think that's bad. I always look for that . . . connection with my own experience because that's what gives you that *real* kind of extra energy for something. You have certain professional instincts, but if you don't go beyond the professional instincts, you're not gonna make it, you know. You've got to connect with it in a very personal way. I think you'll find any editor who does these books successfully really, kind of, is in there. . . . For instance, [with one particular book], I had had a love affair years ago with a guy like that, and I read it and I said, "Oh, now I understand what was going on!"

Each editor said that she would have to believe in a project to sell it, or at the very least, to believe it would hold broad appeal for others (as in the cases of editors who said they would not do this kind of reading outside work). Editors said they looked for written material that demonstrated "a sense of mission," that addressed what they considered to be "*real* problems or needs," material they felt would "touch a nerve." One editor explained that an author's method was as important a consideration as content:

> How a book is done is as important as what the book is about, and you can have a lot of books about the problems women have getting men to commit . . . but only a handful—less than a handful—of those actually *hit.* . . . We like to feel that our books are solid, that they are not just going to be here for six months, that they are going to what we call backlist, which means that after their initial sale, they will continue to sell for three, four, five, or more years.

The composition of lists (all the books a house is publishing), which are compiled twice annually, have an effect upon the projects that are bought because publishers want their lists to show diversity, even within topic areas. One editor described how she tries to compile a varied group of projects, but that more important, she looks for books that affect her personally: "I might know about a trend, and say, 'Oh, we need something to fill that slot,' but many of these books start with just, you read something, and you say, 'my God, you know, that's right!' . . . You have to feel a commitment for a book or it's not—you can't muster up the energy." Editors want projects in which they can sincerely believe.

Four of the five editors I interviewed spoke about connections between self-help books for women and the feminist movement. (The fifth saw no connection between feminist concerns and her work.) One editor said, "you won't find any antifeminist books on my list," but others said that since they hoped to find broad audiences for the books they published, it would be impractical to judge books based solely upon their own personal political agendas. One said that sometimes "you find yourself having to suspend your belief system in order to make an objective and informed decision. . . . Really, your job as an editor . . . is to provide various segments of the marketplace with what they want or feel they need." Sincerity may not always come easy.

While editors attempt to create balanced lists and to fulfill their own personal requirements in selecting projects, they also try to publish books that will hit bookstore racks at the right time. One editor lucidly described the importance of timing in selecting book projects, saying: "You're just constantly reading and looking and trying to keep yourself at least five steps ahead of what's actually taking place in the consumer end of things. You want to be ahead of the consumer. You want to catch a trend before it actually happens. It can also work against you if you get onto a trend too early; you can publish before it's time."

Buying and Selling

Editors emphasized that the amount paid for a project and the number of books in a print run were figures that could not be easily or exactly quantified. Five thousand copies was the lowest figure editors cited, and one million was the highest. Payment to authors could range as widely, they said. One editor warned me that I was trying to get her to quantify something that was impossible to quantify. Publishing was "not a science," she said, and there were no formulas used to determine what would be paid or how many books would be published, though these two figures were certainly related. Decisions about advance payment to authors were strongly tied to editors' estimates of potential revenues. Such decisions were further complicated by competition among publishing houses for a single product, and by publishers' desires to enhance their reputations to attract future sales. One editor explained: "You know, you don't necessarily always buy a book simply to sell lots of copies. Sometimes it indicates a new direction in your program. You know, you may spend more than you think a particular book is actually worth in terms of its net sales to your company, but it's a *statement* acquisition—it says something about where you want to go and it can help attract new properties to you."

Editors see books as commodities in that they are items meant to be sold, but at the same time, they see books as distinct from other products for sale. In other words, selling books is the point of publishing, but it is not the whole point. At none of the publishing companies was market research of any kind undertaken to determine the characteristics of self-help audiences. Two editors, cited below, sum up the reasons they believe market research would be impractical:

If we were doing a product line [then we might do market research]. For example, some of the romance lines . . . used to do market research because they were selling a *product*. Those lines are sold like soap. They're very consistent. And they were able to determine who the reader is. But by the time you get through market research, your book is dead, and who knows what the next book is going to be? Because that market is constantly shifting and constantly changing.

It's not an industry which has ever systematically attempted to quantify or research or study what the American consumer really wants and buys. . . . There's a fundamental problem which is that—one that Procter and Gamble doesn't confront—there are forty thousand new books, including revisions and updates, published every year! So you're not talking about something that's easy to catalog. We're not talking about ten brands of toothpaste. We're not talking about twenty-five brands of cereal. We're not talking about things that will come and stay forever.

Time does not permit testing; both the time frame involved in in-house production and the lifespan of a book once it gets to stores mitigate against experimentation. The first editor cited above emphasized the guesswork necessary in making decisions about projects that could take two years to be published. Though self-help books are products that publishing houses make money from marketing, their producers do not see them as interchangeable and thus deny that they are *products* in the same way that soap or cereal are; editors do not see self-help books as formulaic creations that can be tested and marketed in the same way that toothpaste can. They believe books adapt to changing tastes and desires of the reading audience, and see each book as a unique creation. It is important to bear in mind that there *are* books that these editors do see as formulaic and static—and, thus, researchable—namely, romances.

Editors explained that the process involved in signing a contract on a project and transforming it into a book involves assistance from the publicity department of the publishing house. The editors I spoke with gave varied accounts of exactly where and how publicity people participated in the process, but all five were emphatic about the importance of the publicity department's role in selling self-help books. Publicity people were responsible for arranging advertising, bookstore displays, live appearances like book signings, and radio and television engagements for authors.

Editors saw television as an influential force in the selling of books, though not as influential as many critics of recent trends in publishing believe it to be. Thomas Whiteside, for example, argues that changes in the structure of publishing, book marketing, and retailing have made publishing houses concentrate on producing blockbusters (1980). As trade and mass-market publishing companies become corporate conglomerates, as chain bookstores reach their computerized tentacles into malls across the nation, competition among bookmakers results in a trash-infested industry, catering to the lowest common denominator of reading tastes, he argues. Television, which Whiteside sees as a wasteland of inanity, has had a large part to play in keeping trash afloat; he writes: "As commercial television has inculcated in mass audiences the concept of the personality-author, it has at the same time helped to provide publishers with tempting visions of a new scale on which books of a certain kind, at least might be promoted and sold, through the use of multimedia techniques and the blockbuster approach" (38). Self-help books most definitely fit into the "books of a certain kind" Whiteside mentions: they lend themselves quite well to television presentation, providing both "issues" and "experts" to which audiences respond (as a glance at the contents of recent Oprah Winfrey and Phil Donahue shows would bear out).

Whiteside contends that the beauty of books is being co-opted by the recent relentless capitalistic tenor that he believes has infused the publishing industry. Books, regardless of quality, "are all made to seem strangely alike. . . . all treated as 'product'" (193). Literary merit has fallen by the wayside; Whiteside implies that a golden age when publishing was committed to discriminating good taste and intellectually inspired love of books has been replaced by profit-seeking bureaucracies. "The mass merchandising, the hype, the frenzied pursuit of Number One which the publishing industry has turned to as a central and universal tool is in its very essence anti-art, and even anti-thought," he concludes (193).

Whiteside is not alone in his view of the corruption of the bookmaking industry by the combined forces of television, corporate capitalism, and, presumably, easily led consumers. Walter Powell also sees the profit-seeking conglomerates as money-hungry villains, arguing that chains are changing cultural reading opportunities in America for the worse, and that "if present trends continue," there is no question that "irreparable harm will be done to our public culture" (1983: 62).

This analysis is similar to that made by Todd Gitlin in his dissection of the institutional forces behind prime-time television (1983). Producers, writers, and audience are seemingly powerless against the forces of what Gitlin sees as the obscene mindlessness they have created. Network executives, according to Gitlin, perceive their audience as "uneducated, distracted, and easily bewildered" (87) and out of fear of losing it, continue to benevolently shovel garbage its way. "We swim in [television's] world even if we don't believe in it," Gitlin announces bleakly (333).

In such descriptions of cultural commodity production, producers are seen as carrying out their duties in an institutional setting that absolutely prohibits the challenging of the sociopolitical status quo. The results— the cultural objects created by their endeavors—are seen as overwhelmingly poor examples of creative impulses. The editors I spoke with, however, see themselves neither as powerless trash collectors, nor as participants in a conspiratorial megalopoly whose goal is to reify the political status quo.

Other cultural analysts, too, see the "massification" explanation of production and consumption as simplistic (Lacy 1983; Long 1985; Vaughan 1983). According to Samuel Vaughan, during the same time that mergers have produced mega-corporations, the number of small publishers has increased (1983). Dan Lacy contests the view of television as a hypnotic force captivating potential consumers; he writes that "the total number of books published has approximately quadrupled since television became generally available," and that measurements of book sales (by number of copies) do not show a clear and sustained link between viewing and buying (1983: 121).

Editors were quick to mention that blockbusters enable them also to publish books that they feel have merit, but for which they do not have high financial expectations. Editors believe that recent developments in the bookmaking and -selling industries—such as those Whiteside and Powell point to: increased commercialization, a more explicit focus on books as commodities, larger publishing corporations, the proliferation of chain bookstores, and a reliance for publicity on television shows—do not mean that bookloving is being replaced by greed. Rather, they think that these factors have made their work easier in some ways. One editor discussed resentment on the part of small owner-run bookstores against large chains, which could afford to discount books more easily. She said the issue was complex and ought not be oversimplified into a case of corporate victimization of struggling entrepreneurs:

> Small bookstores are upset by discounting and by what they call the bestseller syndrome. On the other hand, they benefit from the amount of advertising that the bookstore chains do. . . . I've talked too many sides of the issue to really think that it's very black and white. And . . . the chains are a response and a creation of the way publishers have treated and built them. But I think . . . it may be correct to say that the chains—because they are computerized and much more systematic—they can tell you what *is* selling, and they've become an important statistical source for publishers because they brought bookstores to where they never were before. . . . They can, in any given week, tell you what's selling *everywhere*. . . . There's no small bookstore who can do that for you. . . . In that data you capture a lot about where the market is and what the market wants.

Access to statistical data collected by large bookstore chains enables editors to better manage the guesswork they will do in the future, according to this editor, and allows them to see concrete results of the decision making they have already completed.

Editors differed in their assessments of the efforts of the marketing and publicity departments of their companies, but most agreed that it was simply practical to recognize that sales could depend on authors who were also competent spokespeople for their work. Editors said that the marketability of an author could affect the amount s/he would be paid for a project, or the treatment the book would receive from the publicity department, but insisted that it was unlikely that an inarticulate or somehow unpresentable author could cause a worthwhile project to be dropped. Only one editor disagreed, arguing that since self-help books tend to come in waves, and since "often they [authors] don't write their own books anyway," it may be possible to choose between a number of authors writing on the same subject. In this case, it would make sense to choose an author who could perform well on television.

Editors agreed that the publicity department's efforts could encourage the success of a book—could even push a book into the bestseller category—but warned that publicity alone could not make a book successful. "You cannot sell a book people don't want," one editor said. Editors firmly believe that a book does well because it meets a demand, and consequently they do not support any theories of cultural consumption in which coercion on the part of producers or marketers is central (such as those put forth by Whiteside, Powell, and Gitlin). Editors see themselves as providing a service by which they both hope to fulfill book buyers' expectations and to satisfy their tastes.

The role that publicity and marketing departments of publishing houses played in decision making about the purchase of projects varied from house to house. Publicity people's input ranged from clearly delineated participation in editorial board meetings to making more casual recommendations; only one editor said that the publicity department had no formal or informal power in decision making about purchases. Editors believed the input they received from publicity people was often indispensible, and they would actively seek such advice themselves. One editor described how she would arrange for the publicity department to get involved when she had determined that a project warranted its participation:

> For anything that I think will be, you know, a publicity-driven subject—and most self-help subjects are—I will often have a— what we call a—dog and pony show, and I'll get in, you know, people from marketing, people from publicity, and a couple of other editors, and we'll just see how articulate the author is. . . . You want to see whether they can answer questions concisely, and whether they're kind of basically attractive personalities. They don't have to be glitzy or glamorous or cute or anything of that kind, just coherent.

Editors said that it was becoming more common for authors to focus on self-presentation and to include videotapes of themselves as part of the original package under consideration. One of the editors acknowledged that there had been "a lot of objection and commentary about video submission," but said that she thought this development was a reasonable and professionally prudent response on the part of authors and agents to "a very crowded marketplace" where sales could be affected by television appearances. She said that authors were now taking the initiative to market themselves along with—or even before—their submissions were made; "some people go out and produce a video before they make the submission. We don't ask them to do that. They're savvy. They know it's a selling tool. And then we can say to our sales force . . . 'We've seen the author. The author's phenomenal!' . . . And if you're right, they're dazzled. And if you're not, you're in trouble."

Some of the authors who have achieved bestseller status in the past several years have already become performers of one kind or another even before their books come out; and if they haven't, their books are likely to spawn video-engagements beyond the usual book tour. For example, Barbara De Angelis, Ellen Kriedman, and Shirley MacLaine (already famous) created advance publicity for their books in their seminar circuit; Susan Forward has become a radio host; and John Bradshaw's series of lectures runs on PBS.

Defining and Evaluating the Genre

I asked editors—as I had asked readers—to tell me how they defined "self-help" literature, and to talk about how they perceived it to be relevant (or not) to women's lives. Editors' definitions and evaluations of the usefulness of self-help books were similar to those of readers but reflected their particular professional interaction with these books. One editor defined self-help by focusing on the books' potential ability to save users time and money:

> Self-help is a category with many facets that attempts to allow a person to either seek information to help them without the as- sistance of a professional, or to use the information in conjunction with or to help them reflect on the advice that they may get from a professional. But self-help is really a very broad-ranging category. It's everything from how to fix your car . . . how to fix your life, how to improve your relationships, how to make changes in yourself. So you know, so it's an umbrella term that's used to describe a whole wealth of subject areas but with the essential message being on the, you know, can-do aspect of a person. You can do it yourself more cheaply than if you went out and had other people do it for you.

Editors also voiced the same concerns that readers did about the quality of self-help material, often reeling off titles they thought were

"good" and titles (nearly always published by other houses) they thought
were "bad." One editor faulted psychological self-help book authors for
their tendency to oversimplify, and thus to promise to offer answers to
problems that required more than a book could possibly give; she said:
"I think a lot of them are quick fixes and easy answers that don't deal
with the . . . causes sufficiently for someone to change their patterns.
And I think that anyone who is looking for psychological help is trying to
change a pattern, and that's not done by reading a book unless you have
extraordinary gifts of insight and motivation. It usually takes some type
of one-on-one, or therapy."

Profound problems, editors felt, would not be eliminated by reading
alone. One editor said that self-help books exemplified people's desire
to find easy answers to complicated problems; she felt readers were
looking for shortcuts that don't exist. Another said that she thought
reading was often a step in the right direction, even if it were not a cure-
all. "It's easier than going into years of analysis, or years of therapy. . . . I
suppose it's a good thing to have people become aware at any level," she
said. It is not surprising that editors, like readers, are quite supportive of
therapeutic conceptions of health and well-being, and support psychologically based methods of decision making, problem solving, and behavior modification. To editors, the primary question in judging a book's
efficacy is not whether or not they should bottle therapy for sale, but
rather, how well book-therapy could compare to the real thing.

Editors, like readers, said that reading self-help books offered women
the opportunity to confront problems without going public, which consulting a specialist would necessarily involve. "I have one book at home
that has underlinings, marginal annotations that I wrote when I was
really working on a problem," one editor said. This editor also said that
she believed self-help books were helpful even if devoid of sophisticated
theoretical underpinnings, if they could assist people in defining what
their problems were. She said that she would often tell authors: "Even
identifying what is going on in this person's life, even putting a name
and a boundary around the pain or the difficulty that they're in, is such a
gift, that even if you don't have the ultimate solution, it doesn't matter."

As professional readers, editors hope the books they create will last on
the shelves, and are especially concerned with the time frame during
which self-help books will be found usable. One editor defined self-help
books in terms of their longevity:

I think self-help books fall into two categories, the ones that just go on forever, M. Scott Peck, *The Road Less Traveled* [for example] . . . and books that are much more topical and focused. For example, in twenty years I don't know that anyone is going to read *Smart Women, Foolish Choices,* not necessarily because the issue is any less pressing, but because we'll be approaching it differently, the whole demographic men-versus-women, and also in terms of age and emotional development, will be entirely different in twenty . . . years. A book like *Sex and the Single Girl,* the ultimate self-help book of what, the sixties?—I mean, is just laughable in a lot of ways today. So self-help books go through fashions the way other books do also.

All five editors agreed that self-help books must be practically didactic—that they should offer readers a comprehensible program to follow toward achieving desired results, and that this program should address current needs.

Like the readers I interviewed, editors believed that recent social and political changes had created an environment in which women were more likely than in the past to turn to reading for guidance or for a sense of community. One editor enumerated the factors she felt contributed to the current success of the self-help genre:

Well, I think that you're talking about . . . really a tremendous upheaval in terms of women's and men's roles and how women and men dealt with their sexuality. It became acceptable to live out of wedlock. . . . As the population shifted, and there were more women for fewer men of marriageable age, you saw . . . women . . . pursuing careers as an acceptable alternative to . . . getting married. Well, what was there in terms of role models for these women? Almost nothing. So where did they turn? To each other, and for advice, to the self-help books. . . . You also saw, you know, a serious fragmenting of family life. . . . It's not that there had never been divorce. It's not that there had never been single mothers. But when you take a look at statistics and the percentage of the population . . . the fact that the population is so much more mobile, that families and friendships tend to be far more tenuous now than they were twenty-five years ago—and who knows what they'll be twenty years down the road? People have to turn *some-where*. And I think they're turning to these . . . authority figures, the way that . . . maybe you used to talk to your mother, or you used to talk to an older sister, or you used to talk to whoever.

This editor felt that marriage—once an immutable fact for most women—had become an option, and at the same time, norms govern-ing heterosexual interactions had been called into question. Without widely accepted guidelines for behavior, women, especially, were at sea. She said, "I think what a lot of the self-help books are doing are responding to a need for advice, a stability." She saw women's use of self-help books as a means of allaying confusion, and as a search for new parameters for conducting relationships.

Several editors said that part of the reason they thought women were reading self-help books much more than men were had nothing to do with the genre, per se, but was due to the fact that women read and buy more books on the whole. Editors, like readers participating in this research, also said that they believed psychological self-help was espe-cially appealing to women because women are more likely to examine and attempt to ameliorate problems in their lives than men are. In the words of one editor:

I don't know whether this is a cultural or a genetic thing, but I think, as a rule, women are more introspective than men. We have certainly been trained—if there is some kind of inherent pre-disposition among women to be more sensitive, more nurturing, more aware of others' feelings . . . that has certainly been nurtured in us by the culture. . . . I think women have a real hard time in a lot of ways—not to say that men don't—but the women I know seem to be actually looking for answers, and the men seem to feel like why should they bother?

Editors also mentioned that women readers find self-help books ap-pealing because our culture encourages people—especially women—to seek out the advice of "experts," and reading is, as one editor said, "one way to gain access to an expert." Capitalist consumer culture also pro-motes a focus on the self as a product to be improved with the aid of purchases (like books). Ego-centered behavior—which editors see self-help books as advocating—has become a viable subject area in women's reading, one which editors do not see as detrimental to women's development. And even though many of the currently popular self-help books are about forming or conducting fruitful relationships with others, editors thought the commercial success of these books reflected the growing self-centeredness of women. They saw this as a potentially positive or liberatory development.

Several editors complained about books they saw as pitting men and women against each other. One editor said that recently there has been a "whole spate of man-bashing books," and while the messages promoted in such books may be, in part, realistic, she felt they were not representative of the whole picture of heterosexual relations. She told me about a book she had signed recently that offered a "more refreshing message." (The premise of this book was that there were good men out there, and that women were, in part, responsible for the ways in which men treated them.)

Another editor said that she felt certain questions were unanswerable in a general sense, and so she felt self-help books were often deceptive in their claims or promises:

> I don't think there is a book that can tell you how to make a relationship work. . . . Problems people have with relationships tend to be easier to generalize than what makes a happy relationship a happy relationship. . . . I've seen a lot of proposals from people that we've all turned down about what makes their marriage work. It's not what's going to make your marriage work, or my marriage work, or your mother's marriage work, or your sister's marriage work. That's something that's got to be worked out on a very individual basis. . . . You can give people [only] guidelines about solving their problems.

Three of the editors I spoke with said that they would read the types of self-help books they edit as part of their own personal (not work-related) reading. One editor said, "I get exposed to, of course, enormous numbers of books in the course of doing business, and there are definitely books I have taken home because I needed what was in them; there was no professional reason for me to be reading them." Another described how her personal reading could also help her professionally, to bridge the gap between the business world and the realm of the lay-reading public.

One of the editors who said that she, personally, would *not* read self-help books explained that although she "probably shouldn't say so," she thought a person would have to be "sort of insecure" for self-help to appeal to her. She said that she thought people read books in the genre constantly and could become "sort of addicted to it." She did not think this meant that self-help books could not be helpful, and told me that when her mother was widowed, she gave her a self-book on the topic, which she said her mother found "enormously comforting." She said that it helped her mother to feel that what she was going through was normal, and that it let her "see she was not alone." The other nonreader said that she "never responded to the more popular kind of advice books," and that if she were to consult a book for assistance, it would probably be of a more practical, rather than psychological, nature.

Predicting the Future

I asked the editors I interviewed to speculate about where they thought the genre of self-help was headed now, both because I was curious about what they would think as experts in the field, and because I wanted to hear what their actual guesswork would sound like, after hearing them describe the process in detail, but in retrospect. Editors agreed that the two hottest current topics in self-help books were addiction and New Age philosophy. Several had begun working in one or both of these areas. And since these interviews, these two areas have forged a merger of sorts in the "recovery" subject area, which has really taken off. "Already recovery is spinning off into a veritable catalogue of subcategories: abuse, alcohol addiction, incest, food addiction, work addiction, etc." (Jones 1990: 18).

Editors described ways in which addiction theories and therapies were being applied to interpersonal or interfamilial relations. Only one editor with whom I spoke thought this area of self-help was already "glutted"; the others felt it was still burgeoning. They agreed that books focusing on women's relationships with men had become overly narrow since the outbreak of prescriptive literature launched in the mideighties by books like *Smart Women, Foolish Choices* and *Women Who Love Too Much.* They expected a trend toward books written more generally about (heterosexually oriented) family life. Books growing out of the AA (Alcoholics

Anonymous) and ACOA (Adult Children of Alcoholics) programs were mentioned by all five of the editors I interviewed as examples of a growing topic area within self-help. Each editor talked about recent influxes of book projects centering on the premise that dysfunctional behavioral patterns are, at root, addictive and should be dealt with in ways that have been effective in treating alcoholism and other physical addictions.

When I asked one editor why she thought conceptions of problems as addictions were currently in vogue, she said:

> I think that in terms of the chemical addictions . . . the disease theory of alcoholism has had a fantastic role to play in enabling people to deal with addictions as a practical problem, rather than as a moral failure, so that whereas years ago, you know, the *shame* involved in admitting any of that was so overwhelming that people never went for help. Now you can just say—and remove the stigma, the *incredible* stigma from the condition. And I think it's just been a major breakthrough. I think that the ramifications are way beyond alcoholism. I think we're now a society that're really looking at compulsive behavior on every level.

Editors think women and men find the New Age approach attractive because it combines many traditional elements—philosophy, psychology, and history—with an intriguing and exotic flair—occult, Eastern religion, holistic medicine. But women appear to be buying far more of this self-help subgenre than men, if codependency sales are any indication of New Age sales as a whole (Kaminer 1990).

Since my meetings with these editors, I have been watching the bestseller lists, and so far, their predictions have been accurate. Several books on heterosexual family life patterns as addictive or poisonous have risen to success (like Susan Forward's *Toxic Parents: Overcoming Their Hurtful Legacy and Reclaiming Your Life* [1989] and Paul Pearsall's *The Power of the Family: Strength, Comfort, and Healing* [1990]), and New Age influences can be seen in many of the most recent bestsellers, especially in their spiritualism and offering of prescriptive exercises designed to help practitioners gain a sense of self, and then self-love (e.g., Melody Beattie's *Beyond Codependency: And Getting Better All the Time* [1989], John Bradshaw's *Healing the Shame that Binds You* [1988], John-Roger and Peter McWilliams's *Life 101: Everything We Wish We Had Learned about Life in School—but Didn't* [1991]). And whatever happens next in the self-help genre will be shaped by them (and by others like them).

Yet, ironically, if these editors were familiar with Wendy Griswold's cultural diamond, they would see themselves as rather unobtrusive participants in the creative end of making culture. Their vision of their role in making books revolves around the idea that they merely push projects forward, while shaping them to fit the waiting public's needs. The many tasks that build upon one another as a written project grows into a completed work are parts of a profession they see as helping those it serves.

Over the course of their careers (one of the editors I interviewed had worked in publishing for twenty years), the themes their authors have written about have changed—and will continue to change—but in their explanations of their work, editors don't see that they play a part in creating changes. Rather, they view themselves as guides, consultants, hopeful fortune-tellers predicting future reading tastes, who remain quietly in the background.

Editors of self-help books obviously have a vested interest in the reputations of their books; I expected that they would see their projects as addressing legitimate concerns and offering something beneficial and unique to readers. Editors expressed a certain degree of cynicism about the genre of self-help, but their criticisms were most often about *other* books—books with which they had little or no professional connection. They spoke willingly of the shortcomings of reading as a method of problem solving, but their comments did not negate the validity they perceived in the works they brought to press.

Written Defenses:
Keeping Readers Reading

I briefly considered interviewing authors as well as editors. But several televised and print features about authors convinced me that this was unnecessary. The descriptions authors gave of their work when they talked to journalists or talk-show hosts were indistinguishable from the introductory remarks or self-defenses in their books; all they said in person and in print was designed to frame their work as legitimate and special. Authors, even more than editors, must be expected to enthusiastically defend the integrity of their creations or else admit to being money-hungry or sensationalists (or both). Their recapitulations of introductory defenses are, after all, what any good self-promoters would do, and what publicity departments advise and expect. An examination of writers' introductory comments illuminates the ways in which authors frame their arguments, the ways in which they attempt to keep readers interested. Sensibly, authors present their most eloquent and attention-grabbing material first, to keep readers reading.

Self-help authors usually begin by presenting what a few of my readers referred to as their "promise" (which is often—but not always—a toned-down restatement of the aggressive promise made on the cover). In their introductions, authors devote their energy to showing that the topics they will discuss and the analyses they will offer will help readers make changes that are of paramount importance. In some introductions, authors' statements are so ambitious they sound as if foolproof plans for achieving a state of perfection and bliss will be revealed.

In *The Power of Positive Thinking* (1952), now considered a classic of the genre of self-help, Norman Vincent Peale writes: "THIS BOOK IS WRITTEN to suggest techniques . . . which demonstrate that you do not need to be defeated by anything, that you can have peace of mind, improved health, and a never-ceasing flow of energy. In short, that your life can be full of joy and satisfaction" (ix). More recently, but no less ambitiously, Irene Kassorla promises readers of *Go for It!* (1984) that with her help, they will be able to realize any goal or dream. She provides a list of accomplishments that following her program will enable readers to achieve:

- become the person you could greatly admire.
- make a difference in your world.
- be increasingly creative and innovative.
- balance a healthy combination of warmth and assertiveness.
- infuse a sense of joy into your daily activities.
- get the appreciation and approval of those you value.
- develop more endurance and energy.
- explore the full extent of your personal magnitude and power.
  (xiv)

Authors want not only to show the benefits that readers will reap from continuing to read, but also to impress upon them the urgency of the issues to be discussed. Authors want readers to feel they ought not put the book down. Reminders of the momentous nature of the arguments being presented recur throughout self-help books. Steven Carter and Julia Sokol, authors of *Men Who Can't Love* (1987), proclaim, for example, "Today, unlike any other period in our history, the fear of commitment is destroying the fabric of our society" (68).

Self-help authors demonstrate their reliability or expertise in two ways—and commonly through a combination of both: they present themselves as well educated, practiced, and even scientifically sound professionals and/or as authorities who are especially enriched by life-changing personal experiences. Editors see their professionalism as involving an imperative to keep up with trends in American culture; authors explain how they came to be astute enough to chart and analyze these trends. Many begin their books by telling about the personal and/ or professional circumstances that led them to begin writing. These introductory self-revelations are meant to draw readers into a relationship of sorts with the author. They are meant to elicit trust as well as an interest in both the topic and its discussant. It is as if the author were letting the readers in on his or her secrets.

Some professional authors reveal that they were led to pursue careers in psychiatry, psychology, or counseling as a result of having "been there," while others claim to have gained their insights through their practices alone.[1] Some professionals approach the task of writing by maintaining the personae of disinterested experts. They do not expose their own lives in any way, do not use colloquial language, do not address readers directly. For instance, Harold H. Bloomfield et al. (1975) begin *TM: Discovering Inner Energy and Overcoming Stress* by writing: "In our discussion of expanding human capacity through psychophysiological integration we will use the concept of creative intelligence to describe the principle of integrated, or holistic, growth which TM catalyzes. . . . The purpose of this book is to present the significance of TM within a coherent scientific framework" (8).

Authors who maintain a distanced, almost textbooklike tone present their arguments in a manner that asks for respect; they are intent on making their work sound genuinely authoritative. They appear to believe that if they adopt a style associated with scholarly writing or clinical reports, their arguments stand a better chance of being credited. Authors also hope they will not lose the respect of their colleagues by writing books for laypeople; using professional language may help to maintain status.

Some authors appear confused in their struggle to settle upon a narrative style; they erratically combine a dry, professional tone with more informal, personalized language. One such author is Thomas A. Harris, M.D., who explains his purpose in *I'm OK—You're OK* (1969) by writing: "This book is the product of a search to find answers for people who are looking for hard facts in answer to their questions about how the mind operates, why we do what we do, and how we can stop doing what we do if we wish" (13). Harris begins matter-of-factly; he does not attempt to make personal contact with readers: he will help "people" understand how "the mind" works. But then he shifts in the middle of his statement, and includes himself in this category, saying he will examine "why *we* do what *we* do" (emphasis added). Harris wants to sound like a scientist, but he also wants to entice the reader by addressing him or her in a more personable way.

Over time, the purely professional and rather cold narrative style has nearly disappeared from the self-help genre. Most authors have adopted writing styles that enable them to address readers familiarly. An informal authorial voice lends itself to a confession-style introduction. When authors disclose information about their personal lives, they show how their wonder and excitement over their own improvement has impelled them to help others going through the same problems. "Confessional" authors reiterate the same basic process in their introductory defenses of their work: First, they explain how in retrospect, they initially came to realize they had a problem. Next, they discuss how seemingly miraculously, but through their own hard work, they were able to overcome it. This process made them into natural advocates for others with the same problem, people who are less able to fight their problems alone. Finally, in writing about all of this, they become prophets, and set out to explain—on paper—the unique process that has saved them from a lifetime of misery or loneliness.

Authors' revelations make reading seem almost like an exchange, the reverse of the way live face-to-face therapy usually works; here, instead of clients revealing themselves while therapists are disinterested listeners, the therapist speaks to a client who does not respond (directly). Many therapist-writers try to show that they are just like regular people, and that they trust readers with the (sometimes sordid) details of their personal lives.

On the very first page of *Codependent No More* (1987), Melody Beattie tells readers that she used to be an addict and alcoholic. She goes on to explain that after recovering, she became a "codependent"—someone who is closely involved with another person's addictive behavior. Her experiences as an addict, a codependent, and finally as a counselor of both addicts and codependents, led her to write the book. She wants readers to know from the outset that she is not an authority claiming to have the answers to all of their problems. She simply has an understanding to pass on: "I'm not an expert, and this isn't a technical book for experts," she writes (6).

Professional authors sometimes reveal their lack of expertise when it comes to their own lives, in an attempt to gain readers' empathy. In the section of *Men Who Hate Women and the Women Who Love Them* (1986) entitled "A Personal Introduction," Susan Forward confides: "On the outside, I appeared confident, fulfilled—a woman who truly had it all. . . . But at home, it was another story. . . . I soon discovered that [my husband] had a great deal of anger inside him and that he had the power to make me feel small, inadequate and off-balance. He insisted on being in control of everything I did, believed, and felt" (Forward and Torres 4).

Forward writes that she came to realize that she and her husband should be in therapy, that their marriage was suffering from the same problems the women she counseled were describing in their own troubled relationships. However, like many of the misogynist men with whom her clients were involved, Forward's husband would not recognize the problem as she did; he was unwilling to go for professional help. So, she writes, "Finally, painfully, I came to the conclusion that I could no longer stay in our marriage without giving myself up" (9).

Divorcing her husband changed her life. With a heightened awareness of—and interest in—misogynist relationships, Forward began to see patterns in her clients' descriptions of their lives. "Convinced that I had discovered a major psychological disorder, I decided to test the waters further by discussing the topic on *A.M. Los Angeles,* a TV talk show." The show was bombarded with phone calls; Forward was swamped with letters. "I knew I'd hit a nerve," she writes, "The sense of urgency in the letters was tremendous. Women wanted to know where they could find a book on the subject of misogyny." The rest, of course, is history. Forward became a woman with a mission: "I knew then that I had to write this book—not only to help women understand what was happening to them, but also what they could do about it" (11). Narratives like Forward's are evidence that the detached ideal of professionalism for therapy providers has been subverted, at least in print therapy. Professional advice givers are also *personal* experts.

The particular experiences of each author define the contours of the problems and proffered solutions. Like Forward, Colette Dowling felt an urgent need to write,. to make a connection with other women suffering as she had suffered. But Dowling saw her situation (and thus women's situation in general) as developing out of her own inadequacies (and thus women's inadequacies), not the inadequacies of her husband (and thus of men in general). Dowling felt "trapped" within her marriage, her housewifery, but came to feel that this was a trap she set for herself. Her view of her own problem as self-initiated encourages readers who identify with her descriptions to see their problems in the same way.

Dowling writes of her own resistance to the idea that she had been responsible for her own unhappiness and lack of autonomy, thus encouraging readers to recognize—and to overcome—the same denial in their own lives:

> Financially [my husband] was providing everything. . . . It hurt him, he said, that I seemed content to sit back and take advantage of his willingness to help out.
>
> The suggestion that I was not living up to my end of the bargain was utterly enraging. . . . Didn't he appreciate all that I was doing for him, the lovely *home* that I was making, the wonderful cakes and pies? . . . It was true that in our domestic arrangement I was the one who was doing most of the "shit work." It was also true that I had arrogated that role to myself. . . . Inwardly, I *wanted* to be doing the shit work. (8–9)

Dowling goes on to explain that her unhappiness led her to begin writing, and thus her writing helped her to see her own predicament clearly, and to face the fact that she had brought her problems on herself. She sees writing as a potential way of overcoming her loneliness: "Maybe if I described the experience I would find that there were others out there like me. The idea that I might be an anomaly, some kind of helpless, dependent misfit, alone in the world, was horrifying," she writes (13). And, of course, the success of the book indicates that Dowling was correct in her assessment that others like her existed. Authors describe the positive outpouring of identification with which they are met when they begin to discuss their ideas publicly; and in telling, they invite the reader to join the group of vehement supporters even before she has read the ideas in question.

Harold Kushner describes how loss, rather than a crisis in identity, spurred his writing of *When Bad Things Happen to Good People* (1981). The death of his son made Kushner, a rabbi, question not only religious teachings, but the meaning of life itself. In his introduction, entitled "Why I Wrote This Book," Kushner writes vividly of his son's life and death, of his own despair, and of his inability to find enough consolation from friends or in religious books. The books he read "had answers to all of their own questions, but no answer for mine." He decided to create what he did not find for others:

> I am a fundamentally religious man who has been hurt by life, and I wanted to write a book that could be given to the person who has been hurt by life—by death, by illness or injury, by rejection or disappointment—and who knows in his heart that if there is justice in the world, he deserved better. . . . If you are such a person, if you want to believe in God's goodness and fairness but find it hard to because of the things that have happened to you and to people you care about, and if this book helps you do that, then I will have succeeded in distilling some blessing out of Aaron's pain and tears. (4–5)

Men authors of self-help books are less likely to reveal their own stories as Kushner did. Another exception, and one of the first men writers of self-help to bare all, is Mel Krantzler, who begins *Creative Divorce* (1973) by telling the story of his. He was devastated. "I felt like the loneliest man in the world. My internal inventory was zero. Looking back, I could see only failure and guilt—and ahead, a vortex of emptiness, fear and uncertainty. After twenty-four years of marriage, the prospect of living alone seemed intolerable" (10).

This was the old Mel Krantzler, as yet untransformed by the miracles of self-exploration offered by single life. Divorce, rather than acting as the negative force he first perceived it to be, transformed him: "By getting me out of the ruts of my earlier existence," he writes, "the divorce forced me to take a good look at myself, analyze where I was and how I had gotten there, and set the stage for what has been the most exciting and rewarding period of my life so far" (10). Krantzler eventually became an advocate for divorced people, beginning "a new career as a full-time counselor in divorce adjustment problems." His book grew out of his own personal/professional experience, out of his conviction that divorced people could use help finding the yellow brick road that

Krantzler stumbled upon himself: "I saw the need to share this knowledge with other divorced or separated persons who felt trapped and hopeless," he writes (31).

In Carter and Sokol's *Men Who Can't Love* (1987), Steven Carter described how his research for the book initiated self-reflection. In his interviews with single women, Carter heard complaints about men that forced him to confront his own past relationships and his own inability to make commitments: "I liked talking to these women. It was terrific being viewed as Mr. Sensitive, Mr. Understanding, Mr. Nice Guy, but it was a hoax. When I stopped to think about my own relationships, I couldn't help but acknowledge that there had been times when I was no different from most of the 'creeps' they complained about" (17). Carter's self-revelations are different from most in that they are about the process of writing, not about the process that led to writing. Carter wants to show readers how he, too, learned about himself while gathering the material he will present.

Like Forward, Krantzler, and Carter, many self-help authors see themselves as crusaders of sorts. They feel that they are the first to offer a satisfactory definition of a problem, and/or the first to design a successful way out. Dowling writes: "*The question was, why was no one talking about this? How many women might be suffering in silent confusion? Is an inner fear of independence epidemic among women?*" (19, emphasis in original). Dowling names the problem "the Cinderella Complex." In *Women Who Love Too Much* (1985), Robin Norwood writes of her "discoveries" that obsessive love is really based on fear, that women learn to "love too much" in their childhoods, that love can function just like other addictions (xiv–xv). With her new way of understanding relationships, Norwood feels that only a new treatment will be successful; she recommends "Women Who Love Too Much" groups, founded on the same principles as Twelve Step Programs developed by AA (Alcoholics Anonymous) and its spin-offs. Authors strive for what editors see as a unique formulation of a problem or a solution. But they quite often represent this striving as chance revelation—just the chain of events that befell them and their accidentally fortunate methods of responding—in order to downplay the profit that may also be involved. Though editors and authors are not the least bit Marxist in their outlook on the publishing industry, they definitely do not wish to appear to be motivated by money. In fact, self-help authors almost never speak of their books as purchasable commodities, because this would call their altruism into question.[2]

Instructions for Reading

Whether or not authors include conversionlike confessional narratives as parts of their explanations of their crusades, they *invite* readers to listen; they pepper their writing with questions, admonitions, assignments, and advice for all the "yous" out there reading. They urge readers to imagine themselves a part of the telling, to get involved in the substance of the book. Some authors write that they will provide easy answers, while others caution that reading their works may be difficult, may be painful, may entail hard work, but promise that it will be worth it. Authors' assurances of both difficulty *and* ease are used to entice readers. Kassorla, for instance, tries to appeal to readers in a hurry, writing: "EVERYONE READING THIS BOOK HAS THE POWER TO CHANGE. EVERYONE . . . AND ESPECIALLY YOU CAN DEVELOP WINNING BEHAVIORS. YOU CAN START RIGHT NOW!" (xii, ellipses in text). She makes the job ahead sound easy, exciting, and URGENT.

Most authors temper their promises with recommendations of caution. Solving one's problems—an act self-help writers increasingly have referred to as "recovery"—will take time, energy, and devotion: Norwood warns early on: "Should you decide that you really to want to follow these steps, it will require . . . years of work and nothing short of your total commitment" (xvii), and Forward cautions readers of *Toxic Parents* (1989) that "it would be both unrealistic and irresponsible of me to suggest that if you follow the path I outline, all your problems will disappear overnight" (186).

Self-help authors, whether casual or formal in their style, commonly claim scientific backing for the material they present. Authors rely on popular perceptions of the realm of the scientific as factual and undoubtable. In *Psycho-Cybernetics* (1960), Maxwell Maltz proclaims: "Science has now confirmed what philosophers, mystics, and other intuitive people have long declared: every human being has been literally 'engineered for success by his Creator'" (25). In *Body Language* (1970), Julius Fast draws on the works of many experts (including Erving Goffman, Ray L. Birdwhistell, Paul L. Wachtel, and others) to substantiate the "scientific" nature of what he presents. David Burns introduces *Feeling Good* (1980) by writing: "In this book I will share with you some of the latest scientifically tested methods for overcoming blue moods and for feeling good about your life" (1).

Authors' defenses of their work as science are applied to all varieties of self-help advice, from therapeutic techniques, such as those cited above, to spiritual advice. L. Ron Hubbard calls his *Dianetics* (1985) "the Modern Science of Mental Health" and assures readers, "All our facts are functional and these facts are scientific facts, supported wholly and completely by laboratory evidence" (96). (Hubbard does not include any clear descriptions of the research he claims has been done.) Writing from a more traditional religious framework, Peale (1952) claims that even the Bible was a work of science: "These principles [of faith] are scientific and sound and can heal any personality of the pain of inferiority feelings" (16).

Authors also attempt to show that what they have to say will be broadly appealing by assuring readers that they don't have to identify with *every* case study to gain positive results from their reading. Authors stress that their messages may apply to less extreme cases as well, telling readers that even if their lives are not falling apart they can probably learn from reading and "participating" in the suggested exercises. Norwood, for example, implies that most—if not all—women should be able to relate to her book, and that if they can't, they're deceiving themselves:

> If you are a woman who loves too much, I feel it only fair to caution you that this is not going to be an easy book to read. Indeed, if the definition fits and you nevertheless breeze through this book unstirred and unaffected, or you find yourself bored or angry, or unable to concentrate on the material presented here, or only able to think about how much it would help someone else, I suggest that you try reading the book again at a later time. We all need to deny what is too painful or too threatening for us to accept. . . . Perhaps at a later reading you will be able to face your own experiences and deeper feelings. (xvi)

Norwood tells readers that, essentially, there is really no way *not* to relate to what she has to say; by not identifying or disagreeing with her—even by finding the reading boring—readers unconsciously demonstrate a reaction Norwood defines as a psychological device (denial). Most self-help writers are less dramatic in their exhortations to readers.

Sonya Friedman (1985) delivers a more inspiring pep talk designed to keep readers reading; she writes: "Be a smart cookie. Do not go back; do not even stay as you are! Go forward with energy. Go forward knowing that you can reconstruct your life. . . . You have a right and a responsibility to enjoy life, to be excited by it" (17–18). And in her pursuit of identifying readers, Helen Gurley Brown (1982) offers the most gungho, all-inclusive, and most drawn-out come-on of all. She describes the readers she hopes to attract—"mouseburgers"— as people like her, "who are not prepossessing, not pretty, don't have a particularly high I.Q., a decent education, a good family background or other noticeable assets" (2). Brown encourages women to find out if they are mouseburgers by considering a number of questions:

> Of course, we have to determine if you want the same things I have wanted for my book, my craft, to be useful to you. Do you, by any chance, *also* want:
> To love and be loved by a desirable man or men?
> To enjoy sex?
> To be happy in your work—and maybe even famous?
> To make money—possibly a lot?
> To look great?
> To have wonderful, loyal friends?
> To help your family?
> To be free from *most* anxiety?
> Never to be bored and maybe leave the world a better place? (3)

What ambitious heterosexual woman could fail this mouseburger test? It doesn't matter, of course, because Brown aims to reassure readers that they *should* be readers—that they are mouseburgers. As if one questionnaire were not enough, Brown adds a further, more extensive test of mouseburgerhood:

> Please answer True or False to these statements: *You're smart. . . . You are sensitive. . . . You're modest. . . . Envy is not unknown to you. . . . You're more selfish than altruistic. . . . You have a sweet natural sex drive that brings you enormous pleasure. . . . You have drive. . . . You sometimes hurt. . . . It's hard for you to be casual about anything. . . . You want it all, and are "willing to pay the price." . . .* If you answered "True" to at least ten . . . I think you and I are alike. If you answered "True" to even five, I may be able to help you. (3–6, emphasis in original)

Brown differs from many self-help writers in that the conglomerate of qualities she details under the umbrella label she applies are largely positive ones which don't need changing, just development. The reason mouseburgers do not always blossom unassisted is that they are impeded by a lack of confidence or, at worst, they are just a little lazy. Mediocrity can be finely tuned and polished into superiority, Brown promises, enlivening her narrative with personal anecdotes that assure readers they, too, can become successful, happy, and loved if they take her example to heart.

Self-help writers often describe their works as therapeutic texts, which, if readers are diligent, can yield the same results as face-to-face therapy. Louise Hay (1984) gives careful instructions to readers on how to follow her program:

> I have set up this book to take you through a session, just as I would if you came to me as a private client or attended one of my workshops.
>
> If you will do the exercises progressively as they appear . . . by the time you have finished, you will have begun to change your life.
>
> I suggest you read through the book once. Then slowly read it again, only this time do each exercise in depth. . . . Take two or three days to study and work with each chapter. Keep saying and writing the affirmation that opens the chapter.
>
> The chapters close with a treatment. This is a flow of positive ideas designed to change consciousness. Read over this treatment several times a day. (3)

Readers are often subtly informed, as Hay's instructions indicate, that if they don't do the work, they won't see improvements. The work (as Hay's instructions also show) can be quite demanding.

Marabel Morgan (1973) writes of her experiences in reviving her slumping marriage, of her "pursuit of knowledge" which led her to see "certain principles" recur, which she then applied "with stunning results." The ultimate altruist, Morgan gushes: "If, through reading and applying these principles, you become a Total Woman, with your husband more in love with you than ever before, my efforts in writing this book will have been rewarded" (21). Louise Hay (1984) tells her readers: "Know that when you work with these ideas my loving support is with you" (3–4). A bit more humbly, Norwood states in *Letters from*

Women Who Love Too Much (1988) that "simply reading a book, no matter how deeply it affects us, is never enough in itself to bring about the changes we desire in our lives. At best a book can be a signpost, an arrow pointing out the direction in which we need to travel" (4). But Norwood then directs readers back to the first "signpost" she authored, without which her second will not be as useful. She plugs *Women Who Love Too Much* in the preface to its sequel, explaining: "Obviously, in order to gain the most from this book a reader should have already read *WWL2M* slowly, carefully, and hopefully [*sic*] more than once" (xv).

Nobody Does It Better

There is a defensive quality to self-help authors' attempts to show the uniqueness of their arguments. Many authors are critical of competing or preceding self-help books on the same subjects; they want to show that the existing sources are inadequate, and that their work will fill a void. Self-help writers, however, seem to have a short memory and a narrow field of vision; authors discuss others' work not to show how their own fits in—or conflicts with—what is available within the genre (or outside it, in sociological or more academic psychological work) but to *justify* their writing at a particular time when there are likely to be several (or several dozen) other books on the seemingly exact "same" topic. Authors defend the definition of the situation they present as the only accurate one. Unlike the writers at the academic end of the discipline from which self-help books have trickled down, self-help authors often demonstrate a contempt for their colleagues; like readers, they suspect opportunism as a motivating force for a great deal of self-help writing and want to show that they are not part of this trend. Stephen R. Covey writes, for instance, that "an in-depth study of the success literature published in the United States since 1776" showed him that the past half-century had given rise to mostly "superficial" books, "social band-aids and aspirin that addressed acute problems . . . but left the underlying chronic problems untouched to fester and resurface time and again" (1989: 18). Covey feels his book offers the way out of this rut.

Even straight-shooting Robert Ringer feels inclined to separate himself from the other quacks out there proselytizing their own miracle cures. In *Looking Out For #1* (1977), he writes: "There are no ulterior motives involved. I'm not out to convert you to a cause, to enlist your aid in destroying an 'evil,' or to gain your support for or against anything. If you understand that the means to my end is to provide you with a valuable product, then you're already in the proper frame of mind for the realities which lie ahead" (7).

Like Ringer, but usually in a less brash manner, other self-help authors emphasize their honesty, commitment, and sense of vision amid a sea of misguided theorizers or even tricksters. Ironically, in his self-defense, Kushner confronts the views that Ringer espouses, which, by the time of his (Kushner's) writing, have gained a good deal of popularity: "My objection to the 'looking out for number one' philosophy is that it does not work. Take advantage of other people, use people, be suspicious of everyone, and you are liable to be so successful that you will end up far ahead of everyone else, looking down on them with scorn. And then where will you be? You will be all alone" (1986: 59).

More recently, Carter and Sokol write that "current popular non-fiction" addressed to women inadequately analyzes the problems in heterosexual relationships because it examines them from women's point of view, and "at the very best, this is exposing only half of the problem" (1987: 49). They assure readers that their book will be different because Carter has talked to men, and because he, as a man, could supposedly better understand men's motivations. Carter and Sokol do not comment on several similar self-help books that predate theirs, in which authors also claim to reveal men's secret motivations (e.g., Dan Kiley's *The Peter Pan Syndrome* [1983] and Connell Cowan and Melvyn Kinder's *Smart Women, Foolish Choices* [1985]).

Usually, self-help authors direct their objections at specific popular works that precede their own. Occasionally, though, authors offer wider generic critiques. Wayne Dyer, for example, faults psychology for its adherence to the medical model's methodology of viewing people in terms of pathology, or at best—in health—as lacking pathology. He writes: "[Psychologists] have written a lot about striving, but almost nothing about ever arriving anywhere. They see people as always having to improve rather than accepting them as healthy the way they are" (1980: 5). Unsurprisingly, Dyer does not go on to develop his argument into a treatise on how readers could or should remain the same (he would not be writing self-help if he did!). His tautological message is that self-acceptance will enable one to make changes, to fulfill one's potential: in other words, if one thinks of oneself as healthy, one will only get healthier.

Kushner sees the therapeutic framework (upon which most self-help books are based) as an evaluatory and adaptive tool, but not one that offers meaningful insight for spiritual or humanistic development. Psychology couldn't go beyond helping people to adapt to social norms. He writes: "the values of the therapeutic approach tend to be values of adjustment to what is, rather than visions of a world that does not exist. . . . [A skilled therapist] can unblock our ability to live meaningfully, but that is as far as he can take us" (1986: 21).

In the world of the self-help preface, authors celebrate their own expertise, altruism, and fervor for what readers are about to receive. In effect, the message each author hopes to convey can be generalized: I, an ordinary person, found out the hard way, and so I wanted to make it easier for you; and/or, through my (helpful) job as a doctor/ psychologist/therapist, I have come in contact with many who suffer from the same problem, and this book, I hope, will enable me to aide zillions more than I could if I divulged my (helpful) messages only to those who paid to get inside my office.

Both authors and editors see themselves as sort of modern-day prophets, hard at work in the distribution of (human rather than divine) expertise about how to live more fruitfully, more orgasmically, more successfully, more happily. Editors' modest self-evaluations show that they see themselves as silent partners to authors in the creation of books, but descriptions of the intricacies of their work indicate that their judgment and activities govern this process. Authors' self-evaluations are far less modest: in their attempts to entice readers to continue participating in the author-reader alliance, they boldly laud their work, claim grand applications for it, and defend its validity and altruistic purity against a backdrop of competing popular self-help books.

Chapter 5

Shelf Life: Bestselling Unisex Self-Help Books

If you don't decide which way to play with life, it always plays with you. (Shain 1978: 65).

Participants in my study have easily described how self-help books have (and have not) affected *them* personally, but have seemed puzzled when I voiced my own sociological concerns. When I asked questions about how self-help authors handled issues of blame and anger; about whether they read self-help advice as feminist or antifeminist; and about why the genre represented problems as individually—rather than socially— generated and solvable, they responded with puzzled looks. They asserted that, in reading (or editing) the books, they intended to provide or obtain advice and information about how individuals could change themselves. In these same interviews, they described the socially grounded conditions that made self-help books appealing to women, and discussed psychological problems as socially constructed. Ultimately, though, what editors hope to provide and what readers hope to get are not ideas about changing others or changing society.

But because I am a scholar engaged in sociological and feminist evaluation, the social ramifications of self-help authors' conceptualizations of blame, anger, feminism, and individualism are key issues for me in understanding the coherence of the genre of self-help and its impact on women readers. Self-help books are not the only game in town proffering advice to women on how we should live our lives. They are part of an extensive web of psycho-media, which includes women's magazines; women's fiction (or fiction directed at women, like romances); audio- and videotapes that offer advice; and "women's television"—soap operas and daytime talk shows and a specially targeted smorgasbord of cable offerings. Self-help books are simply the most forthrightly instructive of these cultural objects marketed toward a female audience, and can thus illuminate the prevalent images of women created for women (often by women) that are currently bought and sold in the United States.

Self-help books—especially those addressed specifically to women— have come under attack by critics in recent years. (These criticisms are discussed in detail in Chapter 6.) I do not intend to go to battle with the critics who have cast their aspersions on self-help books, in part because I—and the readers I interviewed—often agree with the stylistic and/or substantive appraisals critics offer. But more important, no amount of contesting the applicability of these books to people's lives will render them impotent. The fact remains that these books do appeal, do sell, and do tell a fascinating story about womanhood *and* manhood today. Critics' negative assessments point to the most glaring problems that afflict the self-help genre—oversimplicity, redundancy, encouragement of self-blame. Yet, ironically, these are the traits that have always been characteristic of self-help manuals—since Americans began writing them—and these are traits without which the genre might not exist.

Regardless of whether or not self-help books provide the assistance they promise; regardless of whether or not readers read each and every word and attempt to put authors' plans in motion; and regardless of how long bestsellers remain bestsellers, the continued existence and success of the genre of self-help since its inception say something about the American social psyche. Readers' perceptions about the accuracy (or inaccuracy) of the portraits of women and men offered are crucial to understanding the "consumption" of the genre, and have been con- sidered in other chapters. Here, however, I want to flesh out these portraits and see where they have come from and how they've been shaped over the past several decades. In this and the following chapter, I review the genesis and "development" of the troubled woman and the troubling man (or sometimes vice versa) as they have developed since the 1960s in self-help literature.

I begin (in this chapter) by discussing self-help books whose titles do not imply that they are geared specifically to women, books I call "unisex" self-help, a category which clearly enabled women's self-help. Religious or spiritually oriented self-help books are included within the unisex category. Books dealing with sexuality are a fitting point of transition into relationship-oriented self-help books, for they often are specifically directed at an audience of women. In Chapter 6, I discuss self-help books that are clearly addressed to women or that deal with amending relationships holistically (rather than from a specifically sexual angle). I consider relationship-oriented self-help books to be a category for women because these books are—much more often than not—directed toward, bought, and read by an audience dominated by women. Women, as participants in my study have testified, are held culturally responsible for doing the bulk of the work involved in maintaining heterosexual relationships, so presumably these books are written to appeal to us.

The Objects of Study

I examined self-help books that had appeared on the *New York Times Book Review* bestseller lists between January 1963 and July 1991. The lists fell into the categories of hardcover nonfiction, hardcover advice, paperback advice, trade, and mass market.[1] Lists appearing during the first week of each month were consulted; all self-help books that fall into the categories of psychological self-improvement (at times linked with physical well-being), spiritual development, sexuality, or relationship enhancement were included. (See Table 2 for a chronological listing of the bestsellers included.) Self-help books dealing strictly with financial matters, diet, exercise, health or child care were *not* included.[2] I included bestsellers with a central focus on success in business or health only when authors claim their programs will involve introspection or psychological "growth" (beyond simply the manipulation of the physical self in order to feel better mentally or the teaching of practices that are held to produce success in business).

In making judgments about what self-help is (and isn't), I included books that present the claim—inside or on their covers—that they can offer instruction or assist readers in remedying personal problems. Steven Starker, author of *Oracle at the Supermarket: The American Preoccupation with Self-Help Books* (1989), believes that "intended audience" and "presumed utility" are crucial variables to consider in determining whether a book should be defined as self-help or not. By "intended audience," Starker means a book should be "clearly addressed to the lay reader," and by "presumed utility," he means a book should "[purport] to be of immediate and practical use to the reader, offering instruction in some aspect of living" (8–9). Establishing that books are intended as self-help, of course, involves making judgment calls, no matter how clearly one defines one's standards. Starker writes that self-help books should be "lively, interesting, readable and simplified" for a lay audience; but whether or not a book fits this description depends more on the readers than on the book, in my estimation. I paid less attention to style than Starker does, and relied on more obviously observable phenomena, such as titles (which, more often than not, are dead giveaways that a book is meant—or not meant—to be a self-help book); statements printed on the covers or made by authors in their introductions; and the form of exposition used by the author to present recommendations for change.

Promises and Premises: Covers and Contents

Of course, before they ever become readers, potential buyers must first be sold on the idea of buying particular books. Covers are designed to sell books. Self-help marketers are well aware that people *do* judge books by their covers. Perhaps more than any other literary genre, self-help books feature covers that are meant to attract, meant to sell. Titles are large and bold. Covers generally include extensive advertisements for the contents, which promise the potential reader various life improvements. If the authors are well-known, their names will be featured prominently, and in all cases, if the author has any advanced degree, it will be included.

A detailed examination of one such cover shows the various tactics promoters use to hook readers. A red and purple heart, made of two question marks facing each other, appears on the cover of *Smart Women, Foolish Choices* (not a "unisex" book, but utilized here because it's one of my favorite covers). An arrow through the heart underscores the words "FINDING THE RIGHT MEN." Underneath this caption are the words "AVOIDING THE WRONG ONES." This simple graphic design of a heart that doesn't know why it has been broken suggests that the answers may be found inside. Across the top of my copy of the book, outlined in blue, are the words "ONE MILLION IN PRINT," which assure potential buyers that they will be among a horde of other "smart women" if they decide to purchase the book (and the cover struggles to convince potential buyers that they won't regret the choice!). In bold purple, the blurb on the back cover announces, "THERE ARE GOOD MEN OUT THERE—AND HERE'S HOW TO FIND THEM." The reader is told, in individually bulleted claims, that she can: "*Broaden,* not *lower,* [her] expectations," "Avoid all-too-common types like the Married Rat, the Pseudo-Liberated Male, and the Perpetual Adolescent," "Recognize 'Diamonds in the Rough,'" "Free [her]self from 'love addiction,'" "And understand what *really* makes men fall in love—and stay that way." Underneath these promises to be fulfilled by reading are excerpted quotations from reviews from the *Los Angeles Times* and the *Charlotte Observer,* lauding: "A FASCINATING, HELP-FUL BOOK," and "*valid advice*. . . . You may go from romance junkie to free woman in one easy, insightful reading."

The readers I interviewed are suspicious of cover promises like these, but wishfully attracted by them nonetheless. They recognize that covers are advertisements, and that ads tend to exaggerate and even mislead; but they are attracted by them as a sports spectator might be to a pep rally before a big game. Nonetheless, ritualistic seduction is a big part of buying and selling in our culture: we want to see what's behind door number three. Attraction is not a sure thing, though; the aggressiveness of the come-on may have the opposite effect from that intended by promoters. Titles can allure as well as repel; many women reported being embarrassed about buying such titles as *How to Marry the Man of Your Choice,* and several asserted they would not even consider "silly" titles, such as *Men Who Hate Women and the Women Who Love Them.*

Once inside the covers of bestsellers, I found that their general aims and formal characteristics have not altered over time, though their directions and theoretical underpinnings have varied considerably. Self-help authors allege that their aim is to assist with problems usually described as widely encompassing—if not all-encompassing—flawed patterns in individuals' thoughts or behavior.[3] Authors often begin by defining a set of problematic behaviors, and labeling them and those who practice them. This is usually done in the opening pages of the book; afterward, the problem is dissected, accounted for, and finally, remedies are prescribed.

Norman Vincent Peale, for example, was quite enamored of the break-down technique for self-improvement. In *The Power of Positive Thinking* (1952), he presents "ten, simple, workable rules for overcoming inadequacy attitudes and learning to practice faith" (24–25); "ten

rules for getting effective results from prayer" (65); "six points [toward]
... reducing the tendency to fume and fret" (92); "a ten-point worry-
breaking formula" (131–132); "ten simple suggestions . . . to use generally in solving your problems" (143); "eight practical suggestions" to use
"when a loved one or you are ill" (155–156); "some [twelve, to be exact]
practical suggestions" to use "to fill the mind with attitudes of good will,
forgiveness, faith, love, and the spirit of imperturbability" (164–166);
"seven practical steps for changing your mental attitudes from negative
to positive" (178–179); "ten rules [to] . . . help you to relax and have
easy power" (189); and finally, "ten practical rules for getting the esteem
of others" (100). Many self-help authors have since drawn on Peale's
methodology, and divvied the bits and pieces of the processes they
recommend into carefully numbered steps to make them look easy to
accomplish—or, at the very least, manageable.

Part of the self-help book's promise is that if readers can *understand*
and accept the author's view of the problem—her or his jargon, subdivi-
sions, typifications, and classifications—then they will be able to gain
control over the problem as it manifests itself in their lives. Self-help
authors promise readers they can attain all varieties of happiness; assure
them they can create order in their lives; invite them to seek a genuine
sense of identity; and offer spiritual bliss through (correctly applied)
devoted self-attention. This is basic to *all* self-help books; they rely on the
premise that control over various—and often all—aspects of life *can* be
gained with the proper determination and method. Once readers learn
these techniques, authors imply, everything else will fall into place. This
offer of a method to gain control varies in form, ranging from explicit
guarantees to much more muted implications.

Authors who do not systematically or explicitly guide readers in any
way may still have their works marketed as self-help books. *The Feminine
Mystique,* the earliest example in the wave of bestselling self-help books I
have studied, is more of a political treatise than a program for reform:
Friedan set out to "hunt down the origins of" and to analyze the problem
she names "the feminine mystique." She did not promise to solve
readers' problems, but clearly she hoped to rouse their resistance,
especially with her concluding chapter, "A New Life Plan for Women."
The book, however, was marketed as self-help: the first edition cites Pearl
Buck and Virgilia Peterson on the front and back of the dust jacket,
exclaiming (respectively):

> Betty Friedan has, in my opinion, gone straight to the heart of the
> problem of the American woman, the problem she is to herself
> and the problem she creates thereby for the American man. This is
> a sensible, sound book, and now that the absurd feminine mys-
> tique is set forth so clearly, we can discard it and let a woman be a
> woman.

> I found *The Feminine Mystique* absorbingly interesting, pertinent,
> relevant to my own problems and those of every woman I know. . . .
> What Mrs. Friedan has done is to show both cause and cure. The
> book should be read by every anxious woman in the country.

Comments like these, though not as *blatantly* full of promise as the cover
of *Smart Women, Foolish Choices,* make *The Feminine Mystique* sound as if it
can be applied to the life experiences of any ordinary-yet-"anxious"
woman, and encourage potential readers to categorize it as a self-help
book.

Similarly, the books of Masters and Johnson, which are organized
around laboratory studies of sexual behavior, came dressed as self help.
On the back of *Human Sexual Inadequacy* (1970), for example, is printed:
"WHEN SEX IS A PROBLEM — MASTERS' AND JOHNSON'S BREAKTHROUGH
BESTSELLER." But inside, the style the authors choose is quite clinical,
and probably not originally designed to appeal to a mass audience. I
have included books such as these because their covers imply that they
ought to be used as advice, and because I believe that as a result of cover
promises they were probably bought and used as self-help.[4] Often, as
with the works of Friedan and Masters and Johnson, books gain a
reputation as self-help even if they do not appear to have been written
for a lay audience or to have lent themselves to easy-to-follow step-by-step
application to readers' problems (as Starker believes self-help books
should).

In my own reading of self-help books, I did not approach them as my
participants had—out of need, desperation, a desire to make changes in
my life, as part of a personal quest for specific or far-reaching answers, or
out of "innocent" curiosity. The whole time I was reading, I sought out
ideological patterns and looked for differences. I selected passages to
discuss that I felt were crucial to authors' arguments, as well as passages
that I felt would help illustrate the images of American women and men

sold in self-help books. My focus in interpreting self-help books is on the ideological positions they represent. Since the demands I made as I read are different from those of the women I interviewed, our interpretations are not necessarily the same, just as my interpretations of their reading are separate from my interpretations of my own reading. I don't see our differences as readers as incompatible: that participants feel they sometimes gain from self-help does not mean the genre's portrait of American culture ought not be seen as problematic.

The Emergence of the Genre

The first American self-help books centered on Puritan desires to achieve Christian goodness and success (Starker 1989: 13–15). Gradually, the books turned secular but retained their focus on the relationship between moral behavior and material success. Benjamin Franklin's writings of the mideighteenth century, of course, serve as Max Weber's prime example of the transformation of the Protestant ethic into capitalist dogma. Achieving financial success became a calling; "Man is dominated by the making of money, by acquisition as the ultimate purpose of his life," Weber wrote in 1905 (1958 rpt.: 53). Guides to easy money-making proliferated.

Starker (1989) writes that the highly visible opulence and greed that was characteristic of the Jacksonian period, beginning in the 1820s, spurred a reactive resurgence of self-help books that focused, like Franklin's, more on hard, honest work, and less on the pleasures of wealth. There were many books of this type addressed to children (Starker 1989: 16–18). The publication of self-help books promising that the work ethic would result in financial success continued until it was supplanted by the writings of "New Thought" proponents in the late nineteenth century. In these, the individual psyche took center stage; all action was conceived as radiating from the mind itself. The goal, then, of New Thought philosophers was to achieve a healthy mind. Starker writes:

> It was clear by the latter part of the nineteenth century that the classic self-help tradition, with its foundation in Puritan values and virtues, was no longer relevant to the new American culture and problems. An urban, industrial, and increasingly scientific America

desperately needed a new philosophy to provide hope and guidance to those confused and demoralized by rapid societal changes. . . . Rather than powerless pawns of industry, politics, and urbanism, people were properly to be viewed as important, unique, and full of potential, as local manifestations of Divinity. (1989: 20–21)

Offshoots of New Thought or theories of "Mind Cure" were popularized, primarily through the efforts of Mary Baker Eddy, founder of Christian Science. Challenging the Puritan conception of a vengeful, omnipotent God, Eddy and her followers saw human efforts as paramount. Physical ills were held to be manifestations of the mind, and, with the proper religious redirection and concentration, it was believed that disease— and all sorts of stresses caused by industrialization and urbanization— could be overcome. "The subconscious was conceived to be an invisible source of power and creativity, present in everyone, which could be harnessed by the true believer using meditative/relaxation/ suggestive exercises. . . . Mental suggestions needed only to permeate the individual human mind in order to reach the subconscious and there resonate with Divine Mind" (Starker 1989: 34).

At the same time as self-help books generating from New Thought philosophies were gaining popularity, self-help books for women written by doctors proliferated. These books espoused a rather different ideological orientation; they saw female virtue as residing in frailty, even invalidism. Barbara Ehrenreich and Deirdre English (1978) chart doctors' authority on womanhood in *For Her Own Good: 150 Years of the Experts' Advice to Women.* They write: "The theories which guided the doctor's practice from the late nineteenth century to the early twentieth century held that woman's *normal* state was to be sick. This was not advanced as an empirical observation, but as physiological fact" (110). Passivity was prescribed for women *as* womanliness—the "rest cure," a popular treatment for upper-middle-class women plagued by nerves, stretched this to the limit, advocating complete inertia for weeks at a time (131–133). Though this encouraging of passivity may seem a polar opposite to New Thought's emphasis on the self, both strategies relied on meditation and relaxation. Both conceived of stress as individually induced, and thus personally controllable (rather than resulting from social forces and necessitating social action).

The self-help books of the past several decades revitalize the themes of the Puritan period, along with the New Thought and Mind Cure conceptions of individual agency. Both approaches have been modified by the popularization of psychology, which Starker charts as beginning between the world wars, when psychoanalysis and behaviorism both gained notoriety (1989: 42–43). More recently, self-help books have been deeply affected by the mainstreaming of the (liberal) feminist movement, and by the rise to popularity of conservative politics (Reaganism and the New Right).

Unisex Self-Help Books

The earliest unisex bestselling self-help books of the past thirty years are about gaining control over one's circumstances through a "scientific" understanding of others' behavior. Relying on transactional analysis, self-actualization therapy, and/or gestalt therapy, these books assert that awareness will help readers gear their own behavior toward achieving desired ends. The unisex books fall into two basic categories (which do, at times, blend in a rather confusing fashion). The first group of authors sees "rational" thought as the key to attaining success, happiness, satisfaction. Their discussions make identity a machinelike quality; they believe it can be methodically built or rebuilt with the proper instruction and tools.

What I call "identity-as-machine" books were primarily written by enthusiasts of transactional analysis, which was first articulated by Eric Berne in *Games People Play* (1964), and reiterated even more successfully a few years later by Thomas A. Harris in *I'm Okay—You're Okay* (1967).

The second group of unisex self-help books is much more earthy and emotionally oriented; its authors encourage readers to undertake the careful examination of their feelings, thoughts, and past experiences—especially childhood—in the pursuit of "personal growth." Here, identity is conceived as a rather messy accumulation of emotions and encounters with other people. Identity can be altered through rational introspection which, when undertaken properly, will yield enhancing developments. Early books of this type, which I call "identity-as-growth" books, rely on language popularized by the hippie counterculture, which has gradually been modified into the yuppie language of New Age philosophy. Titles allude to self-enhancing expansion: *Homecoming: Re-*

claiming and Championing Your Inner Child (Bradshaw 1990), *The Sky's the Limit* (Dyer 1980); *You Can Heal Your Life* (Hay 1984), *How to Be Your Own Best Friend* (Newman and Berkowitz 1971), *The Road Less Traveled* (Peck 1978), and so forth.

Identity-as-growth books are presented as vehicles through which readers can achieve self-knowledge and self-love, qualities that are held to be prerequisites for relationships with others. In one of the most well-known of these, *How to Be Your Own Best Friend* (1971), the authors explain, "Your genuine self does not want to do things that are utterly foreign to it; it wants to realize its own potential" (44). In *Joy* (1967), William Schutz contends that attaining this essential self includes the difficult task of shedding the negative influences of others: "[A man] must express and explore his feelings and open up areas long dormant and possibly painful, with the faith that in the long run the pain will give way to a release of vast potential for creativity and joy" (19). Inside each person, the growth books inform, is a special story waiting to happen. Drawing on the Christian notion that each individual is special and unique to God, identity-as-growth books often insist on spirituality as a key to achieving a sense of contentment with one's self, and harmony with the world.

Identity-as-machine self-help books do not take "problems" as their starting point; instead they present themselves as psychological guides for laypeople who are, authors imply, nonreflective, nonanalytical, and thus ignorant, until they read these books. This group of books was meant to appeal in a manner similar to ads in the backs of magazines for "X-ray" glasses that would allow little boys (presumably) to see everyone naked. The premise of these books is that *other* people are operating unconsciously, so gaining an understanding of their motives will put (the exclusive group of) readers way ahead. Life is clearly conceived as a competition, as the titles indicate: *Games People Play* (Berne 1964), *You Can Negotiate Anything* (Cohen 1980), *Born to Win* (James and Jongewood 1971), *Looking Out for #1* (Ringer 1971), *Winning through Intimidation* (Ringer 1974), and so forth.

I Think, Therefore I Can

Identity-as-machine and identity-as-growth books are indebted both to ideas espoused by the Protestant Ethic manuals (like Franklin's) about rational accumulation and to New Thought proponents' notions of positive thinking and self-control. Both types of modern self-help books center on the premise that individuals are responsible for whatever happens to them. Successful relationships will occur as a by-product of successful self-knowledge. Authors detail ways in which people remain seemingly trapped in unfortunate circumstances because of an ignorance the authors claim to be able to cure simply by pointing it out: people do not *realize* their potential power to alter the course of their lives. Todd Gitlin (1987) sees the movement out of which these books grew as a desperate and self-deceptive search for satisfaction and control brought on by the political burnout of sixties activism:

> The impulse to collective expression, blocked on the plane of human action, gets diverted toward the spiritual. . . . With secular revolution discredited as an escape from the "iron cage" of narrow rationality, individual subjectivity promised to reinvent a shattered world: Act *as if* the world were not a prison, and your life will be made whole. If society was impenetrable and politics a simple reshuffling of elite credentials, the self could still be transformed at will—even if, in Zen-like fashion, what was required was the will to wrestle out of the grip of the demon will itself. (426)

Beginning in the 1960s, self-help books revitalized the age-old American notions that material attainment and personal well-being are the results of properly focused desire. Individual destiny is seen as unfolding in accordance with hard work—but a new kind of hard work in which people turn their efforts inward. Authors promise that, with the proper training, thought patterns, intentions, and enthusiasm, readers can become as emotionally and/or materially successful as they (authors) are themselves. But without all this, readers are sure to remain stuck in the same old ruts. Most of all, self-help authors stress, readers must recognize that, either way, it is their choice to do something about their problems or languish in unhappiness!

This belief in people's ability to gain complete control over the conditions of their lives has remained the cornerstone of the self-help genre, even as the original "machine" and "growth" types fizzled out of print. Statements such as the ones that follow, culled from various bestsellers of the past three decades, are typical of the genre:

The self image is a "premise," a base, or a foundation upon which your entire personality, your behavior, and even your circumstances are built. (Maltz 1960: 2)

The problems of the world—and they are chronicled daily in headlines of violence and despair—essentially are the problems of individuals. If individuals can change, the course of the world can change. (Harris 1967: 17–18)

We are accountable only to ourselves for what happens to us in our lives. (Newman and Berkowitz 1971: 22)

All life is a game of power. The object of the game is simple enough: to know what you want and get it. (Korda 1975: 4)

YOU ARE THE SUM TOTAL OF YOUR CHOICES, and . . . with an appropriate amount of motivation and effort you can be anything you choose. (Dyer 1976: 4)

We make our own good fortune. (Brothers 1978: 4)

All power is based on perception. If you think you've got it, then you've got it. If you think you don't have it . . . then you don't have it. (Cohen 1980: 20)

We are each 100% responsible for all of our experiences. (Hay 1984: 5)

I am learning that it is my choice to perceive the world in a more optimistic and positive light because I am learning that it is also my choice to perceive myself that way. (MacLaine 1989: xi)

Become one with your new self. (Siegel 1989: 263)

When you notice an out-of-balance situation within yourself, balance it at once . . . . You are a Master. (John-Roger and McWilliams 1991: 375)

Authors writing out of both the machine and growth self-help ethics are inconsistent, even contradictory, at times, in the moral systems they espouse. Manipulation and selfishness are often described as necessary tactics in successful human interaction, tactics that have earned a bad name through what authors consider to be extreme manifestations. Learning to manipulate others and to put oneself at the center of all encounters and endeavors is, authors proclaim, a means of achieving effective communications skills and happiness in all aspects of life. And yet, authors often define success as the point at which manipulation will no longer be required, and where selfishness will have no meaning.

In *Games People Play* (1964), Berne writes that readers' goal should be to achieve a gameless state of mature adulthood (or a state in which only "good games" are played). However, his whole book is dedicated to an analysis of all the existing games being played. (Berne writes, "This collection is complete to date (1962), but new games are continually being discovered" [69].) Berne's book is designed to attract readers who want to learn how to analyze the behavior of others—others who would, presumably, not be privy to the same analytical skills.

In both of his bestselling (and nearly identical) books, *Winning through Intimidation* (1974) and *Looking Out for #1* (1977), Robert Ringer straightforwardly asserts that *the* goal is winning (in the game of life). According to Ringer, ideally, one ought not hurt one's opponents in the course of the game, but that caveat is overshadowed by his advice not to take losses too seriously because life is simply too short. It follows that one should apply the same attitude to the losses of other players as well, and not feel too badly about bringing them on in the course of the game. Also, Ringer adamantly insists that *everyone* plays to win, and the reader would be wise to catch up with the rest of the gang. Michael Korda concurs in *Power!* (1975), writing: "No matter who you are, the basic truth is that your interests are nobody else's concern, your gain is inevitably someone else's loss, your failure someone else's victory. . . . [So] learning to play the power game is a means of self defense" (4–5). Berne's assertions that we should understand game playing so that ultimately we can learn how *not* to play have been left behind in the dust. And according to Ringer and Korda, it's not how you play the game that counts, either. Winning is all.[5]

On the cover of Julius Fast's *Body Language* (1970), a bland-expressioned woman sits in a chair with her legs crossed, her arms crossed on her lap, holding a cigarette, with captions around her: "Does her body say that she's a loose woman?" "Does her body say that she's a phoney?" "Does her body say that she's a manipulator?" "Does her body say that she's lonely?" On the back cover is printed: "Read *Body Language,* so that you can penetrate the personal secrets, both of intimates and total strangers." Body language, Fast writes, is a combination of learned and universally human actions and gestures. Like Berne, Fast promises insight—secret insight: those whose body language readers learn to decode won't know they are being studied since they don't yet know how to read body language, and thus remain safely unaware of the meanings inherent in their own gestures. "The ordinary citizen who understands body language very well, and uses it . . . can relate [these postures] to the emotional states of the people he knows. In this way he can actually keep a step ahead of other people in his dealings with them. This art can be taught to people for it is a function of careful observation but it can only be learned if one is aware that it exists" (117). The secrets of body language, like the power of Dorothy's ruby slippers in *The Wizard of Oz,* were there all along and we just didn't know it.

According to Fast, a reader's goal should be to utilize his or her knowledge of the body language of others to his or her own advantage (as the prospective male reader might do to gain "penetration" into the "personal secrets" of the generic woman on the cover)—to "reach through . . . personal space, through the masks we set up as protection, to touch and fondle and interact physically with other people" (68)— and also to keep "the masks" in place when necessary, by consciously managing one's own body language to "integrate [successfully] into the world" (79). It is with body language that we protect ourselves from one another, while, at the same time, we long desperately to connect with one another.

Life may be a constant competition, but this desire to commune with one's competitors interrupts it. Some self-help books (in the identity-as-machine tradition) encourage readers to treat this desire to connect as one would a business transaction—rationally, carefully, making sure one's best interests are being served. Others (deriving from the identity-as-growth tradition) urge readers to seek love, because love *means* growth. Readers are mostly prompted by self-help authors to apply a rational economic model to their lives in order to achieve growth; thus machine and growth ethics combine into an enlightened pragmatism, a scientific spirituality.

Body language, psycho-cybernetics, looking out for number one, being your own best friend—all these strategies require self-knowledge. Authors writing from the identity-as-machine perspective see self-confidence as crucial, whereas identity-as-growth authors stress self-love. Within both types of books, the self seems like a treasure being dug up: it is unknown, waiting to be discovered, a reality each individual should become committed to unearthing. If you don't like who you are, the books announce, you don't really know yourself yet. And if you don't like what has happened to you so far in life, it is because you don't like who you are. You can change self-fulfilling prophecies by changing your perception of the self, and thus changing the self itself. Maxwell Maltz writes: "The self-image is a 'premise' . . . upon which your whole personality, and even your circumstances are built. Because of this our experiences seem to verify, and thereby strengthen our self images, and a vicious or a beneficent cycle, as the case may be, is set up" (1960: 2). Identity becomes a kaleidoscope of possibility.

Higher Powers

An occasional self-help author will combine growth and machine ideals within a religious framework and encourage readers to achieve a profitable sense of self and a pragmatic approach to relationships with the assistance of a higher power. As New Age philosophy has become increasingly popular in recent years, spiritual ideas have been woven into self-help authors' messages, or even become the gist of the books (e.g., Bradshaw 1988 and 1990; Hay 1987; MacLaine 1989).

Robert Schuller, Harold Kushner, and M. Scott Peck have each achieved bestselling success for their widely divergent religious perspectives. Schuller's writing is facile cheerleading for God. He combines bits and pieces of the machine and growth ethics; the result is a popular-psychological Christianity, which oddly includes both capitalist and anti-capitalist propaganda. Schuller begins *Tough Times Never Last, but Tough People Do!* (1982) rather inanely, by making a long and drawn-out analogy between people and potatoes (of which I include only a small portion): "People are like potatoes. After potatoes have been harvested they have to be spread out and sorted in order to get the maximum market dollar. . . . It is a law of life. Big potatoes rise to the top on rough roads, and tough people rise to the top in rough times" (31). Schuller promises that he will show readers how to be top potatoes, or "tough people." The "secret ingredient" that separates good potatoes from bad is knowing how to perceive one's problems, he writes. Top potatoes "understand the six principles that pertain to all problems," Schuller explains: "1 Every living human being has problems. . . . 2 Every problem has a limited life span. . . . 3 Every problem holds positive possibilities. . . . 4 Every problem will change you. . . . 5 You can choose what your problem will do to you. . . . 6 There is a negative and positive reaction to every problem" (57–68).

Basically, Schuller recapitulates standard self-help fare: he informs readers that they are responsible for their problems, and that all they have to do is manage them prudently and confidently, and they will not get out of hand. He includes "Twelve Principles for Managing Problems Positively" (which sweetly combine into a little poem); details "Ten Commandments of Possibility Thinking"; proposes ten steps readers can use to win ("Count to Ten and Win"); and ends with a catchy "Alphabet for Action."

But the most crucial step toward success, Schuller writes, is prayer. In each of his books he repeatedly entreats readers to pray. God will love anyone who believes, Schuller informs, and if God loves you, then you will never be alone. The underlying message is that readers cannot expect any sort of success, happiness, or love from God or others if they are not willing to become devout Christians. At the end of *Be Happy You Are Loved* (1986), Schuller writes: "Well then—Love or Loneliness?—it's your choice! The secret of happiness is so simple: Become a "God loves you . . . and so do I" person! Accept Jesus Christ as your Savior and best Friend" (256, ellipses in text). Schuller certainly possesses an ability to come up with gimmicky and peppy slogans, as well as to repeat the same messages in countless ways, but his books lack any real theological substance or specific advice about problem solving.

Harold Kushner, however, has written three books where religious issues are examined humanistically. Unlike Schuller, Kushner does not proselytize obnoxiously; in *When Bad Things Happen to Good People* (1981) he challenges readers to examine their own beliefs as he did when his son died. Kushner posits that God may not be an omnipowerful force who tests the faith of believers and metes out rewards and punishments accordingly, but rather a benign and benevolent power offering inspiration for people to become motivated to help one another. ("God, who neither causes nor prevents tragedies, helps by inspiring people to help" [140].) Kushner concludes that people ought not see suffering as reasonable or just, but rather, that they should work to incorporate its positive lessons into their lives.

In *When All You've Ever Wanted Isn't Enough* (1986) Kushner continues his discussion of the search for sense in a seemingly senseless world. Kushner believes people feel the need to invest their lives with earthy, nonmaterialist meaning: "Our souls are not hungry for fame, comfort, wealth, or power. Those rewards create almost as many problems as they solve. Our souls are hungry for meaning, for the sense that we have figured out how to live so that our lives matter, so that the world will be at least a little bit different for our having passed through it" (18). Kushner reminds readers that meaning will not come without a struggle, that a complete existence requires the direct confrontation of difficulty. Our goals should not be to eliminate or avoid pain, because, he assures, we wouldn't know good from bad times if we didn't have both. Instead, we would "become emotionally anesthetized" (97).

In his most recent book, *Who Needs God* (1989), Kushner continues his examination of the faithlessness he sees as characteristic of modernity. Here he almost pleads with readers in his quest to give others what he has found (but still is nowhere near the proselytizing of Schuller). He writes: "without . . . spiritual nourishment, our souls remain stunted and undeveloped" (11). Kushner asserts that a religious outlook will strengthen the self in a way that secular culture cannot; religion is a "way of seeing" that makes community central (27); it is a faith in the world as sensible, but ultimately, a faith that "transcends reason" (45). Like Bellah et al. in *Habits of the Heart* (1985), Kushner explains that we have gone too far and lost what people presumably once had, a spiritually organized allegiance to one another.

In his psycho-religious treatises, M. Scott Peck, like Kushner, has retained the centrality of struggle as the key to a rewarding and/or meaningful life. In *The Road Less Traveled* which has remained on the bestseller list since 1983, he writes: "it is in this whole process of meeting and solving problems that life has its meaning. . . . It is only because of problems that we grow mentally and spiritually" (1978: 16). Life should be a combination of good and bad experiences, but not of good and evil ones, ideally. As Peck becomes more firmly entrenched as a Christian, he directs his attention to the "not nice" subject of evil.[6] "It is in the struggle between good and evil that life has its meaning—and in the hope that goodness can succeed. . . . Evil can be defeated by goodness. . . . Evil can be conquered only by love," he writes (1983: 266–267). Once evil is eliminated, presumably the healthy struggle with problems will remain to challenge people to achieve personal and spiritual growth.

Religious self-help authors extend secular self-help authors' calls for self-reliance to include reliance on God: without faith, some authors even state, everything else is meaningless. But with it, everything is bound to get better. Other authors conceive of a belief in a supreme power as a sort of extension of self-love. Louise Hay, author of *You Can Heal Your Life* (1987), suggests that readers use "affirmations" to achieve all varieties of health. Affirmations are New Age prayers; they are chants that praise the self. Hay writes: "Let's use the affirmation, 'I am willing to change.' Repeat this often. . . . You can touch your throat as you say this. The throat is the energy center in the body where change takes place. By touching your throat you are acknowledging you are in the process of changing" (49). In Hay's New Age treatise, the body becomes a place of such power that it seems magical.

In *Going Within* (1989), Shirley MacLaine continues on this tack, writing of "higher powers" that are unique to and inside each person. Of her seminars (where she leads collective meditations), she writes: "As I traveled the country I found that thousands of people were opening up and surrendering to their own internal spiritual power" (7). The self, like a rabbit pulling itself out of a hat, is waiting to come out and be known in its divine glory. Part of MacLaine's New Age message echoes the straight spirituality proffered by Kushner; she writes that as a result of modern developments, Americans have "become spiritually impoverished" (43).

In some cases, self-help authors extend personal control over one's circumstances and spiritual growth to include physical well-being. In *Your Erroneous Zones*, Wayne Dyer tells readers: "You can . . . choose to eliminate some physical sufferings which are not rooted in a known organic dysfunction. . . . There is a burgeoning amount of evidence . . . that people even choose things like tumors, influenza, arthritis, heart disease, and many other infirmities, including cancer" (1976:19–20). And now this idea of self-healing, of a damaged self that can cure itself with self-consciousness, recurs repeatedly in self-help works, including: (again) Hay's *You Can Heal Your Life* (1987), Hubbard's *Dianetics* (1985), Pearsall's *Superimmunity* (1987), Seigel's *Love, Medicine, & Miracles* (1988) and *Peace, Love, and Healing* (1989).

Bernie Siegel describe how strong the psyche can be in fighting illness; his books are filled with inspirational stories about people who seem uncontestably on the edge of death, but who miraculously recover. He attributes this to the miracle of the spirit, which, when charged with love for self and others, can do amazing things. Siegel does not promise recovery, but he promises self-knowledge and self-realization, which *may* then help to combat illness, because illness has been encouraged in the first place by "social and psychosocial poisons in our own homes" (1989: 156). Siegel offers self-control that will give rise to self-love, that will perhaps lengthen life—and if it doesn't, will enhance what life is left as well as one's experience of death. Siegel sees bodily ailments, which he sees as opportunities for self-realization: "Allow the disease to heal your life. Begin your journey and become your authentic self now, " he writes (1989: 5). Disease becomes an opportunity for self-transformation, individual revolution.

In Hay's book, the emphasis on self-control has been taken to the farthest extreme. Relying on New Age religious techniques for attaining personal well-being, Hay informs readers that they choose whatever happens to them, beginning even before they are born, writing: "Each one of us decides to incarnate upon this planet at particular points in time and space. We have chosen to come here to learn a particular lesson that will advance us upon our spiritual, evolutionary pathway. We choose our sex, our color, our country, and then we look around for the particular set of parents who will mirror the pattern we are bringing in to work on in this lifetime" (1987: 10).

Saying everything is a matter of choice is really no different from saying everything is fated. Hay has extended choice so far that it becomes suffocatingly constricting. Though Hay's readers may experience her contentions of ultimate and utter control as empowering, Hay dangerously does away with social reality. She holds that even "ACCI-DENTS are no accident. Like everything else in our lives, we create them" (140). Similarly, MacLaine asks rhetorically, "If I had created the pain in the healing in my body, was I also creating the pain and the healing in every area of my life?" (1989: 49). The answer for both MacLaine and Hay—and for everyone else, as far as they are concerned—is yes.

Hay urges readers to figure out how and why they have caused particular physical and mental problems for themselves, by including a comprehensive chart of such problems and their corresponding mental derivations (which she calls "probable causes"). She provides "new thought patterns" which readers can use to correct their self-inflicted maladies. For example, AIDS, she writes, is a manifestation of "denial of the self. Sexual guilt. A strong belief in not being good enough." People with AIDS are urged to utilize the "new thought pattern": "*I am a Divine, magnificent expression of life. I rejoice in my sexuality. I rejoice in all that I am. I love myself*" (1987: 151). MacLaine describes her experiences at the hands of the Filipino healer Alex Orbito, which convinced her "that the physical is fundamentally a coagulation of molecules that are a product of our consciousness" (1989: 227).[7]

This sort of New Age writing relies on earlier self-as-growth philosophical pointers. Both MacLaine and Hay write that the secrets to happiness are love of self and forgiveness of others (which will lead also to love). Hay draws on developmental psychology, stretching it in a new direction when she writes that the parents one chooses have free rein to wreak havoc upon one's psyche in the formative years (from birth to three years old). She urges each reader to baby the "child" who lurks inside her or him and who has longed to come out ever since s/he had been repressed into hiding during infancy: "The way we were treated when we were very little is usually the way we treat ourselves now. . . . *Be kind to yourself. Begin to love and approve of yourself.* That's what that little child needs in order to express itself at its highest potential" (66–67). Hay reiterates the identity-as-growth idea that guilt is detrimental to well-being and broadens it to apply to physical health also, in a fastidious holistic approach that covers absolutely everything.

Along with most self-help writers, Hay casts guilt as an unnecessary emotional leftover from past times; there appears to be no such thing as justifiable guilt in the present. Guilt is not a valid way of feeling because each person is responsible for what happens to her or him, so what could there be to feel guilty about? Nor ought we expect that others should feel remorse over distress they have caused us, because there is no such thing in the self-help world as causing another person to do or feel anything. People do things for their own reasons and do not mean to hurt others. In this vein, MacLaine writes of how seminar participants forgive people who have hurt (raped, beaten, abandoned) them because they learned to "clear" their past perceptions of the events (12). Everyone is the master of her or his own fate. In *One Minute for Myself* (1985), Spencer Johnson explains, "The minute any of us looks to a relationship to satisfy our own basic needs, we begin to experience pain. And we believe it's the other person's fault" (81). Self-help authors offer readers a sort of secularized confessional, where reading itself is the act by which they may achieve absolution. (Authors' ideas about influence become even more complicated when relationships are their stated topic, as we'll see in Chapter 6.)

In *Superimmunity* (1987), Paul Pearsall takes the touchy-feely New Age content of Hay's *You Can Heal Your Life* and transforms it into catchy "scientific" babbling. He writes: "We can control our health: So it is really how we A-R-E—our *attention* to the supersystem, a *relaxed* and constructive imagery, and an adoption of constructive *emotional* and thinking states—that determines the degree to which we control our supersystems" (149). Pearsall stresses bodily connections with mental life (body plus mind equals "supersystem"), making a person sound like a Milky Way of cosmic activity. He writes: "Each thought and feeling is accompanied by a shower of brain chemicals that affects and is affected by billions of cells. This is our immune system, the constant surveillant of intrusion, of even the most minute malfunction of a cell within our bodies" (xi). The "supersystem" is a dramatic battleground for opposing forces within the self; Pearsall offers his method—which basically boils down to the idea that awareness will provide control—as an antidote to intrusive forces that threaten to splinter the self.

In his most recent bestseller, *The Power of the Family: Strength, Comfort, and Healing* (1990), Pearsall reiterates the connectedness of everything in the universe: "Einstein and scientists who follow him demonstrated that we contain the elements of the stars in our bones," he contends poetically, asserting that "the family view is the cosmic view that we are never alone" (1990: xiv). Here, the attack on the self broadens: the institution of the family, which Pearsall sees as the natural protector and nurturer of every self, becomes the endangered species about which Pearsall rallies his enthusiasm.

Self-Help on Sexuality

The sex manuals of the sixties, seventies, and eighties are not, of course, the first sex manuals ever written, and are indebted to their predecessors. Barbara Ehrenreich, Elizabeth Hess, and Gloria Jacobs (1986) write that the "'discourse' on sexuality" underwent a transformation from conservatism and secrecy to a more liberal, even radical, political stance after World War II. Prior to this, sex manuals primarily negated or downplayed women's sexuality, and moralistically denounced variety in sexual activity.

A. C. Kinsey's work, *Sexual Behavior in the Human Male* (1948) and *Sexual Behavior in the Human Female* (1953), ushered in the trend enabling the legitimation of studying sex. Kinsey's work had a leveling effect upon sexual acts, according to Ehrenreich et al., because he was primarily concerned with counting up incidents of orgasm, a methodology that "carried with it the implicit notion that all routes to orgasm are somehow equivalent or at least equally worthy of note" (1986: 44). Kinsey was the first to approach sexuality from the "scientific" angle of a pollster, and helped set the stage for the laboratory work of William Masters and Virginia Johnson.

Coming Together Coming Apart

Masters and Johnson were the first to enter the realm of sexuality and make it palatable, even respectable, to the lay reading public. They did so by maintaining a strictly professional tone throughout their first two books, *Human Sexual Response* (1966) and *Human Sexual Inadequacy* (1970). Masters and Johnson did not present their findings as explicitly useful *for* readers in their own sex lives, nor did they ever acknowledge that readers may have been attracted to their work for personal reasons (beyond a quest for the most up-to-date scientific facts about sex); rather, readers were a tacitly acknowledged audience for the presentation of laboratory findings. Despite the density of the clinical language used in their works, word got out. Nearly every contemporary popular magazine ran articles about or by this dynamic duo (Ehrenreich et al. 1986: 65). With the publication of their third treatise on sex, *The Pleasure Bond* (1975), Masters and Johnson loosened up a bit, and "in association with Robert J. Levin," produced a much more accessible manual.

What Masters and Johnson did for the popular perception of sex was revolutionary in many ways. According to Ehrenreich, Hess, and Jacobs, "Their findings arrived at a time when expert theories of female sexuality ran increasingly counter to women's social experience. . . . Masters and Johnson potentially offered a new social meaning for sex, one that was more consistent with women's emerging sense of independence" (65). Masters and Johnson encouraged heterosexual couples to make their sex lives less goal-oriented, less constrained by traditional notions about aggression, passivity, and performance. Their work helped to promote an image of women as sexually active; to dispel the notion of vaginal orgasms; to proclaim the clitoris as central in women's sexual pleasure; and thus to deflate the primacy of penile penetration in lovemaking. Ehrenreich, Hess, and Jacobs write, "The implication was clear: Women did not need men for orgasmic sex" (67).

Masters and Johnson did, however, contradict their implications of female sexual autonomy (via the clitoris) by asserting the primacy of vaginal intercourse: they write: "To appreciate vaginal anatomy and physiology is to comprehend the fundamentals of the human female's primary means of sexual expression" (1966: 69). Patricia Miller and Martha Fowlkes write that Masters and Johnson's comments on vaginal intercourse "must be read basically as a statement of women's heterosexuality and as a rejection of sexual activity that does not involve the vagina" (1980: 261). A dismissal of the work of Masters and Johnson (such as this) ignores the liberatory potential of their books. Masters and Johnson were, indeed, phallocentric; they demonstrate the confusion that resulted when "old" and "new" notions of sexual practice collided. They held out *both* potentially empowering and traditionally repressive conceptions of sexuality for women.

Ideologically cloudy though it was, the early work of Masters and Johnson enabled all of the sex manuals that followed; indeed, if they did not make it acceptable for Americans to bring their sex books out of the closet, they made possible large and colorful closet collections. For the most part, however, the manuals that resulted did not go any farther than Masters and Johnson had in their analyses of heterosexual dynamics; in fact, most of the authors were overtly conservative in many ways, at the same time advancing what they clearly felt would be perceived as liberal, free-thinking recommendations about sexual behavior.

About sex manuals of the 1970s, Meryl Altman writes: "Pushing repression into some distant, murky, non-historical past, these writers create the fiction of a value-free space—the present—where discussion of sexuality is invulnerable to challenges that it is repressive or partisan" (1984: 117). Indeed, these sex manuals do espouse an understandably schizophrenic ideology of sexual practice. None of the authors advocates sexual contact for its own sake, and yet they acknowledge that many people are engaging in sex in this manner, and imply that such behavior should be considered acceptable. Like parents teaching their children about sex, the sexperts all caution that ideally, the activities described should be done by two people who love each other very much. Authors pose as sexually liberated on the one hand (making informal statements to the effect of: "Anything goes, as long as you want to do it");

but on the other hand, they focus on monogamous heterosexuality (which is nearly always depicted as reaching its ultimate form in marriage),[8] and upon a heterosexual practice in which men's pleasure shares centrality with women's but where men remain, for the most part, on top and in command. Women's capacity for sexual pleasure is recognized, but the sexual objectification of women by men is rarely challenged, and alternatives to heterosexuality are treated at worst as unfortunate deviance, and at best as harmless exotic variations on "real" sex.

Sex manuals draw on the concurrent popular-psychology: sex is an exchange, in which a man and a woman attempt to have their respective "needs met"; ideally, they retain and enhance their unique individual identities and self-images even as they merge physically. Achieving sexual pleasure also necessitates open discussion (gamelessness) and attentive listening. Thus, the same push-pull between a competitive, capitalist view (identity as machine) and a connective, communal conception of human interaction (identity as growth) displayed in the unisex self-help books surfaces here as well.

Ask the Doctor

One of the early Masters-and-Johnson-inspired pontificators was David Reuben, whose *Everything You Always Wanted to Know about Sex* but Were Afraid to Ask* (1969) was a bestseller from 1970 to 1971, followed almost immediately by the success of his *Any Woman Can!* (1971) from 1971 to 1972. Both books were written as dialogues between a knowing doctor (Reuben) and ignorant and/or befuddled, seemingly inept—and certainly inexpert—patients. In *Everything You Always Wanted to Know,* Reuben answers a wide range of questions beginning, phallocentrically, with: "How big is the normal penis?" (5). Then he gradually makes his way through sexuality with (to give a brief sampling): "How does a girl get started as a prostitute?" (251), "What do female homosexuals do with each other?" (269), "Are there any men who would want to wear women's clothes?" (226), and "If these diseases are so terrible, why aren't they better known?" (336). In answer to these questions, Reuben explains that size doesn't matter; that girls become prostitutes because they like sex; that lesbians "were handicapped by having only half the pieces of the anatomical jigsaw puzzle" (269); that indeed, "quite a few" men found women's clothes arousing because they had been overattached to their mothers; and that ignorance of many "terrible" venereal diseases existed because "most victims are Negroes and homosexuals" (336). Despite his claims of enlightenment and an avowed nonjudgmental attitude about sex, Reuben also shows that homophobia, sexism, and racism aren't eliminated by liberal professionalism.

Reuben's second—even more directed and directive—work concentrates on rescuing "THE SEXUALLY MAROONED WOMAN," whom he defines as "any woman who is unwilling or unable to fulfill her destiny as a full-fledged female and thereby enjoy a lifetime of gratifying [hetero]sexual experiences" (1). Reuben's contrived conversation with the sexually marooned patient culminates with advice on how to get married—advice on how a woman can achieve the womanly state for which she is destined as a woman. Meryl Altman aptly describes *Any Woman Can!*:

> The situation is always the same: a woman is unhappy because she is frigid, or because she is promiscuous, or because she is lonely; she cries in the office of the understanding male therapist; he takes care of her; she undergoes treatment; she makes a successful adjustment—and marries. This is propaganda for psychiatry, propaganda for marriage, and propaganda for female dependency on male authority. . . . female sexuality is represented in terms of disease for which proper re-socialization is the cure. (1984: 120)

Though Reuben could see women's sexual liberation as possible only within the confines of heterosexual marriage, he did, nonetheless, see it as a possibility. He actually expresses regret that single women cannot indulge in sexual escapades without stigma.

Keeping the Doctor Away

A less staid—but still phallocentric—approach to women's sexuality was available at the time, authored by a woman who did not guard herself with professional credentials, and who did not even use her name at all. The publication of *The Sensuous Woman* (1969), written by Joan Terry Garrity under the pen name "J," signaled a turning point in tone and style for sex manuals, introducing a new authorial voice, which would remain popular through the seventies. "J" drops all pretense of treating heterosexual sex with kid gloves. "J" is explicit. She writes dirty, using popular language rather than clinical language. She demystifies sex by treating it like any other sport for which players can keep in shape between games.

In 1971, a companion volume to *The Sensuous Woman* addressed to men hit the market. *The Sensuous Man,* written by "M," was identical to its predecessor in style and tone. Both authors begin by reassuring readers that they don't have to be beautiful (handsome), thin (muscular), or extraordinary in any way to become wonderfully adept at lovemaking. The authors assure their readers that they, themselves, are living proof; they aren't the least bit exceptional. "J" writes, "I'm not particularly pretty. I have heavy thighs, lumpy hips, protruding teeth, a ski jump nose, poor posture, flat feet and uneven ears. . . . I am not brilliant and I don't have a magnetic personality" (10). "M" is less specific: "If you are handsome to start with, so much the better. I am not so fortunate" (6).

The goal "J" and "M" set for their readers is to learn to please each other; but their respective advice to men and women is quite different. "J" wants readers to know that only by keeping men happy in bed will they keep men interested at all. A sensuous woman should make her man know "that he is the most remarkable man that ever lived." As part of the bargain, readers are assured they will "reap wonderful benefits . . . such as the *enriching experience of a really joyous and fulfilling sex life*" (11). But should men's and women's sexual appetites conflict, "J" advises that men's pleasure is most important. If readers cannot respond genuinely to men's advances, "J" urges them to perform—to preserve men's sense of maleness, and to preserve men's very presence in their lives. She writes:

> There are times when you can quite legitimately say, "I love you, but I can't make love right now," but no woman of any sensitivity would refuse to make love to a man she cares for, just because she "doesn't really feel like it." You focus like mad on all the fantasies that stir your sexual juices, concentrate on making your body respond to the highest point possible and, if you really can't get to orgasm, to avoid disappointing him and spoiling his plateau of excitement and sexiness, you fake that orgasm.
>
> If you do it well, he won't be able to tell. (179)

Despite her basic assumption that men are worth keeping, they come across in her advice as rather facile, noncommunicative, inconsiderate, and ignorant people. Nowhere does "J" suggest that traditional male behavior should change, but only that women should adapt to it.

"M," on the other hand, writes that men's pleasure has for too long been disconnected from women's. "Our selfish, male-oriented sexual mores are said to discriminate against women and deprive them of sexual fulfillment and freedom," "M" writes, acknowledging that this is "probably true" (27). The problem for men, however, is that every time they have sex with women they face potential failure, not in being unable to satisfy their partners, but in maintaining their fragile male pride, which centers on maintaining an erection. A woman, on the other hand, can never be a failure in this way. "All she has to do is lie there and let the man do his stuff," "M" writes (27). The goal for sensuous men, then, is not simply to give women pleasure, but to learn how to "get it up and keep it up." "M" assumes that women's satisfaction will follow easily after men achieve long-lasting erections.

Both "M" and "J" offer extensive advice on creating and maintaining erections, on avoiding premature ejaculation, and on dealing with male impotence, suggesting that heterosexual practice begins and ends with phallic ups and downs. The early focus of sex manuals on women's "frigidity" or inability to reach orgasm has shifted: now all of the most urgent problems in sex boil down to being men's responsibility. Women are encouraged to participate, but in this phallocentric world, our actions remain secondary.

Sex, Power, and Feminism

Continuing the work of "J" and "M," Alex Comfort's *The Joy of Sex* was published in 1972. Comfort organizes his work like an alphabetized cookbook, which ordinary men and women can peruse in their quest for gourmet status as lovemakers. Comfort writes that the only sexual guidelines readers should observe are not to do things they don't want to do, and to try to please each other. Though Comfort asserts that everyone is basically bisexual (225), his encyclopedic menu centers on the heterosexual couple. Though he acknowledges that group sex and casual sex are becoming more common and acceptable, Comfort feels that good sex is best achieved by a man and a woman in love. They need not be married, but ideally, they should love each other, and presumably, be largely monogamous. He writes: "This book is about love as well as sex as the title implies: you don't get high-quality sex on any other basis— either you love each other before you come to want it, or, if you happen to get it, you love each other because of it, or both. No point in arguing this, but just as you can't cook without heat you can't make love without feedback. . . . Sex is the one place where we today can learn to treat people as people" (9). His monogamist morality precedes the fear of AIDS, which, over the course of the eighties, gradually began to impinge on the sexual mores of heterosexuals and gays. Comfort's prose is accompanied by illustrations (pastel colors and black-and-white) of one loving couple, demonstrating various positions and practices as they are described.

Sex-manual authors of the seventies all indicate that they are aware of the resurgence of the women's movement. Some authors affirm a rather watered-down, facile version of feminism in their works. For instance, in *The Joy of Sex*, Comfort writes, "As to the Women's Lib bit, nobody can possibly be a good lover—or a whole man—if he doesn't regard women as (a) people and (b) equals. That is really all there is to be said" (97). And despite authors' commitment to what Ehrenreich et al. call "equality of orgasm," men enjoy what ranges from a definite advantage to a slight edge in the power dynamics of heterosexual sex. The man-on-top position may have been demoted to one alternative among many, but it is held to be a very special alternative: "If we come back to the good old Adam and Eve missionary position, with him on top, astride or between, and her underneath facing—and we do come back to it—that is because it's uniquely satisfying," explains Comfort (124). And ten years later, within the covers of a book in which he professes to offer enlightened advice to confused men pursuing now-liberated women, Michael Morganstern exclaims: "It's high time someone said something in defense of the 'missionary position.' For too long, people have reviled it as unimaginative, boring, outdated—even sexist. I happen to think it's remained the classic position because it remains the most satisfying to men and women alike" (1982: 91).

Feminist anger against institutional patriarchal forms and their manifestations is denied validity by most sexperts. Indeed, "M" advises that when looking for women, sensuous men should "eliminate . . . Women's Lib militants" (1971: 54). Later, he expands his analysis on feminism, differentiating between "the ultraradical feminists, the dykes and the crazies" on the one hand—whom, he feels, "would settle for nothing short of castration with can openers, scissors, and rusty razor blades"—and on the other, "attractive and rational women . . . committed to Women's Liberation and dedicated to righting the imbalance between the sexes" (179–180). It's not clear how "M" decided which feminists fell into which camps, but he is definitely disgusted by women who are not sexually interested in and available to men, or women who are "unreasonably sensitive" about men's actions toward us. But like Comfort, he urges the sensuous man to respect *his* woman as an equal.

"M" acknowledges that "most men view women solely as sexual objects to be 'used'" (187). "M" believes this attitude is wrong and tells the sensuous man to "treat her as a whole person, and not as a sophisticated masturbation machine" (180). Comfort, however, refutes feminist objections to the objectification of women by men by invoking a rather bizarre eye-for-an-eye suggestion for reciprocity, writing: "The Women's Lib bit about sex objects misses the point—sure the woman and the various parts of her are sex objects, but most men ideally would wish to be treated piecemeal in the same way" (1972: 72). Comfort also minimizes male violence against women, a focus of the then-blossoming women's rights movement. Though he describes rape negatively, albeit glibly, as "a frightening turn-off," he instructs women: "Don't get yourself raped— i.e. don't deliberately excite a man you don't know well, unless you mean to follow through" (248). Comfort upholds traditional notions of women as responsible for male desire, and of men as uncontrollable once they fall under the spell of seductive femininity.

In his bestselling sequel, *More Joy of Sex* (1973), Comfort addresses adolescent sexuality by reinforcing gender stereotypes. He describes how girls may entice boys without even knowing the trouble they are inciting and, in Comfort's view, inviting. He writes:

> The main thing about boys' responses is that girls are often un-aware just how fast a really horny boy can be turned on. . . . Quite a few cock-teasers don't intend to be so, they just don't know enough boy physiology: the sight of nice breasts and a few kisses will produce an erection in most males. If this happens, and she doesn't want intercourse, she should tell him she has her period and offer an alternative. A boy can be given an orgasm by hand and if she doesn't know how, she should let him show her. (111)

Despite Comfort's previously stated conviction that men should see women as equals, he shows much more clearly that he also believes that men's desire is far more urgent than ours, and that it can be dangerous for women (and girls) to spark men's (and boy's) sexual interest especially because we might do so unintentionally. He urges women, from girlhood on, to learn to cater to men's potentially uncontrollable sexual desires.

Comfort keeps coming back to biological differences between women and men, which he sees as instrumental in determining sexual behavior:

> There is something basic in the fact that she has to let him in. . . .
> Sex is external to a man, located in an offshore peninsula like the
> state of Florida, and he puts forth; it's internal to a woman—a visit
> or an invasion—and she has something external left with her. This
> doesn't mean that women unconsciously see all intercourse as a
> violation. . . . Being deeply penetrated by a man you love and trust,
> who treats you as an equal and loves you back, is about the best of
> all feminine experiences—it marks the end of any anxieties about
> who is entering whom. At that point the penis is joint property and
> a lot of infantile fears get resolved. (129)

Comfort seems uncertain about what, exactly, this inner and outer genital orientation means; but he is clearly quite taken with the act of penetration, and believes that women are also (and if we're not, we should be, to help resolve those infancy issues).

Reacting against the then-current masculinist wisdom about sexuality, the Boston Women's Health Collective published *Our Bodies, Ourselves* in 1971. Less a sex manual than a political guide to health and sexuality, *Our Bodies, Ourselves* epitomizes the feminist approach to health care for women that gained visibility and popularity throughout the 1970s. Eleven women who met for the first time in 1969 at a conference in Boston formed the collective. They write that they "had all experienced similar feelings and frustrations toward specific doctors and the medical maze in general" (11). Their continued meetings grew into a book in which they hoped to provide the knowledge about women's bodies which had been denied women by patriarchy, especially as it manifested itself in the institution of medicine. *Our Bodies, Ourselves* focuses on understanding and negotiating sexuality, rather than on improving sex, as past manuals did.

Taking feminist values as her starting point, Shere Hite wrote *The Hite Report: A Nationwide Study of Female Sexuality* (1976) and *The Hite Report on Male Sexuality* (1981). Though these books, like Masters and Johnson's early work, are not structured explicitly as self-help manuals, Hite clearly intends her works to serve didactic purposes. In her preface to the first

Hite Report, she writes: "The intention is to get acquainted, to share how we have experienced our sexuality, how we feel about it—and to see our personal lives more clearly, thus redefining our sexuality and strengthening our identities as women. This book is also meant to stimulate a public discussion and reevaluation of sexuality" (1976: 11). And in the preface to her second volume, Hite set out "to find out what American men are feeling, thinking, and doing" (1981: xiii). In both works, Hite seeks to uncover the relationship between gender socialization regarding sexuality and sexual practice.

Hite's books were marketed as definitive and newly revelatory sex manuals in the tradition of Kinsey and Masters and Johnson. Reviews on the back cover of the first *Hite Report* proclaim: "Women who read [this] are likely to be reassured . . . and men should be pleased to have so much specific information about what women really want" (*Newsweek*); "The biggest sex study since Masters and Johnson" (*The National Observer*); and "read *The Hite Report* if you want to know how sex really is right now" (*New York Times Book Review*).

In the first *Hite Report,* women respondents reveal that they are decidedly disappointed with their sex lives, while men sound incredibly callous, inconsiderate, even violent (men sound like this even in their own accounts, in Hite's second volume). Few of Hite's respondents are happy with the status quo of heterosexual relationships, Hite writes, because the power imbalance between men and women in American culture provides an unhealthy environment for creative expression in every conceivable way. She writes, "We must begin to devise more kind, generous, and personal ways of relating which will be positive and constructive for the future" (1976: 11).

The Magical Mystery Tour

Irene Kassorla's *Nice Girls Do—* (1980) is addressed to women and centers on women's receiving, rather than giving, pleasure. Kassorla believes that everyone harbors sexual guilt and has repressed sexual fantasies as a result of parental messages against sex that we received in infancy and/or childhood. She writes that women, especially, are taught in early childhood that sexual pleasure is wrong. Kassorla urges readers to engage their sex partners in her therapy, which she calls "the pleasure process," assuring that "In the PLEASURE PROCESS you will learn how to orgasm in countless ways and in countless numbers" (16). She counters male-oriented approaches to sex, such as those of Comfort and "J," by advising women: "*Don't assure* your partner that you are happy and satisfied when it isn't true; *don't pretend* to be in ecstasy when you can't wait until he dismounts. And above all, *don't feign* orgasm or there isn't a chance for you to learn how to be a happy and healthy person sexually" (87).

Alice Kahn Ladas, Beverly Whipple, and John D. Perry combined efforts two years later to revolutionize sexuality with their presentation of four mysteriously new "scientific" sexual phenomena in *The G Spot and Other Recent Discoveries about Human Sexuality* (1982). They write: "The evidence we present indicates that women and men are more alike sexually than had been previously imagined. This may help to remove barriers between people and bring about a greater understanding of human sexual behavior" (xv–xvi). Based on research which is only vaguely described throughout the book, Ladas et al. herald a new sexual era centering on women's "G spots" (G stands for Grafenberg, the doctor who first proposed that such an area existed). G spots, the authors explain, are "relatively small and difficult to locate" areas— invisible to the eye and mostly indistinguishable by touch—on the front interior vaginal walls, which are best stimulated by "firm upward pressure" (44). Their descriptions of the G spot include convincing jargon but end up quite vague: they write that "the G spot is probably composed of a complex network of blood vessels, the paraurethral glands and ducts, nerve endings, and the tissues surrounding the bladder neck" but that "the cellular structure of the G spot is, at this time, unknown" (42).

Ladas et al. claim to have supervised an experiment in which four hundred (unidentified) women volunteers were examined by doctors or nurses. Each and every one of these women had G spots! When stimulated, Ladas et al. write, these women's G spot would swell and become hard, and this could result in an orgasm more intense than clitoral orgasm (and often followed by ejaculation of a mysterious clear or milky substance). Ladas et al. suspected that all women had G spots but just didn't know it yet.

Ladas, Whipple, and Perry were well aware of the implications of their research. They knew they were reviving the Freudian concept of a vaginal orgasm that was best achieved through penile penetration, and they knew about the opposition the Freudian phallocentric ideology of female sexuality had met with from feminist critics and laboratory researchers. They knew that the validity of Freud's vaginal theories had been publicly shattered by the research of Masters and Johnson, most notably. So they couched their argument within an all-inclusive theoretical framework, framed it with hard-science words and deceptively nonjudgmental language, and also accused Masters and Johnson of disregarding any evidence of G spots they found. But, they assured confused readers, all the previous theoreticians, according to their "unifying" research, could be right in the end. There were vaginal (G spot) orgasms. There were also clitoral orgasms. They weren't going to say that one type was better than another; they were only going to present the evidence.

One man wrote in: "*Since my wife learned about the G spot and female ejaculation, she refuses to allow me to play with her clitoris with my finger or my tongue. . . . Now she insists that we have intercourse without much foreplay (which I enjoy a lot) and she berates me for being a bad lover because I don't help her to ejaculate*" (1982: 168, emphasis in original).

Strangely but surely, women who knew how to work their G spots tended to demand the exact sexual behaviors that Hite's women so resented men wanting: allegedly, these women were obsessed with vaginal penetration, and they wanted it fast and hard. Women with G spots even climaxed *too* quickly for their partners. For most men partners of G-spotted women (unlike the man cited above), the new discoveries were wonderful and had led to unimaginable heights of sexual compatibility, the authors contend.

Ladas, Whipple, and Perry's "discoveries" of the newfound physiological similarities of men and women strongly implied that women were just like men, and all the previous attention to women's special sexual needs was rather needless. To counter the phallocentric implications of G-spot centrality, Ladas et al. include testimony from lesbians, who, they state, are more likely to know about their G spots and to ejaculate than heterosexual women. (It is easier to locate G spots with fingers than with penises, they assert; but the majority of the comments they include from "subjects" attest to women's preference for the latter as G-spot stimulators.)

Another "discovery" which Ladas et al. explore is the excitability of the prostate gland in men, which can, they recommend, be best stimulated anally. Ehrenreich, Hess, and Jacobs contend that "*the G Spot* . . . presented the insidious notion that women's clitoral obsessions were driving men to homosexuality." The recommended position for optimal coital stimulation of the G spot, they point out, was "suspiciously similar to one used for anal sex" (1986: 184).

The discovery of the G spot caused a spot of media hoopla that accompanied the success of Ladas, Whipple, and Perry's book. The sensation died down as quickly as it had erupted, and sex manuals went back to proffering advice on various means of clitoral stimulation and fellatio. Occasionally, an author will mention the possibility of the G spot's existence, but only in a most tentative manner.[9]

Separating the Men from the Women

A decade after "J" and "M" proffered their brand of definitively raunchy sexual wisdom to masses of eager would-be sensual men and women, a second pair of gender-specific manuals, followed by a unisex manual, were released to guide sexually confused heterosexuals through the 1980s: Alexandra Penney's *How to Make Love to a Man* (1981), Michael Morganstern's *How to Make Love to a Woman* (1982), and Penney's *How to Make Love to Each Other* (1982).[10]

After a friend told Penney about a sexual encounter with a man during which she was encouraged to take an active part in setting up the nightly activities, Penney became inspired to investigate men's concerns about sex. She began by reading sex manuals (including those by Comfort, "J," and "M"). Penney discovered that men were culturally programmed to be the directors of sexual activity, and yet, ironically, their needs had become neglected in the process: "Most everything . . . seemed to take for granted that the man was basically the initiator in sex, that he should be sensitive to a woman's needs, take a lot of time, and help a woman achieve an orgasm or even many orgasms if she needed them. But what, specifically, did *men* need besides an erection and a good climax? What were the finer pleasures that men responded to? No book or person had ever clearly revealed to women what making love to a man was all about" (1981: 19).

Penney believes women have experienced a sexual revolution, that our pleasure has become central in heterosexual love making, and that in the meantime, no one has been paying attention to the poor men. Men's pleasure has been taken for granted, even ignored altogether: "Think how many women suffered in silence until men learned what women needed physically and emotionally," she writes (21). Now, apparently, men have rightfully earned another turn. As "J" had done a decade earlier, Penney asserts that women should take action and return the favors we have been reaping from sexually sensitive men. Penney agrees with "J" that a woman need not be exceptionally beautiful to please men well in bed; but she should be very clean, carefully dressed, and well coiffed. Penney describes many ways in which women can set the stage for sexual encounters, favoring lots of candle-lit bathtubs preceded by carefully prepared favorite meals (his). She reminds women that "the quickest way to a man's heart is through his stomach" (69).

Ehrenreich, Hess, Jacob write that *How to Make Love to a Man* "expressed, more than any other manual, the growing physical alienation between heterosexuals" because Penney translated sex into such a carefully orchestrated performance, in which men's pleasure and women's pleasure were distinctly different phenomena. "This was theatrical sex, so tightly scripted that there was little room for spontaneous heterosexual impulses to destroy a scene" (1986: 101). The "close-your-eyes-and-think-of-England" approach to sex becomes unimaginable; Penney tells readers to plan sexual encounters compulsively, and to make sure everyone has a good time while they're at it.

Morganstern writes that his sequel for men, *How to Make Love to a Woman* (1982), was designed to help men cope with the confusion brought on by the combined forces of the women's movement and the sexual revolution of the sixties and seventies.

> There's been so much change . . . that most men don't know quite what to think anymore. . . . When we first began trying to give women what they wanted (and for years before that), they wanted a MAN—in capital letters. They wanted to have their dinners paid for, their chairs held, their doors opened, their cooking complimented, their virginity preserved, and their rings quickly. . . . Then, suddenly . . . things began to change. In what seemed like only a matter of days, women wanted none of the above. Instead, they wanted free sex, no children, equal pay, our places in law and medical schools, and our jobs afterward. (2)

It wasn't that women weren't having enough attention paid to our pleasure, but that women were becoming more difficult to give pleasure to, because we were so aggressive, competitive, and changeable. We might gradually lay claim to and swallow up all the goodies in the world, Morganstern imagines, since "free sex" set us off on our power-hungry insatiable quest.

Morganstern describes his own confusion about how to treat women. He laments that romance seemed to have disappeared with the onset of women's equality (which he believes has been achieved). But he reassures his readers that his "hundreds" of interviews with women indicate that "romance has returned" (5). Men need not be intimidated by women's progress; indeed, he writes: "Recognizing the full potential of women doesn't have to mean giving up old sex roles" (7). Femininity, he consoles his readers, is alive and well underneath the business suits and lab coats women have donned.

Penney writes that the letters she received from readers and the questions she was asked during the tour promoting *How to Make Love to a Man* led her to write *How to Make Love to Each Other* (1982). Women and men seem to have different basic concerns about each other, she writes, concerns which she hopes to reconcile with her work. Women are concerned with keeping men interested in the relationship, while men are concerned with keeping women interested in sex (17–18). In her new book, Penney reiterates the graphic techniques she presented for women to use on men in her first book and supplements these with corresponding instructions for men. She urges women to "*let him know* that you are truly interested in sex," by "*sending sensuous signals*" especially by catering to men's interest in "visual effects," which could range from wearing black lacy underwear to buying soft-core pornography. Penney urges men, on the other hand, to focus on "romance, romance, romance, romance"; she tells them to "really *listen*" to women and to "talk" to women (119–124). Penney's unisex manual confirms Morganstern's assertions of a return to the comforts of traditional ways, with a dollop of discussion thrown in—despite the scary, yet necessary, changes brought on by the women's movement. Men, it seems, were smart enough never to change their minds; they still wanted the same thing: women dressed up in slinky costumes like those in pornographic magazines to cater to their imaginative tastes.

Beyond Body Parts

Paul Pearsall's *Super Marital Sex* (1987) is an interesting blend of egalitarianism, conservatism, and New Age philosophy. Pearsall promises readers that he has already been successful in helping one thousand heterosexual couples to revitalize their sex lives with his super marital sex program at two Detroit hospitals. Pearsall writes that he is indebted to Kinsey and to Masters and Johnson, and he recycles some of their advice in his own book. But he also promises more for couples who are monogamous and who follow the program: "Super marital sex is the most erotic, intense, fulfilling experience any human being can have. Anonymous sex with multiple partners pales by comparison, an empty imitation of the fulfillment of a sexuality of intimacy and commitment to one person for life, a 'fourth perspective' based on an entirely different model of sexual functioning, physiology and interaction between husband and wife" (xvi).

Pearsall promises no less than a religious experience of newfound sensuality. Couples can have "psychasms" together, which, he explains, are much more sophisticated and enriching than all that old muscle-spasming people settled for back in the seventies. Pearsall recommends achieving "psychasms" by practicing "the posture of the future" (sitting facing each other, with legs overlapping, against two separate stacks of pillows, basically) and making contact between the back of the penis and the clitoral area. The key to super marital sex, according to Pearsall, is that telepathic communication takes precedence over mere genital sensation, and thus, phallocentrism is seemingly banished. Attention to the *process* of sexual interaction supplants the goal-oriented nature of the old kind of sex. One husband-convert told Pearsall: "I can tell you now that it just cannot be described. We insert the penis sometimes, I ejaculate sometimes, we have orgasms, psychasms, breastasms, I tell you, we just merge. . . . If you would have told me that erection or insertion was not necessary weeks ago, I would have thought you were going crazy" (224). Pearsall's subjects come alive in a way that Masters and Johnson's never did: they praise his methods left and right, even as he denies them an intense focus on bodily reactions. Pearsall wants sex to be free and beautiful, an out-of-body experience with curative powers for marriages that have grown unhealthy and/or dysfunctional.

Sex manuals have traveled from the laboratory-grounded, highly physical explanations of sexual phenomena of Masters and Johnson back into the laboratory from which Paul Pearsall's "psychasms" emerged. Sex has gone from technical to earthy to theatrical to otherworldly. None of the more recent bestselling sex manuals received the same attention or caused the same controversy as the earlier books (written by Masters and

Johnson, Reuben, Comfort, and Hite). The incognito, mysterious sexperts "J" and "M" who beckoned to American women and men with visions of broadened and naughty sexual experimentation have been replaced by the highly visible, high-strung, Pepsi-touting "Dr. Ruth," whose primary concern seems to be whether adolescents are using contraceptives. Recently, avoiding pregnancy has taken a backseat to people's fears of contracting AIDS; "safe sex" has supplanted good sex in public parlance. As Pearsall, the only sex-manual author of the past five years to gain bestseller status, imparts, *morally* good sex is for married couples only.

Unlike unisex self-help books, which propose more general programs for successful living and self-reflection, sex manuals—except for the more politicized feminist ones—do not pretend to tell readers how to live their lives. But the ethos that each successive author conveys regarding sex is closely related to the moral frameworks that authors of unisex self-help books outlined for their readers. Sexuality becomes a player in the game of identity building: sex manuals incorporate both the machine and growth models developed by self-help authors: one could learn techniques to gain sexual success that centered on clearly delineated action (pressing the right buttons), and/or one could expand one's horizons as a person through the creativity of sexual experimentation.

Despite the author's claims in each ensuing manual that s/he had the answers to sexual problems, the proper techniques, or the key to attaining the necessary frame of mind for sexual success, the men and women depicted in the sex manuals keep drifting apart, resenting each other, fighting or stagnating, despite each successive author's attempts to bring them together. And when these men and women get out of bed—as they do in the following chapter—their animosity toward each other takes center stage. It is in self-help books addressed to women that heterosexual relationships in their totality are deconstructed most fully.

Chapter 6

The Tangled Web:

Self-Help Books about Gender

Whatever the apparent cause of death, I want to reiterate that loving too much can kill you. (Norwood 1988: 218)

During the summer of 1987, a Barnes and Noble bookstore in Greenwich Village displayed Forward and Torres's *Men Who Hate Women and the Women Who Love Them* (1986), Norwood's *Women Who Love Too Much* (1985), and Cowan and Kinder's *Women Men Love, Women Men Leave* (1987), along with several other recent arrivals of this ilk in its window, with the caption "Women who read too much" in large lettering. This display seemed to me to be both ironic and peculiar, given that bookstores usually attempt to *attract* customers, not make fun of them for the books they might buy. Lisa Ann Marsoli and Mel Green's sardonic little paperback, *Smart Women, Stupid Books: Stop Reading and Learn to Love Losers* (1987), hit the bookracks (albeit briefly) at about the same time that I saw this display. Its authors direct their clever insults differently than the bookstore window designer: they parody the books themselves, rather than the women who buy them. They begin: "It's not your fault! Men are stupid and smart women know it! It's time to stop worrying and start enjoying them [men] for what they are—which will always be less than you want. This book welcomes you to the age of the 'user friendly relationship'" (1).

Commentary on self-help books addressed to women has made its way into editorial columns, feature stories, even comic strips.[1] At nearly every turn, the recent wave of self-help books addressed to women has met with disdain or mockery from nonusing reviewers who are appalled at the simplistic limp prose; the tautological nature of authors' arguments; misrepresentation of what (in the opinion of the critics) women want or need; a skewed presentation of current sexual dynamics; and/or offensive recommendations for change.

During the summer of 1987, "Cathy," the ultimate neurotic American woman comic-strip character, was reading a pile of self-help books on the beach. In the first frame, she explains to her boyfriend Irving, "IT'S A WHOLE NEW LINE OF BOOKS THAT HELPS US STUDY THE NEEDS AND MOTIVATIONS OF THE OPPOSITE SEX SO WE CAN WORK TO CREATE MORE MUTUALLY FULFILLING RELATIONSHIPS." Cathy pauses. "WHAT ARE YOU READING, IRVING?" He replies, "*HOT ROD WORLD.*" In the next frame, Irving, still smiling under a pile of mangled books, protests, "I THOUGHT YOU WANTED TO UNDERSTAND ME." Cathy, walking away—can of diet soda in hand—retorts, "I ALREADY KNOW TOO MUCH." Cathy's creator (and namesake), Cathy Guisewite, draws attention to the unreciprocated nature of women's efforts to "understand" men, and implies that there may be very little, indeed, worth understanding—or, perhaps, that ignorance would be more blissful than knowledge of what men are about. Self-help books can be only a waste of time, she implies, like the men they claim to decipher.

In February 1988, Berke Breathed's syndicated comic strip "Bloom County" showed Opus the Penguin (a male character, incidentally) staggering under a pile of self help-books (with titles including *Everything You Don't Know about Yourself, Hug Yourself, Women Who Love Bad Dogs,* and *G-Spot Blues*), while exclaiming: "AREN'T THEY WONDERFUL? A VERITABLE TOWER OF PSYCHOBABBLE! MY GOODNESS, IT'S GREAT TO LIVE IN AN AGE WHERE THE EMOTIONALLY DISTURBED CAN SO EXPERTLY TREAT THEMSELVES!" In creating an analogy between self-help books and the biblical tower of Babel, Breathed depicts the usage of self-help books as a fruitless and silly exercise—as yet another example of the misuse of faith by the faithful.

In the less overtly comical area of journalism, experts have been cited in feature stories, voicing the various charges that are often leveled against current self-help books: In a *New York Times* feature article on self-help for women, Susan Reverby explains that "women read these books because they are having genuine difficulties in relationships. . . . But what they get are simple psychobabble answers" (Lawson 1986). Hannah Lerman believes the books lay all blame and responsibility for making relationships work on women readers: "This fantasy feeds on women's low self-esteem and on their being programmed to think they have to perfect themselves endlessly" (Lawson 1986). Betty Friedan exclaims that "'women shouldn't be such patsies' for romantic advice books. 'They aren't going to get anything out of them'" (Lawson 1986). *Vogue* writer Susan Bolotin exhorts, "It's time that women said no to the majority of self help books. . . . It's time they said no to feeling responsible for everybody's happiness. It's time that women put blame on the unisexmen who deserve it and thank (and love) the ones who don't" (1987: 254). In a *Mademoiselle* review, Paula Caplan concurs with the view that though self-help books profess to help women, they ultimately end up blaming us: "Too many of these books are saying 'The real cause of the trouble is you, sweetie' " (Landi 1987: 247). Gerald R. Rosen warns, more charitably, that "well-intentioned instructions can turn out to be structured in such a way that nobody follows them. . . . If you combine that possibility with the exaggerated claims, publishers are selling products that nobody might be able to use and that might leave them feeling more upset with themselves for failing" (Hinds 1988).[2] And *Newsweek* writer Laura Shapiro writes that "the new advice books offer an accurate picture of a substantial predicament—but few ideas for resolving it" (1987: 65). At best, critics doubt the promised effect of self-help books on readers and see them as a waste of time. At worst, they label them as politically backward, narrow, and even potentially damaging to more gullible readers.

Objections to authors' writing styles are often raised in derogatory reviews of recent women's self-help bestsellers. Bolotin writes off the subgenre as "drivel," bemoaning authors' "sing-song" contradictory advice and titles "with the cadence . . . of a pitching sailboat about to keel over" (254). In a group review of four self-help books addressed to women (by Norwood, Forward, and two by Cowan and Kinder), Joyce Maynard complains that the books run together, writing: "I feel a bit like a person who has sampled every flavor at Baskin-Robbins and can no longer distinguish between chocolate and coffee" (1987: 92). Shapiro likes Forward's style, but says "most of her colleagues . . . write as though their readers [are] simpleminded and subliterate" (1987: 65). Reviewers claim the books lack sophistication, originality, and individuality; thus, how can they be expected to assist their readers in gaining these qualities?

It is clear from my participants' comments that readers do not necessarily turn to self-help books because they expect the books to deliver all they promise. Readers read because they hope to find some comfort, some insight, some information in self-help literature. The same stylistic maneuvers that journalists find intellectually offensive comfort many readers; others, though, may indeed perceive the writing as being intellectually beneath them. Though reviewers see self-help books for women as providing pat answers which recur from one work to another, authors often take readers through complex (sometimes contorted or contradictory) arguments before making recommendations.

Self-help books for women are filled with labels that authors have applied to people in their attempts to codify behavior. Readers may come to wonder, after being bombarded left and right by these catchy phrases, whether there are connections to be made between them. Is the "woman who loves too much," "the man addict," or the "mouseburger" the kind of "woman men leave" because she is caught up in the "Cinderella complex," the "Wendy dilemma," or "the feminine mystique?" Why does she get involved with men suffering from the "Peter Pan syndrome," with those "who can't love," or even with "men who hate women" in the first place? How can she become a "liberated woman,"a "total woman," a "smart woman" who doesn't make "foolish choices," or a "smart cookie" who doesn't "crumble"? Can she eradicate her "man-addiction" and cure his "commitment-phobia" simultaneously? If such women do exist in droves, as the popularity of current self-help books might suggest, what is the meaning of such male-orientation in what has been called the postfeminist period? And if the women and the men in each book are all the same people, why are there so many books?

Common bonds are everywhere to be found in this branch of the self-help genre because, for the most part, authors confront the same issues in their quests to disentangle the web of problems they believe women experience in intimate relationships or in our attempts to form them. Men and women do emerge seeming quite incompatible. In fact, reading these books one after another sent images from Thurber cartoons flitting through my mind—images of men and women alternately smirking at and cowering from each other while crouched behind the living room furniture, as they engage in out-and-out outrageous warfare (1931: 389–399).

The Perils of Childhood

Self-help books that attempt to decipher and improve heterosexual relationships present a strange picture of women and men. Based on the same popular-psychology that characterizes the unisex self-help books and the sex manuals, those addressed to women are unique in that they focus on problems of gender in American life—though often, attention to this subject is not the authors' *stated* area of interest.

Self-help books about relationships lead readers down a twisted and overgrown path to the breeding ground for heterosexual relational problems: childhood. Quite simply, the message being spread is that our parents screw us up. And since women are the ones who do the bulk of the parenting in this culture, mothers reap most of the blame for screwing up children in self-help books. Barbara Katz Rothman writes (of literature with a more scholarly bent than self-help books):

> Every now and again, someone discovers that children are raised by women, and writes a book about it. The point of the book is to blame mothers, or mother rearing, for the evils of the world, most especially for the evil that men do. The basic argument . . . is that boy children, because they are reared by mothers, have to separate themselves, consequently rejecting the mother and the womanliness in themselves, and dominate women and the world. (1989: 211)

Self-help authors are continually rediscovering women's complicity in the shortcomings and wrongdoings of their children. Sometimes, authors take a different—yet ultimately as derogatory—tack and claim that the mindlessness of mothering work leads to a lack of personhood, a void of identity in women. Women and men raised by mindless mothers can grow up to be social misfits. Self-help authors implicate fathers as causing problems also, but the root of men's problematic behavior as fathers lies in their upbringing, so the vicious circle leads back to mothers. In other words, as Rothman describes, men are usually let off the hook because they were raised by women.

Most self-help writers see separation from mothers as a crucial step in achieving individuality and growth in adult life. This kind of thinking raises a number of questions: If separation is the only means of achieving adulthood, should all connections be seen as immature or dangerous? And if all connections *are* immature or dangerous, what kinds of interactions should we strive for? If our parents' ties to us threaten our growth, how should we prevent ourselves from doing the same things to our children? Authors seem oblivious to the implications their arguments raise; however, as their narratives unfold, they often provide presumably unintentional "answers" to these questions.

The formulation of women's problems as maternally induced is also problematic in terms of the books' *raisons d'être:* why would self-help authors—who are often women themselves, and more often than not, people who see themselves as feminist in some manner—blame *women* so vehemently, while claiming to be able to help them? Wouldn't contempt, however mild, for one's "clients" be antithetical to the whole act of offering help? Part of the answer to these questions lies in the premise of the self-help genre that we cause our own problems. Readers are taught that to change whatever it is they want to change about their lives, they have to buy into the idea that it is within their power to do so; this concept forms the core of most unisex and gendered self-help books. To see themselves as in control of their problems, readers must, to some extent, accept that they have played a part in creating them. Without such an acknowledgment, there can be no hope of improving. Also, blaming client-readers for their problems can be seen as a possible outcome of therapeutic relationships, in which the "expert" hands down knowledge to the ignorant patient below; some authors indicate (by their tone) that they view their "relationship" with readers in this manner.

Authors' assertions of reader-blame range from overt to subtle to contradictory descriptions of women's participation in our own and others' pathologies. In some books, women certainly sound like masochists; in others, we are depicted as unintentionally acting as our own worst enemies. Authors do not touch on the possibility that reading self-help books that encourage readers to blame themselves may be a masochistic activity itself. And readers, as I've discussed, do not view this activity as masochistic, but realistic, and even self-nurturant. All self-help authors advise that other people's behavior cannot be controlled, while assuring readers that a change in their own behavior will force others to change. The problem must first be traced to its source in readers' lives, so that readers proceed with an understanding of how they, because of their upbringings, have become adults who get into problem situations with others.

Most self-help authors are not clear in their articulations of who should accept blame for problems or responsibility for their amendment. Authors often don't appear to *want* to blame mothers—or women in general—at all. But their explanations become muddled because they have not resolved conflicting frameworks for evaluation; sociology and psychology, various strands of feminism and antifeminism, conservative and radical thought collide. And though some authors do question and critique the mutually exclusive gender spheres they present, radical proposals for change—such as the abolition of gender as a social and sexual construct altogether—are not advanced. (Such ideas are perhaps more than the market could bear.) Even authors who claim to believe wholeheartedly in gender-exclusive realms of behavior for men and women get confused about who is to blame for problematic relationships when they set out to advise women.

Because girls and boys are treated differently in infancy and childhood, many self-help authors begin, we emerge into adulthood with contrasting beliefs and behaviors which often become irreconcilable when brought together. When we are babies, our mothers dress us up in pink or blue depending upon our gender. They pin our hair up in barrettes if we are girls, or buy us baby bow-ties if we are boys. They tell us to cross our legs, or not to play with dolls. They teach us to cook, clean, and care profusely, or they teach us not to. And thus, women—as mothers—are the social construction-workers of gender, for both future men and future women.

Because mothers teach their girl children compliance and passivity, they do not fare well as role models for girls in self-help authors' formulations. (The idea that mothers could function as role models for boys is not even considered.) Fathers, through the examples they set, enable their sons to become similarly distant or authoritative husbands and fathers themselves. But fathers are not seen as initiators of gendered behavior for men; rather, they are depicted as mere transmitters, re-ifiers, passive agents, really, in the work of maintaining gender. The prevailing message authors convey is that the destructive aspects of gender identity are born at home, beginning at birth, and that these proliferate like sneaky viruses which cannot be curbed without heroic effort.

Self-help authors do not portray women's gender socialization of children as *social* work; their conception of the indoctrination process focuses on *individual* behaviors about which generalizations can be made. Occasional references are made to culture or society and to the institutionalized nature of socialization, but on the whole, self-help authors seem to conceive of society as a mass of family units, each diligently doing its part to contribute to a uniform whole. Unlike Candace West and Don Zimmerman (1987), who write about "doing" gender as a deeply embedded social activity, self-help authors treat gender as a psychological given: each of us learns prescriptions and proscriptions pertaining to our particular gender, based on our specific parents' quirky pasts. As we have inherited these rules for behavior, so we will pass them on to our children, unless we redirect our efforts and break the chain—through reading.

Faith in Gender

Most authors are unwilling to give up the idea that a certain amount of difference according to gender is a desirable or "normal" result of "normal" development. Authors concern themselves primarily with extreme cases. But they also describe these extreme cases as quite plentiful, even epidemic. Thus, authors imply that it may not be that something has gone too far in the process of child rearing, but rather that something is wrong with the very core of child-rearing practices themselves. Though they may, at times, lean toward a grand indictment of American family life, ultimately authors are trapped within the narrow psychological frame they have so carefully crafted.[3] Thus, individual mothers are held responsible for the individual men (the commitmentphobes, the misogynists, the drunkards, the lovers-and-leavers) who will become problematic in relationships with other women's individual daughters. And individual mothers are seen as creators of the individual women (the clingers, the overinvesters, the passive-aggressives, and so forth) who will become problematic in relationships with other women's individual sons.

Self-help authors create a bizarre portrait of women in which we are omnipowerful and yet powerless. Men are no less peculiar. They learn to feel powerful—especially over women—from the mothering they receive, yet paradoxically, they also learn that mothers are ultimately the powerful ones and that men are, consequently, powerless. Perhaps strangest of all, the majority of the mismothering mothers and their daughters and sons don't have the faintest idea about what's going on, according to self-help authors. That's where the books come in.

All this confusion contributes to the contradictory nature of self-help authors' recommendations for improvement or problem solving. Authors usually acknowledge that men should be different, and yet they believe that men might very well be unchangeable. Women, however, *can* change. Authors urge women to adapt by adopting men's strategies for conducting involvements, even though such strategies seem, in their own narratives, to be rather inept. Ironically, then, the same women being reduced to (wronging) mothers are instructed to emulate the distanced jerks they have (wrongly) been creating. This is the composite, and often confusing, story that self-help books report about heterosexual relationships. Each book may not reproduce all of this amalgam, but steady readers will be exposed to many—if not all—aspects of this composite.

Participants in my study would sometimes demonstrate their belief in the validity of this composite view when they talked about what they had learned from books they considered influential in their lives. For instance, Val said that she had read *Women Who Love Too Much* to see if she was "one of them," and found out "I kind of was, although I hate to admit it." She read *Men Who Hate Women and the Women Who Love Them* to gain insight into a man she had recently broken up with; "he is definitely one of them," she said. She drew on the contents of the book to explain why she selected the book in the first place:

> I was concerned about that [loving too much] because my husband had had many affairs, and I am concerned about my children and how they are going to form relationships. . . . I mean, you know, why—*why* did I choose a man who was going to double-cross me? I probably did that intentionally, very honestly. . . . I think that was her [Norwood's] point. . . . I felt I was a product of a family of women who loved too much, because my mother covered for my father, and I had done the same thing. . . . And I also didn't want to get trapped in the same thing again.

The readers I interviewed often demonstrated their support for the idea that one's behavior in relationships is patterned on one's parents' relationship with each other; several participants described their struggles to transcend or deemphasize parental (especially maternal) influence in their lives. I am not disputing that this idea—of the generational transmission of behavior patterns—is sensible, or real in its consequences for those who feel it to be forceful in their lives. Certainly, we do learn from and imitate our parents in ways that we experience as both beneficial and detrimental. But this idea alone, if developed in certain manners (which I explore in this chapter) can result in an antisociological way of understanding social interaction that reproduces itself endlessly and, I believe, unproductively.

The Problem Gets a Name

The recent spate of self-help books for women began with the pioneering work of Betty Friedan. Though they have been influenced by unisex self-help books over time, current self-help books for women still concern themselves with the core issues that Friedan raised in *The Feminine Mystique,* published in 1963. Friedan, writing to an assumed audience of middle- and upper-class housewives, urges women to seek meaning outside their homes and separable from their families, by joining the male-dominated labor force, which she idealizes into a panoply of challenging, autonomous, personally satisfying, and remunerative professional pursuits.

Friedan's starting point for the deconstruction of women's homebound lives is the activity of mothering. She criticizes psychological research for its negative focus on mothers (189–205) and then begins her own attack. In her efforts to show the ill effects of the traditional gendered division of labor within middle-class households, Friedan enthusiastically denounces women's work as housewives and mothers. Full-time housecleaning and child rearing are depicted as degrading and stultifying activities, which, at their worst, could and would produce children who lacked the skills necessary for healthy adulthood, Friedan believes.

The psychological task of separating from the Mother was held to be of paramount importance by Friedan. This important developmental accomplishment could be frustrated by mothers who were (unconsciously) determined to live vicariously through their children (since their own lives lacked purpose). Friedan writes: "These mothers have themselves become more infantile, and because they are forced to seek more and more gratification through the child, they are incapable of finally separating themselves from the child. Thus, it would seem, it is the child who supports life in the mother in that 'symbiotic' relationship, and the child is virtually destroyed in the process" (289–290).

The closeness of mother and child is the lynchpin of Friedan's argument that full-time housewifery should be ended. Women have been socially programmed for this relationship, but it ends up hurting everyone. She implies that the symbiosis in which most mothers engage with their children could create emotionally immature, promiscuous, and/or academically unsuccessful children. Friedan believes that a boy might become a homosexual as a result of his desire to flee the all-consuming mother, "who attaches her son to her with such dependence that he can never mature to love a woman, nor can he, often, cope as an adult with life on his own" (275). Friedan bemoans the increasing visibility of gay men in the sixties and lumps homosexuality together with a litany of societal ills created by "parasitical mother-love" (276). Ironically, she considers it more immature for men to choose men as lovers than to choose women—whose childish and dangerous methods of loving she devotes her efforts to detailing. Though Friedan questions some long-standing institutions, others (heterosexuality among them) remain unchallenged by *The Feminine Mystique.*

Overinvestment in her children could lead a mother to beat them, as well as to accept beatings herself from an angry husband. "There is no doubt," writes Friedan, "that male outrage against women—and inevitably, against sex—has increased enormously in the era of the feminine mystique" (273). Men's anger at overinvesting mothers, Friedan implies, is somehow justified. She calls for action to stop all the miseries being inflicted upon and by women: housewives must extricate themselves from the "comfortable concentration camp[s]" that are their homes (307).

I do not mean to deny the feminist sensibility of Friedan's work. Clearly, as readers' letters to her indicate, her work was experienced as incredibly liberating for many women. By examining the ideological inconsistencies and underlying conservatism in *The Feminine Mystique,* I do not mean to imply that its status as a feminist literary milestone was not earned; rather, I hope to show some fascinating ways in which Friedan—and many other early feminists—deconstructed her—their—own arguments. I don't think the ambivalence with which writers like Friedan described women's predicament was consciously articulated.

Now, in retrospect, it becomes easier to read. Friedan's work (and other feminist writing to follow) endorse both a view of women as wrongfully imprisoned *and* as builders of our own cages. This ambivalence between two compelling and equally unsatisfactory extremes—blaming women for everything and seeing women only as victims—remains with us in current feminist literature. What we have gained with time, I think, is awareness of the difficulty of describing how hegemony plays itself out in everyday life.

Recapitulating and Refining the Problem

Germaine Greer offers an interesting twist to Friedan's argument in *The Female Eunuch* (1970). She encourages women not only to leave home, but to pull our houses up from the ground as we go. Greer casts patriarchal capitalism as the problem impeding women's liberation in a way that Friedan does not. Greer wants revolution for women: "The old process must be broken, not made new," she writes (352). Despite her clearly articulated sociological frame, Greer's anger at women's situation still spills over onto the "victims" themselves. Like Friedan, she sees mothering as a warped institution, and the mother-child bond as an "introverted relationship of mutual exploitation" (70). Relations between men and women in *The Female Eunuch* sound far more embattled and embittered than those Friedan presents. Like Friedan, Greer shifts her sympathies back and forth, identifying alternately with women and with men.

Friedan and Greer both assert that men would prefer women's liberation to women's oppression because women would be better, more interesting people if we were free, and men would enjoy being with us more. Greer's idea of freedom is more radical than Friedan's; but in both cases, the question of who will do the housework and child rearing after women liberate themselves is handled only vaguely. Friedan implies that women ought to be able to hire help, and she never confronts the fact that this would no doubt mean that *different* women would be employed to be oppressed by the feminine mystique. Greer also mentions hiring help and throws in a few references to communal living, or what she calls "cooperative enterprises," in which privatized marriage and parenthood would become socio-psychological constructs of the past.

In *The Total Woman* (1973), Marabel Morgan reacts against the budding feminist movement which had, by the time of her writing, enthusiastically incorporated the works of Friedan and Greer as doctrine. Despite her political and religious ultraconservatism, Morgan's advice is strangely tinged by feminist fallout and even predicts a coming trend in feminist writing that insists on valuing what women have traditionally done. Underlying Morgan's reiterations of the biblical imperative that men take charge of everything and women comply with their righteous dominance is an opposing strand of thought. She encourages readers to control their marriages in subtle ways, by carefully manipulating their husbands into a situation where they would *feel* all-powerful, but would really be playing into their wives' hands and would buy them all sorts of gifts and adore them unceasingly. Morgan stresses the goodies that would accrue for scheming willing victims of hegemonic rule; women would come to know our place so well that it could not help but improve. Men, it seems, would be oblivious to women's maneuvers, and if we plan carefully enough, our acting would become real.

Shortly after Morgan's antifeminism became a bestseller, a new trend of antifeminist feminism erupted out of the women's movement. The passivity of women and the complicity of men in ensuring women's passivity that enraged Friedan and Greer and fueled their powerful writing devolves into a self-centered whine in Colette Dowling's *The Cinderella Complex* (1981), which is basically a reiteration of Friedan's core argument. Dowling sees mothers' socialization of girls as detrimental to women's futures; she writes: "girl babies learn that help comes quickly if you cry for it. . . . *Bit by bit* [a boy baby] *learns to become his own emotional caretaker*" (105, emphasis in original). According to Dowling girls were being taught fear of real life—outside the home—by our mothers, and would undoubtedly grow up and teach this fear to our own daughters, and so on.

It would seem that a less attentive mother would produce a more independent daughter—that is, that it would be beneficial if mothers would mother girls the same way they mother boys—but not necessarily. Dowling describes how an underattentive, betraying mother, in league with an "intense, overbearing father," would create a daughter who had "difficulty in growing up and getting free" (122). Either way, in Dowling's view, mothers take the blame and daughters are damaged by mothers, because the intense mother-inflicted mother-daughter bonds are so difficult to break, and without a break, independent identity cannot be gained.

So, according to Dowling, women are trapped by our mothers, and like our mothers, we will go on to ensnare men, who, like our fathers, we hope will protect us (as the handsome prince did Cinderella, too). Dowling describes how women unwittingly make family life into "a web of children and relatives and carefully selected friends in which the husband is ensnared, a stiff and shiny-winged fly" (147).

It remains unclear in Dowling's portrait of a normal—yet maladjusted—woman's development why men would put up with such manipulations. And Dowling never explains why women did not turn to other women, rather than men, for protection. It would seem a logical developmental step since mothers were the ones who originally shielded girl babies from the traumas of real life, that women would seek mothering from women in later life, especially since men don't know how to do it. But like Friedan and Greer before her, Dowling takes heterosexuality for granted and does not pick up on the implications of the utility of lesbianism which are included in her own argument.

In self-help books, men and women suffer differently from an inability to separate from their mothers. Men, it seems, simply go in search of replacement mothers, with whom they continue the dialectical battle of obtaining motherlove while defining themselves as men in opposition to their new mother figures—wives. Even at their worst, it seems that men's overconnections with their mothers would cause women far more harm than they would the men who engaged in them. On the whole, self-help authors see men as able to integrate their search for reviving the comfort of the womb with a rewarding and worthwhile life in the real world.

Women, however, are viewed by self-help authors as stunted in our growth as individuals when we do not separate from our mothers, and as understandably inept at achieving separation because of the mothering we've received. Close ties with unrelentingly clinging mothers are portrayed as draining, and, ultimately, emotionally unrewarding for all concerned parties. Rather than seek replacements for mothers in lovers only, as men do, women look to a whole host of significant others to latch onto, especially daughters. Nancy Friday describes this phenomenon in *My Mother/ My Self* (1977): "Being cute and helpless, clinging, clutching, holding on for dear life, becomes our method for survival— and ultimate defeat" (61).

Though our mothers may cause many of our troubles, they are also the source of all good, according to Friday, who is one of the few authors to include explicit appreciation of motherwork in her book. (Perhaps it is because Friday devotes an entire book to mothering that she has enough space to consider it from more than one side.) In praise of mothering, Friday writes: "We get our courage, our sense of self, the ability to believe we have value even when alone, to do our work, to love others, and to feel ourselves lovable from the strength of mother love for us when we were infants—just as every single dyne of energy on earth originally came from the sun" (55).

Smother-mothering, which even Friday's kind words do not erase, remains a problem through the seventies and into the eighties within the self-help genre. The flip side of smother-mothering, undermothering, comes into its own in the eighties. Women who don't pay enough attention to their children's needs can cause just as much damage as those who are overly attentive. Early self-help writers who addressed women (such as Friedan and Greer) didn't write about undermothering because it didn't fit into their formulation of the problem; to them, less mothering would have been a desirable end for women and children.

As the subgenre of self-help books for women ages—while women have entered the paid labor market in greater and greater numbers— the character of the neglectful mother emerges with more regularity in self-help narratives. Susan Forward and Joan Torres (1986), for example, detail how a lack of mothering can lead to misogyny in men: "In addition to withholding love and attention and thereby frustrating her son, a cold, rejecting mother will often punish him for his normal needs of her. From this he gets the message that his *neediness is unacceptable and shameful.* . . . Many misogynists use bullying and macho behavior toward women to defend against these unacceptable feelings of vulnerability" (119). In other words, women can often be held responsible for misogyny if we are underattentive mothers. There seems to be no happy medium. Boys can become damaged in the process of separating from their mothers, Forward and Torres explain, when they are unable to do so smoothly or easily. "Unlike a girl, who can stay close to her mother while she finds her own identity, a young boy must pull away from his mother in order to grow up as a healthy adult" (111). Here Forward and Torres see boys as much more damaged by mothering than girls are: the Freudian concept of identification with the parent of one's gender as a necessary element in properly maturing as woman and men resurfaces.

Mothers who hamper boys' efforts to separate from them also contribute to the production of misogyny in our culture, according to
authors. Such overmothered boys will eventually suffer from deeply
internalized fears of women's all-consuming passion (to smother them)
as they become men. The theme of women entrapping men recurs
throughout the relationship-oriented self-help books of the seventies
and eighties.

Authors may or may not themselves believe that women are out to
ensnare, envelop, or engulf men, but they strongly believe that *men* feel
women are out to gain power over them. Forward and Torres write that a
typical misogynist "harbors a hidden belief that if he loves a woman, she
will then have the power to hurt him, to deprive him, to engulf him, and
to abandon him" (99). Before she can destroy him, a misogynist will
defend himself; he "sets out, usually unconsciously, to make the woman
in his life less powerful" (99). He wants to weaken her, to make her
completely dependent on him in order to disempower her with the
force of his hatred; he may even abuse her physically to gain this end.
Their explanation of how misogyny works resonates with Susan Griffin's
analysis of the ideology behind pornography (1981). At the root of the
"pornographic mind," Griffin writes, is men's fear of their own feminine
side (culture's fear of eros). At the root of Forward and Torres's argument, femininity comes dressed up as everyone's mother. According to
Forward and Torres, each man will view every woman with whom he
comes in contact through the lens of the first woman in his life, whom
he both loves and loathes for her power—as well as for her lack of it.

Fathers can reinforce misogynist behavior, Forward and Torres write,
by being women haters themselves or by not setting an appropriate
masculine example at all. "Tyrannical" fathers teach their sons to follow
in their footsteps, while "passive" fathers leave boys to rely all the more
on their dangerous mothers. Both sorts, according to these authors, thus
fail in their instrumental and essential role of facilitating separation
from the mother. Somewhere between tyranny and passivity lies the
proper realm of fatherhood, Forward and Torres imply; but they never
explain exactly what this is.

Fathers can also hurt daughters, and a corollary to the argument that
men look for their mothers in the women with whom they become
involved is voiced by Forward and Torres (among others): women look
for our fathers in the men with whom we become involved. Self-help
authors see parental influence as working in one of two ways for women:

some believe each of us seeks whatever treatment we received from our fathers, however unhealthy it was, because that is how we think relationships are supposed to work; other authors believe we strive to attain the love we never felt in childhood, which—because the lack of it has been festering in our heads over the years—can never be delivered by any mortal man. Either way, it seems, women are doomed to be unhappy in the heterosexual relationships we form.

Norwood (1985) and Forward and Torres (1986) both describe how some women choose men who are detrimental to their health (emotional *and* physical) because their fathers neglected or abused them when they were younger and may well have also neglected or abused their mothers (with whom they overidentify, because they have not forged a mature separation). On the other hand, Cowan and Kinder (1985) write that it isn't that women are choosing the wrong men, but that we have unreasonable "distorted" expectations that formed as a *reaction* to our lack of fatherlove (37).

What remains unanswered in Cowan and Kinder's explanation is why fathers would be distant and unloving enough to create such a large scale problem in their grown-up daughters' lives if most men are not really inadequate. Cowan and Kinder seem to view men and fathers as two distinct categories. They waver between letting men off the hook and tentatively implicating them—along with women—in relational problems. But the reasons for men's inadequacy—however they manifest themselves—can be traced back to mothering. Boys learn that dependence upon the Mother, however wonderful it might feel, is a very dangerous and antimasculine characteristic. Normal male development necessarily involves fear and/or resentment of the Mother, which will later become generalized against women as a group, according to Cowan and Kinder. They write: "In adulthood, when men are drawn to intimate attachments with women, they experience both pleasure and fear—the pleasure of being nurtured . . . and fear that these deeply ingrained feelings of helplessness and dependency will overwhelm them" (67).

Self-help authors rarely address women readers *as* mothers. (Fathers are never addressed, of course, because they are not expected to be reading these books.) The position of the child in the mother-child relationship seems to lend itself more readily than that of the mother to an argument centered on the self's struggle to achieve identity.

Psychologist-writers consider the experience of childhood to be far more influential in achieving a sense of self than the experience of mothering children. Also, the examination of women's passivity easily initiates a discussion of the role of the child, because though mothers may be seen as passive women in many ways, they are not considered passive *as* mothers.[4] Even mothers' apathy is perceived as active behavior by its recipients, according to the popular-psychology voiced by self-help authors.

Authors occasionally feel uncomfortable about implicating mothers too much in the neuroses of their children, and a few offer caveats to temper their arguments. For instance, Nancy Friday writes: *"Blaming mother keeps us passive, tied to her.* It helps us avoid taking responsibility for ourselves. All any mother can do is her best" (83). But for the most part, authors are not overly reticent about pointing fingers at the "generalized mother," the source from which life and all its problems spring.

Creatures of Culture

Most self-help authors at least acknowledge culture as a co-creator of the problems that mothers cause, but this is primarily lip service. Forward and Norwood each comment on the undesirable power dynamics inherent in a culturally imposed dependence of women on men:

> Our culture reinforces this idea [that men's masculinity depends on their ability to dominate women] by depicting women as appropriate targets for men's hostilities. In literature, movies, and television, women are used by men as shields, foils, and hostages. They are raped, beaten, and shot with frightening regularity. Pornography implies that a woman's inherent seductiveness justifies any sadistic and/or sexual act a man wishes to commit against her. (Forward and Torres 1986: 121–122)

> Everything happens in a context, including the way we love. We need to be aware of the damaging shortcomings of our societal view of love and to resist the shallow and self-defeating immaturity in personal relationships that it glamorizes. We need to consciously develop a more open and mature way of relating than what our

cultural media seem to endorse, thus trading turmoil and excitement for a deeper intimacy. (Norwood 1985: 64)

Though both of these authors implicate social mores in the continued subjugation of women, these mores appear to *reinforce* the parental misdeeds the authors spend much more space chronicling, rather than to have *caused* them. They both discuss media as if they are somehow disembodied from everyday behavior or other institutional structures.

In a similar vein, Carter and Sokol (1987) briefly mention the cultural messages fed to girls that teach us to expect that someday our princes will come, sweep us off our feet, support us financially, and protect us from the experiences of adulthood: "Your only fault is that you have been sociologically groomed to respond favorably to a man who acts like the Knight in shining armor, the hero who is going to pull you up onto his horse and take you riding into the sunset," they write (35). If cultural explanations had remained central to these authors' expositions, women's "only fault" of successfully absorbing messages that are part of "normal" socialization would seemingly leave us blameless. This, however, is not what happens; psychology prevails.

The most sociological treatments of gender-based power imbalances come from Harriet Lerner (1985) and Deborah Tannen (1990). Lerner offers recommendations for individual change on the part of women but reminds readers that "if we do not also challenge and change the societal institutions that keep women in a subordinate and de-selfed position *outside* the home, what goes on *inside* the home will continue to be problematic for us all" (224). She reiterates Kate Millet's early feminist slogan, "the personal is political" (223). And Tannen doesn't write straight self-help so much as social analysis that blurbers laud as didactic. For Tannen, "Recognizing gender differences frees individuals from the burden of individual pathology" (17). She ventures to the other end of the spectrum, really, from blaming women or men: no one's morally wrong in interactive impasses; men and women just demonstrate different *styles*. And "if we recognize and understand the differences between us, we can take them into account, adjust to, and learn from each other's styles," Tannen explains optimistically (17). Unlike most self-help authors, Tannen presumes men will act to forge a new way of communication despite the cultural training that has rendered them—by her own account—basically mute.

Acknowledgments of cultural forces aside, at the root of psychologically oriented self-help books about relationships is the idea that there are certain patterns of behavior in which we engage primarily because we share psychological characteristics, rather than because of the social nature of the patterns. Our minds don't work healthily because we are psychically, rather than socially, flawed. Theodore Isaac Rubin presents a prime example of this reasoning in *One to One: Understanding Personal Relationships* (1983), writing:

> The intensity and quality of relationships are dictated largely by the character structures of the participants. These patterns sometimes change in response to the relationships themselves or to the influence of unpredictable outside forces, but such changes are seldom profound or permanent. This is the result of the relatively fixed nature of the character structure of each participant and the tenacity of interpersonal transactions once they become established and familiar. (viii)

Attention to our own individual situations will help improve the world in the long run, Rubin states, because malfunctions at home are the basis for malfunctions in the societal system at large: "We must increasingly understand these core relationships if we wish to remedy a very sick society," he writes (x). This one-way relationship between individual psychology and social dynamics on a large scale is reiterated repeatedly in New Age books. Assertions of individual power as the basis for self *and* social change may be experienced by readers as invigorating and inspirational, but they also imply that exposure to self-help authors' advice makes living in the dark inexcusable. Once a reader sees the "truth" (the writing in the book), she should get to work on herself. If she doesn't, it means she is not fulfilling her true potential as a human being, authors write, reiterating the central message of identity-as-growth unisex self-help books.

The bottom line of the childhood-centered theories espoused by self-help authors is that if our parents, especially our mothers, behave appropriately, we will grow up happy. (And what, exactly, good parenting should be may very well elude self-help readers because there are so many fine lines hazily marking the divisions between over- and underdoing it.) If our parents, especially our mothers, behave inappropriately, we will be damaged in some way. Authors are vehement about the inescapability of our parents as models for future personality development. Parents are both inescapable predictors of what we will become, and psychological impediments we must try to clear from obstructing our paths to personal growth. Even if we survive childhood with a relatively intact identity, however, the battle for selfhood is by no means over.

Negotiating Gender and Selfhood

Adult men and women are like two distinct species in self-help books. The same pattern that surfaced in the sex manuals recurs in relationship-oriented books, but here books about men and women are addressed primarily to women seeking to understand themselves and the men with whom they are involved. (Perhaps sex is important enough for men to warrant reading about, but the more mundane, nonorgasmic aspects of relationships are *women's* work.) Authors range widely in their attitudes about the severity of the operational differences between men and women that cause problems when they get involved with each other. A minority holds that men and women are basically motivated by the same desires and impulses; it is simply that these manifest themselves differently. Most, however, believe that motivations, behavior, desires, needs—in short, everything—separates men and women. Joyce Brothers exemplifies this view in *What Every Woman Should Know about Men* (1981):

> Are men and women really so different?
> They are.
> They really are. I spent months talking to biologists, neurologists, geneticists, research psychiatrists, and psychologists—the scientists who are opening new frontiers in the study of humankind—in preparation for this book. . . . What I discovered was that men are even more different from women than I had known. Their bodies are different and their minds are different. Men are different from the very composition of their blood to the way their brains develop, which means that they think and experience life very differently from women. (4)

Similarly, Barbara De Angelis opens her book, *Secrets about Men Every Women Should Know* (1990), with the quip, "Have you ever wished that men would come with instruction booklets?" (xv). She then, of course, offers her very own ("May [this book] help you create the loving relationship with a man that you've always dreamed of" [xvi]).

As a result of growing up amid the complex and detrimental configuration of parental authority described by self-help authors, most women become male-identified: we center our lives on others—especially men. As a result, we experience problems with self-esteem and identity. Men, however, become self-centered as a result of normal development. To many self-defined feminist self-help writers (such as Friedan, Greer, Dowling, Friday, Norwood, and Forward and Torres), women's primary desires to form relationships with men and to keep these relationships at center stage are seen as the base upon which all problems between men and women rest. Men, according to self-help authors, don't put relationships first in their lives, don't obsess over problems in relationships, and don't fall to pieces when their relationships do. And rightly so! authors exclaim. If women could only emulate men, authors seem to believe, and could only deemphasize the importance of our relationships with men, we would be better off in every way. The problem with these recommendations, as I see them, is that women's approach to forging connections is assumed to be more detrimental than men's distance. Studies of marriage repeatedly attest to the fact that women are dissatisfied with men's inability to participate in maintaining intimacy, and show that at the same time, men are quite dependent upon women for the emotional caretaking that they seem unable to reciprocate (e.g., Bernard 1972; Riessman 1990; Rubin 1976). And yet, repeatedly in self-help books, women are depicted as overly invested, and men as stable in their distance from us.

Women's insecurities and miseries revolve around the mother-propelled myth of male salvation, encouraging us to become so dependent on men we lose any hope of real selfhood. Male salvation may have been necessary once, when people lived in caves and men's protective strength was all that stood between the weaker sex and "the wild," but now, Dowling writes, the time is ripe to purge ourselves of the princess fantasy, because it holds women back from realizing our true potential.

Dowling's message for American women is: Get a life! (my paraphrase). She describes women's attempts to explain our situations as a result of patriarchal rule as a misguided endeavor to displace blame, maintain the status quo, and remain sheltered. Women's oppression is imposed from within, she announces. In her analysis, then, oppression ceases to exist; there can be no such thing as self-oppression, really, because there is simply *no reason* for it. Women are simply creating and maintaining problems, holding ourselves back from the opportunities awaiting us: "Women are continuing to choose low-paying careers. . . . Women are not just being excluded from power. . . . We are also actively *avoiding* it," Dowling asserts (36). Or worse, women are hoping to cash in on free handouts with exaggerated complaints of unfairness or discrimination (131).

Women are not proper adults, according to Dowling; we are childlike in our dependence on men. But adulthood, to Dowling, is really a masculine phenomenon. Dowling describes women who have engaged in successful male adulthood—by pursuing careers—as possible Cinderella Complex victims waiting to happen. These women are "phobics"; they lack fulfillment and a true sense of identity. They cover up their fears with a "counterphobic facade." They give the appearance of being strong and invulnerable; they have "an inner need to feel superior" to men and tend to overachieve because they can't face up to their deep feelings of inadequacy and helplessness (66–68). After reading *The Cinderella Complex,* one might wonder whether any woman can grow up free from the neurotic problems Dowling describes; it seems that we are all in need of therapeutic realignment.

In a departure from the prevalent focus on the dangers of involvement, Helen Gurley Brown, author of *Having It All* (1982), does not see women's problems as a result of complex psychological misdeeds from the mother-controlled past. Rather, our difficulties are caused by a lack of self-confidence that will be easy to shake under her direction. What Marabel Morgan did for married women working at home, Brown does for single women who have ventured into the paid labor market. She presents her advice in the form of a schmoozing pep talk for women who are interested in "Having It All," finding access—as Brown claims she has—to "love, success, sex, and money."

Brown encourages women not to develop manlike qualities in order to find our true identities (as Dowling thinks we should), but to exploit (stereotypical) "feminine" traits if we want to achieve success on a par with men—in business or in bed. Brown recommends masking her method of cutthroat competition with pandering smiles and sexual innuendo. She defends the wily manipulation of (horny) men as simply good business sense, and perfectly ethical, because everyone involved will gain from women's performance: "To be a pleaser and a charmer is *not* selling out; it is investing in happiness (yours!) through the process of making other people glad to be around you," she writes (33). The business world should not be stripped of sexual tension and made into an androgynous arena, but rather sexuality should become a useful part of the games being played, Brown feels. If men and women work together, according to Brown, sexuality will enter the workplace; it would be naive to imagine it could or should be kept out. To Brown, opportunities for sexual fulfillment are everywhere, and women everywhere are ripe for fulfilling. "As for not sleeping with the boss, why discriminate against *him*?" she writes (35).[5]

Brown sees relationships between men and women as challenging and fun, energized by sexual tension, rather than embattled and embittered—as past advisers had portrayed them. The real enemy for women is other women, not men, and the real goal is personal fulfillment, not revolution. "You will be in full bloom when other women are losing their husbands, children, and confidence," she writes (29). Women ought to treat men as boyish and harmless objects of acquisition, all of whom are eligible for seduction. Brown urges women to carefully plan our pursuit of men for our own gain.

According to Brown, all a woman needs to do to "have it all" is to be clear about her goals, and to put them into action diligently. Brown revamps the work ethic for women. Achieving success becomes far more simple as Brown conceives of it, compared with the advice prior authors offered readers; it is no longer bound up with deep psychological issues, but merely a matter of strategy. Brown sees gender not as problematic, but as a thrilling manipulant in "new" techniques for pursuing an exciting life.

The Inside Story: Men Experts

Men authors reveal deep-seated beliefs in the viability of gender stereotypes and often display these views at the same time that they attempt to show how sensitive and politically aware they are. When describing the romantic failures of his case studies, Steven Carter, coauthor (with Julia Sokol—but Carter narrates the book in the first person, and Sokol's voice is not discernible) of *Men Who Can't Love* (1987), repeatedly stresses the seeming superiority of the women he consulted: "I began by interviewing approximately fifty single women. All of the women were attractive, desirable, contemporary women who had a lot to offer any man" (20). Though Carter asserts that he "used the same criteria" in selecting men for his "study" as he did for selecting women, he describes the men as "intelligent, normal," and "well educated," but he uses none of these adjectives to describe the women. Underneath Carter's alleged nonsexist methodology, one can sense that sameness for men and women really means difference.

Similarly, Cowan and Kinder temper their finger pointing with flattery in their opening chapter, "Being Foolish." They write: "We find, so often, that the *more intelligent and sophisticated the woman, the more self-defeating and foolish her choices and her pattern of behavior with romantic partners*" (1985: 6, emphasis in original). Readers are urged to identify with these superior, and yet misguided, women—women who have been helped by the authors to extend their intelligence and sophistication to the realm of romance.

Like women authors, men authors of relationship-oriented self-help also detail male fears of female entrapment. Dan Kiley, author of *The Peter Pan Syndrome* (1983) and *The Wendy Dilemma* (1984), describes how the combination of men's fears of commitment with women's desperate needs to connect often result in a fine mess for all those who participate. Men are far less likely to be judged as suffering from the "PPS" than women are to be found maladjustedly practicing Wendyish behavior. About potential Peter Pans, Kiley writes: "You have to be careful in labeling an adult male as a victim of the Peter Pan Syndrome. . . . The presence of one or two attributes of the PPS doesn't make a man a victim any more than being unconscious makes a person dead" (1983: 15). But Kiley informs women readers, "The question is not *whether* you mother your man, but *how often* and *whether you're aware of it*. Remember, women fall into the Wendy trap without realizing it" (1984: 10). Kiley must assume that women are the ones reading both of his books, and he hopes to enlist us as agents of change, by encouraging us to apply the "Wendy" label, so we can begin to cure ourselves.

Though Carter and Sokol take men as their starting point, their conclusion is the same as that of authors who make women's perspective central, in that they believe it is women who must amend our behavior if heterosexual relationships are ever to succeed. As dynamics between men and women indicate, women's methods simply are not working, the authors assert. Women put men off with our desperation, scare them away with our demands. Women who, at first glance, appeared to Carter to "have a lot to offer any man" were foiled because they didn't understand how to deal with these normal men (1987: 19). Normal, everyday guys, it turns out, are often "commitmentphobics," Carter explains.

Carter and Sokol do not show how to turn an uncommitted man into a committed one, as they originally promise they will; they show only how to identify, respond to, and ultimately leave such men—because it is unlikely these men will be capable of change. A true commitmentphobe, according to Carter and Sokol, needs professional help yet has personality traits that make it unlikely that he will be willing to seek it. Drawing on Barbara Ehrenreich's *The Hearts of Men* (1983), Carter and Sokol describe men as deeply threatened by marriage (or any long-term commitment that resembles marriage). They write that a woman who "acts like a wife" will merely reinforce male indifference in the men she pursues, because men don't really want someone looking after their needs, and don't really want self-sacrificial understanding and nurturance. Yet the same men are torn by a conflicting need to rely fully on women (owing to the time when they were dependent upon their mothers), according to Carter and Sokol. The upshot of the dialectical nature of men's needs is that they are unable to be intimate in the ways in which women are. Thus, the kind of intimacy that Carter and Sokol believe women desire is held to be impractical, as well as nearly impossible to achieve.

Carter and Sokol encourage women to tailor our behavior to men's needs in a way that they believe will foster independence for us, but in a way that also ensures that women will never have our style of loving reciprocated. And yet, ironically, the authors *seem* to be in favor of reciprocal love and gender equality—as long as the intensity is carefully muted. They recommend that women reduce our overinvolvement to a healthy disinterest, finally advising: "Just . . . don't ask anything of him" (242). The way to gain control is to do less than nothing, to let go altogether: "Think of it [your relationship] as a sickly plant. . . . If you just keep trying to water it, it will drown," they write (226–227). Clearly, if women are the waterers in this analogy, men—not relationships—are the waterlogged ferns. Christopher Lasch writes that in recent cultural commodities (such as self-help books) "an everpresent undercurrent . . . is the insistent warning that closeness kills" (1984: 98). And indeed,

Carter and Sokol seem to believe this to be true, because the men they knew certainly experienced women's love as threateningly dangerous.

In *Iron John: A Book about Men* (1990), Robert Bly validates men's rightful separation from women with rather different methods than most self-help authors. The dust-jacket synopsis of the book hails Bly's endeavor as a turning to "the most ancient stories and legends to remind men and women of welcome images long forgotten, images of a vigorous masculinity both protective and emotionally centered." But the emotionalism being eschewed remains the realm of womanly attachment; even so, early on Bly carefully denies that this is an antifeminist work ("I want to make clear that this book does not seek to turn men against women, nor to return men to the domineering mode that has led to repression of women and their values for centuries. . . . [This book] does not constitute a challenge to the women's movement" [x]). Bly calls for a resurgence of male ritual with pop-anthropology rather than pop-psychology: men need to celebrate the "Wild Man" within by bonding with one another nonsexually. Bly reifies traditional notions of gender divisions by recounting men-only rituals designed to consolidate and affirm masculinity without acknowledging that such ceremonies all affirm the otherness of femininity and, more often than not, are designed to consolidate male power against the realm of the feminine. This argument presumes a cultural essentialism that differs little from biological essentialism. Though clearly Bly grieves the lack of connection many men (including he) experience in their relationships with their fathers, an unconscious but damaging motherlove (which seems to encompass heterosexual relations with women also) plays a considerable role in the frustrated establishment of the all-important male bond.

Books by men experts sound an unequivocal warning for women: if we really care about men, we must do so differently. With *Iron John*, the different methods of interaction central to traditional stereotypes of gendered behavior are sanctioned as sacred: ironically, women's achievement of the capability for intimacy means that men have been overloved into losing their most prized connections.

Getting It Right:
The Economy of Therapy

How can self-help reading women differentiate between loving too much and loving just the right amount? The answer lies in identity development, which self-help authors unanimously see as the key that women should utilize to avoid overinvolvement with others. Women are urged to become more "masculine" in the application of our affections—less other-directed, more self-involved, and more reliant on our newfound reading-inspired sense of self-satisfaction.

Authors continually bombard women readers with the message that if we don't care about ourselves, no one else can be expected to care about us either. The first step for any change comes from the identity-as-growth philosophy: learn to know and love oneself. Though in and of itself this sounds reasonable enough, it becomes troublesome in the extreme. Self-help ideology promotes the notion that we can gain complete control over whatever happens to us; we simply have to elect to begin the process of change that will inevitably mean a better life. Until we do so, we are "not fully mature human beings, but rather . . . dependent and frightened children in adult bodies" (Norwood 1985: 255).

As Dowling had done earlier, Norwood reifies the view of women as dependent snivelers, reluctant to give up the security of protected life. Women's love, under such circumstances, Norwood explains, is not the real thing, but another example of neurotic behavior: "Most of the 'giving' we did when we were loving too much was actually manipulation" (260).

Over and over again, authors reiterate that underlying any healthy relationship with another person is a strong sense of self. If a woman has a strong identity, she will not experience a desperate need to get involved with men. If she does not experience this desperate need, she will be more likely to (accidentally) meet a man with whom she can form a good relationship. If you weren't looking so hard, self-help authors tell their readers, you'd find what you wanted. And once you find it (by actively not seeking it), the relationship will be better than you could have ever possibly hoped for (in the past, when you were busy hoping), because you will be less personally invested in it. (That reading is part of the looking is not acknowledged.)

Lynn Shahan, author of *Living Alone and Liking It* (1981), writes that selfhood, by its very nature, is threatened by involvement. She tries to cheer those who find themselves on their own by commending them for the important self-developmental work they will have the opportunity to undertake:

> Living alone offers you an unparalleled opportunity for developing a solid personal identity. . . . Experiencing solitary living gives you a chance to know yourself intimately; a chance to draw upon untouched personal capacities; a chance to find out who you are and what your strengths are. . . . There are people who never have the chance in their busy, peopled lives to meditate, to ponder their mistakes, or to examine the direction their lives are taking. Stagnation sets in and personal growth is stunted. In contrast, the person who lives alone can capitalize on an optimum opportunity for self-awareness. (26)

What imperils women's identities in our involvements with men, according to self-help authors, is that we feel rather than think. Forward writes that "women have to learn to assess their feelings, and to differentiate between thoughts and feelings." She sees women's problems as stemming from overinvestment in the emotional realm of life; this poses a danger toward maintaining a sense of self. "Once you have your emotions under control, logic, instead of fear and anxiety will dominate your life. You will begin to think clearly about yourself, your relationship, and where you are headed" (1986: 172). Thoughts, presumably, are easier to manage and control than emotions are; and proper thought-control can lead to power over dangerous or dysfunctional feelings. Thus self-love becomes self-control, and control over self offers the illusion of order. If everyone would do the same, authors imply or state outright, self-love would solve the world's problems.

In a classic example of the early feminists' search for rationality, Dowling encouraged women to apply market-economy evaluative techniques to our constant reassessment of ourselves and our involvements. Dowling writes that a liberated woman should take stock of her life the same way a man would take stock of his finances: "*Keeping a running balance is not just good financial policy: it's good emotional policy. . . . Does the energy output meet the gratification income, or is there an unbalance? Am I spending more than I'm getting, and if so, how can I get more? . . . Keeping a* running balance in my psychic account makes it less likely for me to retain a distorted, unrealistic picture of things" (p. 222, emphasis in original).

Author after author advises that the ideal relationship is one in which neither partner gives more than the other: an economic balance is essential. In their bestselling guide to negotiating, *Getting to Yes* (1981), Roger Fisher and William Ury write that "any negotiation primarily concerned with the relationship runs the risk of producing a sloppy agreement" (8). Though their book seems to center on formal, professional decision making, they claim that their methods are easily applicable to all relationships. Thus, they urge that "competitors" (in this case, men and women) take care not to allow our involvement with each other to get in the way of rational bargaining. Janet Woititz encourages readers of *Adult Children of Alcoholics* (1983) to ask the following questions in evaluating their relationships with others: "What is in this for me? What is the payoff? Why do I maintain this relationship? Who is this other person to me?" (87).

Even in economically balanced involvements, expressiveness is strongly valued, especially in the relationship-oriented self-help books' trajectory through the seventies and early eighties. Merle Shain (1978) tells readers that all healthy—or what she calls "feeling"—relationships share the following qualities: "expression of feelings, wisdom and maturity, an orientation to struggle, an acceptance of deprivation, a tolerance for fair fights, passion, and room for apology and gratitude" (215). Participants in intimacy should be moderate in their displays and expectations, according to Shain, and should understand that any relationship will have its crests and peaks, which "wisdom and maturity" will help partners to weather.

Shain writes, "We are all afraid of being swallowed up by love, of ceasing to exist except through someone else, so we rush toward love with open arms and hide from it when it comes to us" (12). The fear of—and desire for—unity with others is a lifelong struggle for and against a return to the comforting and all-powerful—thus intimidating—womb. Shain, like many other self-help authors, urges her readers to seek love but to be careful consumers. She cautions, "We have only so much emotional currency, it isn't an unlimited supply, so you've got to invest it wisely if you want to make it grow" (98).

The use of financial language in authors' discussions of self and relationships began in more purely identity-as-machine self-help books and gradually spilled over into identity-as-growth books. Robert Bellah et al. (1985) see this sort of language as representative of a therapeutic ideology that stresses personal profit, and that is unable to recognize any collective power not based in individuality:

> A deeply ingrained individualism lies behind much contemporary understanding of love. . . . Such a utilitarian attitude. . . . is one solution to the difficulties of self-preservation in a world where broader expectations may lead to disappointment or make one vulnerable to exploitation. Then love becomes no more than an exchange, with no binding rules except the obligation of full and open communication. A relationship should give each partner what he or she needs while it lasts, and if the relationship ends, at least both partners will have received a reasonable return on their investment. (108)

What Bellah et al. call the "therapeutic attitude" derives from the more powerful ideology of capitalism. Capitalism creates a culture where the purchase and consumption of goods are held to be activities of paramount importance, but where benevolent rhetoric proliferates regarding profitlessness—volunteerism, a thousand points of light, and so forth. In a culture where some women seem able to permeate the bastions of male power and attain autonomy and prestige, and yet where a majority of female-headed families live beneath the poverty level; in a culture where inequity in sexual interaction has supposedly been leveled, but where women repeatedly see ourselves represented on the covers of pornographic magazines and in headlines reporting rape; in a culture where men have "role models" as disparate as Rambo and Bill Cosby—it is no wonder that identity complexes and ideological confusion have afflicted women and men. Daily we encounter anticapitalist capitalism, antifeminist feminism, antipatriarchal patriarchy, and their inverses.

Bellah et al. continue their discussion of how therapy has influenced our culture by relaxing their indictment; they write that it must be taken into account that "the therapeutic view" also incorporates "expressive individualism, an expanded view of the nature and possibilities of the self." This means that "love then becomes the mutual exploration of infinitely rich, complex, and exciting selves" (108). What happened to the therapeutically recommended relationship as individualistic need-meeting exchange? Ultimately, the argument they offer about the infusion of therapeutic ideology into our culture is no less confusing than that offered (about maintaining relationships) by the most enthusiastic practitioners of the therapeutic ideology—self-help authors themselves.

The result of such confusion (in terms of the advice authors offer) is that women are urged not to get too close to others, for fear of losing, or never finding, what is most valuable within ourselves. Lasch (1984) sees the contradictory fears and desires involved in personal interaction as an indication that identity is uncertain. He sees this as a problem endemic to our particularly "narcissistic" culture, the hallmark of which is "a self uncertain of its own outlines, longing either to remake the world in its own image or to merge into its environment in blissful union" (19). Self-help books offer evidence of the dilemma Lasch highlights. At the root of his concept of narcissism is insecurity. Men involved in heterosexual relationships, according to self-help authors, are torn between their own feelings of inadequacy in relation to women and their conflicting fears of women's power to engulf them, like giant womb-monsters. Women involved in heterosexual relationships suffer from a different form of insecurity: we don't know who we are, and don't know where we stand in relation to the men in our lives.

Since relationship-oriented self-help books are often written by therapists, it is not surprising that authors often recommend therapy as a beneficial option for their more troubled readers. Authors realize that many readers have "come to them" in lieu of consulting a professional in the flesh, and thus their recommendations are always couched in casual and nonthreatening terms. Some authors also try to demystify the experts, by cautioning readers against certain types of therapists. For example, Forward and Torres write: "Unfortunately, misogynists are alive and well in all professions, and psychotherapy has more than its share" (243). They try to educate their readers to be careful consumers: "*Don't be afraid to shop around.* . . . More important, *don't be afraid to trust your instincts*" (242, emphasis in original). Oddly enough, Forward and Torres trust the same women who are helplessly drawn to misogynist men to instinctively pick a good therapist.

Norwood urges women-addicts to go for help, either by enlisting a professional therapist or by joining a self-help group. She ends *Women Who Love Too Much* by describing how interested women could set up their own self-help groups, based on the principles for "recovery" she details. Norwood recommends that if women do decide to consult therapists, we select women therapists because "we share the basic experience of what it is to be a woman in this society, and this creates a special depth of understanding." Also, in therapy with a woman, she writes, the reinforcement of the root of women's problems, what brings women to therapists in the first place—dangerous heterosexual dynamics—can be avoided. Norwood, herself a therapist at the time she wrote *Women Who Love Too Much*, encourages readers to question the authority of therapists.

Taking Responsibility

While relationship-oriented self-help borrows from the "identity-as-growth" tradition, the ideas that one creates *only* one's own circumstances and that obligation to others grows rightfully only out of self-love, the responsibility for change (of bad relationship patterns) is implicitly or explicitly laid on women's shoulders. This seems a no-win situation for women. As in the male-authored sex manuals, even a movement devoted to women's development (feminism) becomes part of the problem.

Carter and Sokol imply that men avoid involvement with women because of what women have become as a result of the women's movement (1987: 68). So, in response to those readers who thought that women were the ones oppressed by patriarchy and its insidious ideology, Carter and Sokol explain the situation differently. As a result of the sexual revolution and the women's movement, men have found the keys to unlock the prisons forged by their marriages to women. They write: "Metaphorically speaking, men have been let out of the cage. And regardless of how warm and loving that environment could be, to the man it is still a cage. So, like any other animal who sees a cage, his first instinct is to run" (70). (Meanwhile, women wait, holding the doors to the cage open, and wondering what the problem is.)

Despite Carter and Sokol's claims that there are nice, good men out there who do want to form relationships with women, their descriptions of these men's basic characteristics make men—in general—sound like sex-crazed, thoughtless idiots. For instance, they describe a man's actions when he is first interested in a woman: he acts quite attentive, thoughtful, and caring; *but,* they contend, "he is simply acting on impulse, with no thoughts about what his actions mean or how they will be interpreted" (217). In other words, apparently, he is merely engaged in mindless sexual conquest, and is basically insincere.

But egalitarianism and reciprocal communication aside, authors seem to be saying, these guys are incorrigibly led around by their penises. Women have to be very careful about sex, according to self-help authors. This advice transcends the recommendations of caution for women that are included in sex manuals. Cowan and Kinder caution "smart women" against "sexual aggressiveness" with men, writing that "the need to perform sexually is at the core of some men's fear and defensiveness toward women who are sexually assertive, and women need to understand this to deal sensitively and successfully with men" (1985: 76–77). In their second book, *Women Men Love, Women Men Leave* (1987), Cowan and Kinder applaud "a natural swing back toward more traditional sexual values" (95) and reiterate, "When a woman is sexually aggressive . . . it can be very intimidating to a man" (97).

Carter and Sokol advise women to play the traditional roles of sex-stoppers, indicating their belief that men may be interested in women only for the challenge of orchestrating a sexual encounter: "Don't rush into bed: The more he is pushing, the more you should be slowing him down" (1987: 207). They advise women to control sexual behavior because men cannot be expected to. *"Make sure you've always got one foot on his brakes and another on yours,"* (210), and: "Know that he doesn't think the way you do. Before saying the kind of things he says, you would weigh your words very carefully. Don't assume that he is doing the same thing" (213).

Cowan and Kinder do not tell women to practice the stereotypical feminine activity of resisting sexual intimacy, as Carter and Sokol did; rather, they suggest vaguely that women ought to be careful about "timing" should we choose to play the parts of aggressors. Clearly, they see traditional gender roles as beneficial to sexual relationships; and according to conventional arrangements, women are supposed to first wait and then refuse men's advances. The double standard is alive and well here.

Women authors are not necessarily more radical than men authors, and often confirm this view of men as sex-starved and play down women's interest in things sexual. In *What Every Woman Should Know about Men* (1981), Joyce Brothers writes: "Whatever a man thinks about sex, you can be sure that he thinks about sex almost constantly" (142). For Ellen Kriedman, who has written separately for audiences of women and men in *Light His Fire: How to Keep Your Man Passionately and Hopelessly in Love with You* (1989) and *Light Her Fire: How to Ignite Passion and Excitement in the Woman You Love* (1991), sex is a wholly different phenomenon for each gender. For men, sex is exciting sportlike interaction, often involving playacting and costumes: "Just remember, your goal is to shock him and make him feel as though he is with a completely new woman," she advises (1989: 126). This after recommending "FIFTY-ONE WAYS TO KEEP HIS FIRE LIT" (117).

Kriedman counsels men quite differently, explaining that sex for women isn't really sex as they know it: "Sex for her is kindness, gentleness, devotion, commitment, caring, patience, and compliments. . . . It's telling her how much she means to you. It's going shopping with her. It's helping her with the chores. It's noticing she has a new dress or hairdo. It's asking her to dinner. It's whether you phoned to say you'll be late. It's bringing home a card or a gift" (1991: 162). The freeing up of women's sexuality has become so diffuse that it is nonsexual (and nonsensical): we really want to be flattered and hugged more than anything else, apparently. Echoing "J," De Angelis confirms in her advice that women ought to try to want what men want, at least some of the time.

Sex is generally seen as a tool that has to be very carefully controlled by women, one that can easily work against us. Margaret Kent, author of *How to Marry the Man of Your Choice* (1984), cautions: "If you either have sex too soon or delay too long, you will lose the man for marriage" (213). She adds, "since sex is the greatest gift you may offer a man, you must carefully build it up beyond other natural pleasures to have it work to your advantage" (217). Like Brown and Morgan (and also "J" and Penney), Kent sees relationships between men and women as best achieved through carefully orchestrated interaction, a seemingly direct contradiction to advice of authors who see relationships as resulting only when women aren't trying so hard. But what women are consistently urged to do is to try *not* to try, to learn to appear effortless in our relating, while always keeping on guard.

Sexual relations are often beside the point according to self-help authors. Many authors advise that it is much more important that women and men get along outside the bedroom, and that good sex is useless if there is no basic rapport. Rapport is difficult to gain. Forward and Torres's descriptions, for example, depict relationships between men and women as precariously constructed over a hotbed of seething resentments. Women tend to turn anger in on themselves, while men are apt to extend their anger outward and direct it against women in displays ranging from "obvious intimidation and threats to more subtle, covert attacks which [take] the form of constant put-downs or erosive criticism" (5). Men, then, suffer very little, while women are subject to all sorts of psychological and physical ailments as a result of men's anger toward them (153–157). Part of why men don't suffer as much as women (from their obvious problems) is because men, generally speaking, are childlike and childish in their interactions with women. They become romantically involved with women seeking a sort of infantile symbiosis with a mother figure in the first place, according to Forward and Torres. When men's childish needs are being met, much of their suffering is alleviated.

Forward and Torres urge women to remember that we are dealing with people who look like adults, but who have never learned to act like them. Adult behavior, in their formulation of the problem, eventually ceases to be a masculine quality. Brothers writes, similarly: "if a woman is aware that there is a child hidden within every man, it is a giant step toward understanding the male mystique" (49). Self-help authors explain that when women begin to change, the child-men with whom they are involved will not accept alterations in the relationships easily, but will fight to maintain the old order because it makes them feel safe and secure. In *The Dance of Anger: A Woman's Guide to Changing the Patterns of Intimate Relationships,* Harriet Goldhor Lerner writes, "*There are few things more anxiety-arousing than shifting to a higher level of self-assertion and separateness in an important relationship and maintaining this position despite the countermoves of the other person*" (1985: 26, emphasis in original).

While reading many self-help authors' descriptions of men's behavior, it is puzzling why any woman would stay involved with such men, much less *love* them. As they are depicted in self-help books, men seem to want things only their way, and to be very averse to changes or compromise. They often can't communicate on any level, except maybe sexually—and then only sometimes (other times, they may be sexually inept, disabled, or abusive). Authors do not stress the cultural patterns underpinning men's inabilities to interact; rather, they favor psychological explanations, which don't really show what women might have to gain from staying in such relationships, or how men might benefit from persevering in such immature patterns of behavior. It appears, then, that women are too emotionally helpless to break our cycle of suffering (passed down by our mothers); that men are incontrovertibly obsessed with their love/hate dilemma with women (mother figures); and that a real cure for dismal heterosexual relations is not in sight.

You Might As Well Face It: You're Addicted to Love

Recently, women's cravings for commitment in our involvements with men have been described as addictions by self-help writers. Inspired by the methods employed by the AA (Alcoholics Anonymous) movement, and beginning with books about the effects of alcoholism, specialized self-help books began promulgating the notion that psychological phenomena fit into the same frameworks as physiological disease. This trend in self-help books has burgeoned into an enormously successful subgenre of New Age literature called recovery. Woititz's *Adult Children of Alcoholics* (1983), a slim volume, gained unexpected success and set the trend for books of this type. Though addiction models use the language of pathology, this language is undercut by a dedication to upbeat or nonjudgmental language (e.g., "survivors" instead of "victims," "feedback" instead of "mistake," "shame-based identity" instead of "bad self-image," and so on). In exemplary fashion, Woititz instructs readers that normalcy does not exist, no matter how hard they have worked to emulate their perceptions of it, writing: "Normal is a myth like Santa Claus and the Brady Bunch. It is not realistic to talk in terms of normal, since it is something you have been fooled into believing exists. Other concepts like functional and dysfunctional are more useful. . . . The task, then, is not to find out what normal is, but to discover what is most comfortable for you and for those who are close to you" (55). The words "functional" and "dysfunctional" have a distanced, clinical ring to them, and Woititz insists that these terms are not universalistic in meaning; a plurality of functional relationships could exist, and none would be preferable to any other. Designed to soothe and seductive in its invitation to revelatory self-knowledge, recovery language signals a change in semantics, though not in purpose.

In *Codependent No More* (1987), Beattie writes about all the people whose behavior enables addicts to maintain their addictions. Being codependent means being addicted, in a sense, because the dynamics of the relationship with the addict become necessary to the codependent as well. In other words, codependents might be said to be addicted to other people's addictions. I have classified Woititz's and Beattie's books as relationship-oriented because their starting point is dysfunctional relationships readers are having with alcoholics, or with other practitioners of obsessive behavior.[6] Codependents are urged to forge a separation from the addicts to whom they are attached—at least emotionally—and to take responsibility for only their own behavior. Woititz writes: "If the child of the alcoholic, not unlike the alcoholic, is ever to mature, there must be accountability. Part of having a strong sense of self is to be accountable for one's actions. No matter how much we explore motives or lack of motives, we are what we do. We take credit for the good, and we must take credit for the bad. The key is to take responsibility for all our behavior" (21–22).

It was not until Norwood's *Women Who Love Too Much* (1985) became a bestseller that the problem of addiction was stripped of its chemical origins and moved into the realm of heterosexual interaction.[7] Recasting interactional problems between men and women as addiction-related, as Norwood does, legitimizes them, in a sense, by deemphasizing the responsibility of the sufferer (called survivor no matter how badly victimized she has been) and by framing the problem with the medical language of pathology. Like physical addicts, psychological addicts and codependents can't be blamed for their problems, advisers explain, but they can be held responsible for orchestrating their own cures, once they realize they are addicts or codependents. Addictions become individual problems, which can be ameliorated only by individual action. People are held responsible for healing their "dysfunctional" addictive situations, just as they were held responsible for *solving* their *problems* before. Kaminer writes that "addiction and recovery look a lot like sin and redemption" (1990: 27). Reading is offered as a conversion or faith-bolstering ritual.

Norwood could not emphasize enough how important it was that women face up to the severity of our problems. Addictions may not sound nice, she knew, but there they were. Like a reliance upon alcohol, women had been reliant upon men to vanquish our monumental fears. Like alcohol, men wouldn't work as a solution to life's trials and tribulations. Norwood invites women to measure ourselves against a checklist she provides so we may determine whether we are, indeed, "man junkies" (39–40), and invites readers to accept the label of "addict" before moving on to treatment. She writes, "I am thoroughly convinced that what afflicts women who love too much is not *like* a disease process; it *is* a disease process, requiring a specific diagnosis and a specific treatment" (208).

In an interesting parallel, Carter and Sokol extend disease status to men, rather than women. They argue that men, rather than being seen as the victimizers of women (as Forward and Torres argue), deserve readers' empathy, for they are pitiful creatures engaging in "phobic" behavior, and they can't help doing what they do. "Commitmentphobia is a true phobia, replete with all of the classic physical and psychological phobic symptomatology," they proclaim (1987, 55), wielding medical language to endear commitmentphobes to readers' hearts. Kiley does the same sort of fancy labeling in describing the "Peter Pan Syndrome"; women's problems are not quite as dignified when entitled "the Wendy Dilemma."

Norwood encourages women man-addicts not to blame themselves for their problems. She writes that self-blame is the way in which women who love too much try to feel that they have power over their situations (when they really don't). Women want to feel in control more than anything, according to Norwood, and self-blame is a method that only masks the problem, and which cannot lead to any real power.

All in all, the woman who loves too much is asea in contradictions. She longs for—but deeply fears—the right kind of men; she is afraid of "her own feelings" and thus relies on the man in her life (and the wrong kind of man, most likely, given her inability to judge properly) to feel *for* her, "taking her excitement from his excitement." She may even have some strange sexual habits and/or hang-ups, since she can't distinguish between "love and sexual excitement" or between "fear and pain" (39–40). She sounds every bit as confused and conflicted as the men described by Kiley, Cowan and Kinder, and Carter and Sokol. But unlike these men, *she* has presumably picked up a self-help book. And if she can identify and admit that what she suffers from is man-addiction, she will have taken the first step toward recovery.

Norwood concludes, with other self-help advisers, that the very nature of passion is dangerous (for women especially), viewing it as a need that forever builds on itself, and which, therefore, should be limited by women. Norwood views romantic love as dangerous obsession, echoing earlier feminist concerns about marriage as imprisonment.

In the past several years, the addiction-codependency-recovery triumvirate became degenderized. Most notable, the work of John Bradshaw locates these "issues" within the family (1988, 1990). Bradshaw reiterates Norwood's thesis when he writes: "I define codependency as a disease characterized by a *loss of identity*" (1990: 8). The goals "uncovery," "reclaiming," and "healing" that Bradshaw promotes imply that a core self exists, obscured by all the troublesome or traumatic experiences one has had. When one strips off all the layers of misfortunate experiences with exercises provided by Bradshaw, one achieves what he calls "self-creation" or "homecoming." If one delves down deep enough, Bradshaw assures, something salvageable (a "wonder child," e.g.) will finally emerge. One will reach a state of "bliss" that signifies "non-attachment," dispassionate passion, and "undependence" that will restore one to one's self (1988: 134–135).[8]

Fighting for Passion

Many self-help book authors do see potential good in passion. Leo Buscaglia has maintained that love should be exuberant and of primary importance in people's lives throughout his successful career as a self-help writer. In his first bestseller, *Love* (1972), Buscaglia laments the "world's" seeming resistance to real connection between people: "To live in love is life's greatest challenge. It requires more subtlety, flexibility, sensitivity, understanding, acceptance, tolerance, knowledge and strength than any other human endeavor or emotion, for love and the actual world make up what seem like two great contradictory forces" (191). Buscaglia reiterates this "love is all you need" theme endlessly in his works, encouraging readers—despite the stream of contradictory advice out there—that to undertake "the challenge of human relationships" (as *Loving Each Other* [1984] is subtitled) will be the most productive step they can take as human beings. One of the maxims Buscaglia offers in *Loving Each Other* is: "Don't be afraid of giving. You can never give too much, if you're giving willingly" (152). In a way, Buscaglia encourages love in a religious sense (as Christlike and giving) which counters the caveat emptor approach that others have recommended, or the complete self-immersion of recovery writers.

Buscaglia objects to the cool calculations recommended by Dowling and others; but in other ways, he agrees with them, repetitively informing readers that in order to get others to love them, they must first love themselves, for instance. He urges readers to end destructive relationships and begin productive ones, as other self-help writers do, but never presents a cogent analysis of why certain relationships fail and others don't. He omits any consideration of gender-related issues in heterosexual relationships, also. Where Buscaglia differs from other self-help writers is in his analytical frame: he has none. Instead, he offers readers upbeat and sugary sermons on how nice loving, trusting relationships can be. Apparently, these pep talks are in great demand. Buscaglia has spent more time on the bestseller lists than any other self-help author writing during the past quarter-century; in fact, he had three books on the bestseller lists at the same time during 1983, 1985, and 1986.

Despite their pessimism about change on a large scale, feminist authors call for fairness in relationships and hope for happy endings. Forward, for example, reiterates Shain's definition of an ideal relationship as mature and evenly balanced. Men and women who achieve such a relationship together have to transcend traditional gender behaviors. She writes: "A good relationship is based on mutual respect and a relatively equal balance of power. It involves concern for and sensitivity to each other's feelings and needs, as well as an appreciation of the things that make each partner so special. . . . Loving partners find effective ways of dealing with their differences; they do not view each encounter as a battle to be won or lost" (1986: 175). As always, in the self-help genre, the war between men and women can come to an end only when we all believe we have the power to stop it.

In her examination of the changing American ideologies about love, Francesca Cancian (1987) proposes that "androgynous love" that "emphasizes mutual support and implies that self-development requires committed relationships" would be a workable alternative to the split between men's and women's styles of loving (107). Cancian suggests that a mutual therapeutic orientation between lovers is likely to be egalitarian, and thus, that interpretations that see the therapeutic ideological influences on relationships as lamentable are incorrect. Self-help authors are generally optimistic about egalitarianism as a possibility, though their descriptions of heterosexual relationships plagued by seemingly insurmountable problems of gender tend to negate this hopefulness. What Cancian recognizes that self-help authors tend to ignore is that the underlying supports for an "interdependent" future cannot occur without extensive social and economic change; "so much energy [devoted] to intimacy and self" cannot bridge and does not address "the gulf between private and public life" (150).

Conclusion

Self-Help Culture

Such a drive to self-knowledge . . . is a protest against the dehumanization of society made by women on behalf of everyone, because it is
women who find themselves most discomfited by the gap between who
they are and what they are supposed to be. (Oakley 1984: 2)

Only connect! . . . Only connect . . . and human love will be seen at its
height. Live in fragments no longer. (Forster 1921: 186–187)

Are the various readings of women's relationship with self-help literature that have been presented here compatible? Is the social world these
narratives speak of a tidy whole? The answer, of course, is no. No,
because divergent readings are simply divergent, like interpretations of
Rorschach inkblots. But the answer is also, in some ways, yes. Yes,
because sense can be read into—and woven between—these divergent
readings. Here, I want to combine the various strands of this story (about
women and self-help reading, you'll remember, rather than murder on
the Irish moors) together into a coherent synthesis. Remember that in
trying to render my interpretations of self-help reading sensible, I have
imposed an order upon the phenomenon. I've moved from readers'
perceptions to editors' perceptions to authors' perceptions to books'
offerings, while using the frameworks offered by reader-response theory
and feminist qualitative research methods as tools for analysis, and
borrowing Griswold's "cultural diamond" as a structural agent. Now, in
these last pages, I want to convince you that the order has been effective,
that divergent readings can be read into one story, and that my
reading—this story—works.

 Steven Conner writes that postmodernist discourse centers on critical
hedging: "What is striking is precisely the degree of consensus . . . that

there is no longer any possibility of consensus, the authoritative announcements of the disappearance of final authority and the promotion and recirculation of a total and comprehensive narrative of a cultural condition in which totality is no longer thinkable" (1989: 10). So the questioning of authority and little else is held as authoritatively true. This seems hypocritical because postmodern writers obviously want to be authorities, and yet seem bent on erasing the idea that truth can ever be gained (while engaged in the very act of writing the truth about a lack thereof). Circles and circles of mirrors and mirrors yield the ultimate truth that truth is a socially constructed event. I would argue that to admit that truth lies only in social construction is responsible, not hypocritical.

Various—and admittedly circular—constructions of a cultural activity have been aired here: readers see heterosexual relationships as problematic because women are overinvested in them, while at the same time, they take responsibility for analyzing relationships through their self-help reading (which often tells them that because they are women, they overinvest in relationships). Similarly, readers are dissatisfied with men's participation in intimacy, and their self-help reading validates this dissatisfaction while urging them to divest their attention from these relationships.

Some readers see women's socialization in this culture as detrimental: in learning gender, we learn limitations that men (likewise learning gender) learn to surpass. Self-help reading enables some participants to confirm this view; indeed, they may see their own self-help reading as yet another indication that women are limited by dependence on authority. Other readers' remarks about men show that they feel heterosexuality would work more productively if men were socialized to be more feminine. Their self-help reading confirms the strength women evince in caring; indeed, woman-authored self-help may serve as an example of this sort of woman-to-woman (or woman-to-women) care. For most readers, care is the core of both the problem and their search to remedy or temporarily relieve it. Women care abundantly; men, not enough. Self-help books usually enlarge this into women caring too much (and some readers concur on this view); men's methods become models for us to follow (especially within, but not limited to, books authored by men). Many women feel cared for simply reading such explanations. Hedging becomes inevitable: more than one story exists here.

When people began to question me about my "findings" in this project, I experimented with different ways of answering. I found out that most people, like positivist sociologists, want responses to be cut-and-dried descriptions of cause and effect. (The postmodern tendency to hedge may be spreading but is by no means accepted everywhere.) After politely listening to my ramblings about meaning and how it gets made, people would often say, "Well, does reading help these women or not?" or "Is self-help reading a good thing or a bad thing?" If I would say that these were not really the questions in which I was interested, people would be disappointed, thinking (I imagined) how impractical and inessential this sort of academic work was. But if I would say that I was interested in what self-help reading had to show about our culture (and vice versa)—and would go on to tell about how I read self-help books; how I read women's reading of them; how it all came back to reinforcing or challenging the way gender plays itself out in our lives and the ways in which we learn to play it—this would please people a little more. They would say how interesting this was but would still be disappointed (I imagined) not to have something more tangible to grasp, such as evidence of what will happen as a result of all this cultural consumption, or a clearer endorsement or condemnation of self-help books themselves.

Sometimes I would cut right to the chase: my short-version answer was that I found that our culture is really screwed up, though most people seem well-intentioned. ("For that they gave you a Ph.D?") This, after all, *is* what sociology is all about: finding and naming the power divisions that problematize social life. I also like to think that the awareness interpretive sociology hopes to foster can help us to correct what is wrong with our arrangements. Writing about culture is done in the hope of understanding it better; but it is also done to make more culture and to articulate alternatives. (This book hopes to be a self-help book too!) This stance may be nothing more than an altruistic pretense to which progressive academics may cling: nevertheless, I cling. Of various possible constructions, we choose those (or hope to realize those) that seem morally intelligible, *truthful* in their rightness. So the relativism that circular postmodern arguments urge does not render moral judgments defunct. Any critique—even a relativist one—is a socially constructed and moral stance.

The short-version description of my findings did not satisfy because it sounded obvious. People want to hear something they don't already know, or at the very least, they want to hear it in a lingo that is partially foreign to them. Just as the women readers I interviewed wanted to believe in authors' authority, so most people want to believe academic expertise yields a special view of the social world's secrets. The longer version of my "findings" was spoken in the language of sociology, yet in terms of content, the longer version was the "same" answer as the short version (just as the Rorschach interpretation "a furry bat with fuzzy teeth hanging upside down by its toes" is the "same" as "a bat"). At least, this was how both answers were meant by me, the creator of them. But as with any communication, reception determines the message far more than creation does. The long version worked better because I was telling people a story they didn't know about a reality they did know in a language they respected because it sounded official.

This is part of what makes self-help books work, too: readers' perceptions that an aspect of life-in-general has been aptly described by someone with some claim to expertise satisfies them, for the time being. Self-help authors' narratives about heterosexual relationships and personal identity are truthful depictions of real life when they echo readers' conceptions about what is true in a style that renders such conceptions valid for the readers. This is part of the reason readers keep going back for more.

But women also read self-help books because they are *there;* they are everywhere. Reading self-help books fills time and space in the same way that turning on the television can make the house feel less empty. (The main difference is that self-help books reflect a more active purchase: we have to buy the books and bring them home with us, whereas television sits ubiquitously in most of our living rooms, so easy to turn on.) Even women who don't make a habit of self-help reading are exposed to the ideology wielded by self-help authors. Everyone—whether she (or he) reads these books or not—has some idea about what stories they tell.

So questions such as Which comes first, the appeal of the self-help book or the potential reader looking for advice? and Do we make culture, or does it make us? are moot. These "alternatives" are really the same, in that they are inseparable parts of the same reality. We are infused with culture because we live in it. We make and revise culture (as we live in it); but it also has a life of its own. "More than ever, the realm of everyday consciousness becomes one whose significations are indistinguishable from the images, spectacles and messages that circulate through mass media and mass culture" (Polan 1988: 45). We each experience and make cultural life through the particular configurations of the cultural life we enter into personally. Cause and effect have no place in this analysis: self-help culture *is* our culture.

Self-help authors' ideology regarding identity and interaction fit together quite coherently with other media manifestations of advice for women. Excerpts from bestselling self-help books often reappear (or preappear) in women's magazines. Even when bits and pieces from specific books are not published, similar self-help articles abound, offering advice that centers on managing relationships as well as improving self-image. Many authors are experienced in self-help dispensing media other than print. Problems that seem to manifest themselves in the lives of women are dissected daily, weekly, monthly in live appearances and on television and radio.

In soap operas, the therapeutic culture proclaimed by self-help authors permeates, and offers itself up to consumers as an effective methodology for self-analysis; Ruth Rosen writes:

> Problems are not only personal; they are also interpreted—and cured—through psychological insight. Therapeutic redemption has replaced religious salvation. Evil is no longer unexplained; it is understood through an excess of psychobabble. Characters continually ask each other how they "feel" about everything. Couples are encouraged to "communicate" . . . because marriage will falter without "open discussion." . . . The danger of psychological repression is ubiquitous. (1986: 62)

Though soaps themselves are not therapy in any traditional sense, they offer ministories that dispense therapy with approval. Tania Modleski sees the appeal of soap operas as lying in "expectation [and] . . . in (familial) disorder," while they simultaneously "offer the promise of immortality and eternal return—same time tomorrow" (1982: 88–89). So like self-help books, soap operas are reassuring both in the very reliability of their recurrent existence and in their reification of the therapeutic model of problem solving. And like self-help books, soaps entice users by dispensing hope for a better future, while ultimately diffusing any radical reevaluation of the status quo. Both cultural forms rely on tension between an ideal world which centers on care, and a reality which denies its importance. According to Modleski's reading of soaps, they "convince women that their highest goal is to see their families united and happy, while consoling them for their inability to realize this ideal and bring about familial harmony" (92).

Similarly, in her evaluation of readers' involvement with romance fiction, Janice Radway concludes that since romance reading enables women to conceive of a perfect world where men are "neither cruel nor indifferent, neither preoccupied with the external world nor wary of an intense emotional attachment to a woman," repetitious reading is born "not out of contentment but out of dissatisfaction, longing, and protest" (1984: 215). Several of the participants in my study consciously recognized that one of the reasons they keep going back to self-help books is that they remain unsatisfied. Reading self-help books provides temporary respite from problems, even as it focuses on problems as its topic. Like romance reading, the act of self-help reading protests the conditions that create the ideology most often voiced in self-help books.

While I was working on this project, incidents on two television shows influenced my thinking about how self-help reading made sense within American culture. In recreating these events, I am deliberately stepping at least four levels into the infinitely mirrored circle of cultural practice: this is media (print) about media (television) about media (print) that claims to describe social life (which is shaped by both print and broadcast media).

The first television incident occurred on the "Phil Donahue Show" and convinced me that self-help literature enables people to measure themselves against a backdrop of comforting stereotypes. Part of the appeal of self-help literature lies in the reassurance of hearing about the worst-case scenarios, and realizing one is better off—so my readers have told me. Authors of self-help material have an uncanny ability to present flat and predictable extreme cases, extreme cases who, with their help, can become nonextreme. Nowhere are extreme cases paraded with more enthusiasm than on daytime talk shows. Here, this technique is elevated to ritual.

Cowan and Kinder appeared on "Donahue" promoting *Women Men Love, Women Men Leave*. As part of the show, the audience and callers could question two women, whose first names appeared on the screen along with identifying captions that read, "Has Successful Relationships

With Men" and "Has Unsuccessful Relationships With Men." So, I thought, is this what it all boils down to? There are two kinds of women in the world today? That such a simplistic and strange version of reality is not laughed off the screen may indicate that this reductive manner of explaining behavior works. The calls and the audience-generated questions to these women were not jokes.

But why would such conceptualizations of gender and relationships appeal? This particular "Donahue" was rather mild in its portrayal of the peculiarities that erode heterosexual relationships. In a more strident vein, Oprah interviews couples who have had extramarital affairs, no longer trust each other, and come on television to tell the world; Phil hosts a fashion show featuring transvestites and dresses up in a housedress and a frowsy hat, taking calls from repulsed men and tearful wives-of-transvestites who want to hear their voices on national TV. Oprah interrogates women who have no moral qualms about sleeping with married men. Phil questions men who have led—some of them, until the morning of the show—double lives, replete with double families. Sally Jesse Raphael devotes a show to husband-beaters. And the audiences participate, enthusiastically and angrily, in turn—but always loudly (and always dead seriously). Why?

Watching the show where Cowan and Kinder handed down their expertise to an audience of women, I thought yet again about the messages of self-help books in terms of their defensibility. This is the line most critics take in evaluating what offends them culturally: they say such cultural objects appeal to the lowest common denominator, that they exist to feed their audience's (or "the masses'") desire for pure sleaze and/or inanity. And while this line of attack has its appeal, it misses something. Yes, there is a lot to condemn, a lot that is objectionable about our culture—and in this particular instance, about self-help books and other media presentations geared to appeal to women. But users are not sopping "trash" culture up like the superabsorbent paper towels that pay for "Donahue" or "Oprah" to stay on the air. Rather, they are constructing meaning as they view, just as readers construct meaning as they read.

Television shows like this—and their radio equivalents—are invitations to what might be called a visual- or audio-reader to be a participating voyeur in the privacy of her own home, to identify and to cringe, to admire—but more often to feel superior to any number of human exhibits. Such shows work well as advertisements for self-help books, not only by featuring "experts" who write self-help books, but by creating an atmosphere where oddity can be celebrated and booed, where normalcy can be contested and affirmed.

The other television event that influenced my cultural analysis of self-help reading also concerns the making of the mundane into the ridiculous, but in a much more ironic and self-conscious (postmodern) manner. Consider this (paraphrased) conversational exchange: on "Late Night With David Letterman," filmed in front of a studio audience, a comic named Julie Brown talks to her "host" about what she has been doing lately. "I joined a women's group," she says. "There are so *many* these days—there's 'Women Who Love Too Much,' 'Smart Women, Foolish Choices.' The one I joined is 'Kill, *Kill* All the Men.' The audience laughs. Brown continues talking to Letterman. "We believe there's nothing wrong with any woman anywhere," she explains, straight-faced. "If a woman does have a problem, it's a man's fault."

"Kill, *Kill* All the Men?" Letterman asks, sardonically.

"Kill, *Kill* All the Men," Brown affirms.

I see how the televised audience responds—with laughter—but how can I know what they find funny? Is the perceived humor (as I "get" it) the same as the joke Julie Brown intends? Is Brown satirizing those who produce self-help culture, those who consume it, or both? Is she making fun of feminism or making fun of women?

Brown and Letterman's exchange is designed to amuse. It has undoubtedly been rehearsed and then recreated to sound like extemporaneous conversation that two acquaintances might have after not seeing each other for a while. (This is very different from Phil's or Oprah's rapport with their guests, who usually come on to defend themselves to the audiences—live and at home—while Phil and Oprah facilitate.) Letterman's viewers are encouraged to incorporate Brown's words into their understanding of heterosexual relationships (at least for the time being). In this way, they have something in common with readers of self-help literature being sold on a way of seeing things by authors. But of course, unlike readers, Letterman's audience is encouraged to laugh, to see how ridiculous heterosexual relations have become, especially as represented by self-help books (which spurred the growth of self-help groups like "Women Who Love Too Much").

The atmosphere on "Late Night" shares with "Donahue" a reliance on tension. The test on "Late Night" is for guests to receive laughter and not to let Dave get away with too many jokes at their expense; the test on

"Donahue" is to gain the support and avoid the wrath of the audience. Letterman's audience is much more compliant: these people clearly want to enjoy themselves. Their enjoyment is offered as an incentive for the television audience; we are who the repartee is really designed to amuse. Their laughter urges us to laugh too, to commune with the people we see laughing on the screen, just as in reading self-help books women are encouraged to feel a sort of kinship with the "case studies" described, and with the other readers reading the same books in the privacy of their living rooms. But really, by the time we watch, this studio is empty and dark, and Letterman's fans cheering on at the show in the flesh are probably themselves transformed into living room viewers like us (watching Letterman and Brown, themselves seated in a living room/office set as fake as their repartee). A false connection is urged, just as the connections encouraged by self-help reading are often ultimately experienced as empty, and thus these activities reproduce themselves.

The key to the generic humor of "Late Night" seems to be the underlying assumption: hey, we're a crazy species. Aren't we full of shit in all our—supposedly—most sincere moments? Rather than search for sincerity, the show parodies its very existence. What "Late Night" offers is the opposite of what people look for in self-help books. But both of these cultural objects are about the same thing: sincerity and its lack. (And on "Donahue," members of the audience look for sincerity in the most unlikely places: they want to understand the parade of deviants that their host brings to show them. Failing this, they dismiss the losers with sincere contempt.)

The feeling that our culture lacks sincerity has escalated in the past quarter-century: both "Late Night" and self-help books capitalize on this. Arlie Hochschild sees our doubts about sincerity as sensible in a culture that commodifies everything from toasters to smiles (1983). Politics since Watergate and the seemingly unproductive protest culture of the sixties contribute to feelings of apathy and ineffectiveness about the democratic process. American commercialism has even come to embrace the *mistrust* of potential buyers in the game of making a sale: people really like the Joe Isuzu commercial because it acknowledges that car salesmen are sleazy liars. Like "Late Night," this ad applauds us for knowing the game's a rip-off, and in so doing, hopes to get us to believe sincerity lurks behind the acknowledgment that it doesn't exist.

This approach "admits everything," in the words of Mark Crispin Miller, and "exults in its own process of manipulation" (1986:188). What has become most genuine of all is the medium's own self-referentiality. Miller writes that television "purports to offer us a world of 'choices,' but refers us only to itself" (193). Self-help makes the same sort of offer: it will teach us how to make the right choices (instead of "foolish" ones), but we will have to keep coming back. Like television, the genre is self-referential, and like television audiences, readers of self-help books have been shaped by the ideological underpinnings of this literature that sells us the idea of a newer, purer, healthier self.

Self-help books don't "admit everything," though. As authors' self-descriptions as ultraaltruistic personae demonstrate, they would never confess to writing for money. Nicole Woolsey Biggart describes a similar sleight-of-mind: people involved in direct selling organizations are taught (by those who sell them on becoming salespeople) *not* to see what they do as selling. She writes that "by transforming selling into a nurturing function such as 'teaching' and 'sharing,' many distributors come to see their economic activities as primarily an act of caring" (1989: 116–117). This conception of a materially based exchange as free of the market mentality of capitalism appeals to buyers also. Readers, for example, want self-help authors to be genuine friendly experts and see "money grubbing" as antithetical to offering valid advice. They buy therapy in various forms, but don't want what they get to be tainted by the transaction. Persistent is the feeling that therapy, commercialized, robs us of sincerity.

Despite its consistent celebration of the free market as the American way, our culture constantly denigrates capitalist greed, either by pretending buying and selling are really giving and taking, as Biggart describes, or by treating those who sell as if they've crossed over into impropriety.[1] As Barbara Ehrenreich writes in her description of resistance to the welfare state: "The ancient Christian insight that money and markets are the province of the devil cannot be entirely abolished, only repressed" (1987: 187). We know—even Republicans know—that a pure profit orientation has a very ugly and vulgar cast to it. So we pretend it isn't there: dress it up as something nice, or pretend it doesn't matter, that it's beside the point.[2]

In American culture, selling masquerades as service, whether it "admits everything" or not. We will buy what looks to us as if it will care about us. Women make especially good consumers because we are good at caring but often don't get enough in return for our efforts. Even objects that can't "speak"—in the same way that media can—signify that they care. Certain cereals and margarines care about us, about our health and our looks. Ditto various concoctions of makeup: they care about keeping us sincerely youthful. Condoms now care about keeping us safe from disease and death. Deodorants care about our maintaining inoffensive odorlessness. Frozen foods want to make us less harried; they care about our having just a little more time for ourselves. We need to buy a lot of stuff that cares about us because although, ultimately, we know we *cannot* buy care, we nevertheless will settle with buying approximations of it. Our buying takes us in circles, because part of what sells us on buying is the fragility of the self that the media (self-help books included) advertise: it constantly needs to be bolstered, even remade.

Self-help books propose to help women find out about ourselves, to teach us effective ways of being. Authors operate on the assumption that we don't know how to do this on our own, and that this is understandable because we have been routinely mistaught. Gender disparities underlie self-help authors' analyses of self-knowledge for women: identity, for women, is especially difficult to define. Sometimes, according to self-help authors, we need a lot of changing; at other times we need self-acceptance. Acceptance, in fact, becomes a sort of paradoxical basis for accomplishing change. Identity becomes a messy compilation of past experiences that need to be sorted through and reprioritized. The changes advocated by self-help authors for women have changed very little since Friedan wrote *The Feminine Mystique* in 1963: women have been encouraged to place less value in involvements with others and to pay more attention to personal development. Lasch writes that uncertainty about identity is part of participating in consumer culture: it makes us make ourselves into commodities "offered up for consumption on the open market" (1984: 30–31). Self-help teaches women marketing strategies to use on ourselves.

In a similar vein, Robert C. Allen describes soap operas as both "commodity and commodifier" (1985: 45–60). Audience members are quite literally sold to advertisers, just as editors must decide whether to "buy" the alleged marketability in each book proposal they see. Self-help books, because they are didactic guides, commodify readers while they read, by urging them to make themselves into objects of analysis and improvement. The authors, of course, do not explicitly advise self-objectification, but achieving the goal of reading—whether learning how to pursue ideal growth, becoming an ideal woman, or attaining the ideal relationship—involves the purchase of whatever new ideal self the author is peddling.

One of the participants in my study, Lauren, talked about how self-help books offer self-conceptions readers can "try on." A process that aptly characterizes self-help ideology is the makeover, which has special salience for women in this culture. If you don't like it, change it; dress up your assets and hide the ugly parts. The message being conveyed by media that tell women how to make ourselves over is not covert: self-help books, magazines, television, and advertisements all encourage women to see ourselves as mutable, correctable, a product of various influences in constant flux.

In self-help literature (as well as other media), men, in contrast, are rarely variable—no matter how much women might wish they were. It must be noted that men participate in one comparable act of cultural consumption through which they seek to explain (and simplify) women: pornography. As many of the essayists in *Men Confront Pornography* show (Kimmel 1990), pornography enables men to engage in fantasies where they are *never rejected* by women. In this way, the romance version or the idealized soap or self-help version of manhood is similar to the pornographic version of womanhood. But unlike the depictions of men in romances, soaps, or self-help books, the women in pornography have little power. The possibility of the women in pornography deciding to reject the viewers they serve never exists; these fantasies for men rely on the denial of women's agency. Indeed, this may be a large part of the appeal of pornographized womanhood. Men imagine—via pornography—a system of caring that leaves them invulnerable, and in which women focus solely on men's satisfaction (and in which women are ecstatic in their male-defined purpose).

In the self-help world, the same sort of antagonism—between what men and women want that users of pornography acknowledge in explaining its appeal—resurfaces again and again. The resolutions offered mostly confirm men's desires (as voiced through pornographic fantasy) as realistic: men are seen, in self-help books, as wanting only their own satisfaction and as being unable to achieve reciprocal relationships (especially out of bed). In self-help books for women and in pornography for men, men are depicted as wanting to be cared for, but wanting also not to have to care in return. The care that titillates men in pornography is bodily service, whereas the care women want from men (as expressed in self-help books) is all-encompassing and involves reciprocity. When there is reciprocity in pornography, it attests to men's power; in self-help, the whole point of reciprocity is to transcend ego-boundaries and inequities in power through intimacy. Because self-help literature shows reciprocity to be so difficult to attain, men are cast as obstacles that women work around as we attempt to forge meaningful relationships in what appears to be very much like a war zone.

It is no wonder that defensiveness has come to signify the demeanor in which ideal relationships ought to be conducted, now, at a time when social problems are commonly referred to as wars to be fought (e.g., the war on poverty, the war on drugs, the war on AIDS, the war in the Gulf for "a new world order"), and when ideas about individual actions producing (earning) individual consequences have been mainstreamed into American thought and emphatically embraced by Republican leadership. The prevalence of addiction-rhetoric assists in de-socializing social problems, so that anything that goes wrong can be broken down into individual cases of pathology, which, when treated, will yield many singular cases of recovery. But recovery is always described as an ongoing struggle; thus, it unwrites itself: the self can never truly be recovered, and we can't truly win this war either. But the books continue to fuel the hope that somewhere, within the depths of the self, sincerity can be found and capitalized upon. Oddly, though, the recovery process is often held to emerge best from a group process, in which self-discovery and spiritual revelation is the goal for each participant: a sort of atomistic togetherness.

Addiction presents a convincing image of our problems because it recognizes the salience of disguised yet uncontrollable consumption in American culture. If addiction means insatiability, then addiction is the goal of consumer-oriented culture. Ehrenreich writes: "We have come to understand human needs as limitless, just as the cornucopia of goods and services offered by the market appears to be endlessly abundant. In this view, greed is central to human nature, and it is also fully consistent with the expectations of society" (1987: 185). In warning us against obsessive behavior, the self-help genre offers a critique of the very conditions that create its success. Remember Bonnie, who described self-help books as being "like a drug." Addictive behavior, when extended from substance abuse to behavioral characteristics, seems especially applicable to women, who are already seen (by this genre and in this culture) as compulsively centered on relationships.

Self-help books tell us about relationships based on commerce. Underneath, though, is this thing called love that we pretend (and self-help helps us to continue to pretend) can be unaffected by a culture based on consumerism. Women's return to self-help books boils down to the belief that there is, on some level, a "natural" quest for connection, and for purity of self. But how can we find such things through a vehicle that encourages us to try to be real, and to try to disengage from our connections in order to forge them better? To borrow a manner of speaking from the discourse of semiotics: self-help books claim to show women how to get from "cooked" to "raw"—from culture to nature—and this simply can't be done through more or better cooking. We can't gain sincerity by learning it: this doesn't mean, though, that we can't learn to *feel* more sincere, or that we can't learn to feel sincerely better.

I am not going to conclude that the reason for all of this raw cultural consumption (of overcooked goods) is that women are lonely, because that's not all that's going on (and men are lonely as well). But women do feel culturally alienated—so participants in this study have said. And women and men are often alienated from each other, as well. And so women, because they bear the brunt of the responsibility for connections, turn to the forms that exist for assistance, reassurance, and sometimes amusement: books, television, whatever it takes. And there is a lot to choose from, a lot to buy.

It's rather bizarre that while we are so alienated, we have also come to believe so wholeheartedly in talk—talk shows, therapeutic talk, heart-to-heart talks—as a curative measure in our personal lives. Such talk fails us when it does not challenge the general faith in psychological rhetoric and reactionary political developments that encourage us to conceive of individual action as either a cure-all or the cause of all problems, and to believe we are entitled to buy the answers to our problems.

Buying self-help, whatever form of media it takes, is about alienation *and* hope; about personal dissatisfaction *and* societal inadequacy; about wanting to conform to achieve magical happiness *and* about wanting to create new arrangements. Reading—even what has been deemed "trash," like self-help books—has generally been considered to be a more creative activity than watching "trash" television; the assumption is that reading offers us more room to be imaginative or contemplative than watching does. Maybe this is because when we read we make up pictures in our heads, and television gives them to us. Or maybe it is because of the pervasive attitude that television seduces viewers and then renders us senseless with its inane offerings. But I see no qualitative difference in the forms, in and of themselves (temperaturewise or healthwise). No medium automatically rots intelligence or enlightens; the messages, their sources, and our openness to them are what counts. Any reactionary message can be subverted or resisted, if subversion and resistance *are* culturally possible. A culture may generally thwart such possibilities, and media may help or hinder, depending upon how they are shaped and who shapes them (as both makers and readers).

In general, the ideology of self-help books, like the capitalist and patriarchal ideology that is dominant in our culture, denies connection and community-based action. Self-help books rarely recommend socially oriented solutions, yet they don't kill off readers' hopes for connection, either. Readers also do not approach these books clamoring for social change; but there is certainly the sense among participants in this study that social change would be desirable, even as it seems so unlikely in our current culture (and cultural consumer goods such as self-help books). What is most remarkable, then, about the applications of this genre is that readers feel it allows them to tap into a community of sorts; they "feel less alone" when they read. Ultimately, I believe, the form of the self-help book does not prohibit new or radical formulations of problems; but currently, its extension of therapeutic and individualistic solutions provides only an illusory cure for what ails us, collectively, as a culture.

Appendixes

TABLE 1. Demographic Information

Name	Age	Race	Mar.	Rel.	Ed.	Emp.	Inc/# Supt'd.	Freq.	Types read
Mona	37	B	div.	Episc.	college	sales	15–30,000/3	rare	gen
Emily	46	B	mar.	Bapt.	some coll.	counselor	45–60,000/4	mod.	gen
Marianne	36	W	div.	Prot.	some coll.	secretary	under 15,000/1	mod.	rel
Val	34	W	sin.	Luth.	some coll.	secretary	30–45,000/2	often	gen
Carol	36	W	div.	Cath.	some coll.	secretary	15–30,000/1	often	gen
Sandy	26	W	mar.	Cath.	m (ed)	teacher	60–75,000/2	mod.	gen, fem
Sarah	27	W	sin.	Jew.	msw	social worker	15–30,000/1	often	gen, na
Allison	26	W	sin.	Cath.	college	sales	30–45,000/1	rare	gen
Nell	40	W	mar.	Cath.	m (hist)	administrator	over 75,000/2	mod.	gen
Amelia	37	B	div.	Prot	college	manager	30–45,000/2	mod.	gen, rel
Liz	28	W	sin.	Cath.	college +	admin. asst.	15–30,000/1	mod.	gen
Joan	52	W	div.	Episc	m (ed)	teacher	45–60,000/2	often	gen, fem
Nancy	41	H	l.w.l.	Cath.	hs	tel. int'er	15–30,000/1	rare	gen
Abby	27	W	l.w.l.	Jew.	msw	social worker	45–60,000/2	mod.	gen, na
Evelyn	57	W	div.	Jew.	college	secretary	15–30,000/1	often	gen

continued

TABLE 1. *Continued*

Name	Age	Race	Mar.	Rel.	Ed.	Emp.	Inc/# Supt'd.	Freq.	Types read
Lauren	23	W	sin.	Jew.	ma +	grad student	under15,000/1	mod.	gen, rel
Rena	59	W	mar.	Jew.	ma +	ret'd teacher	60–75,000/2	mod.	gen
Anna	31	B	l.w.l.	none	mfa, msw	social worker	15–30,000/2	mod.	gen, ast
Celia	36	W/AmIn	mar.	Cath.	some coll.	p.prof. (teacher)	30–45,000/3	often	gen, na
Hillary	30	W	sin.	Jew.	msw	social worker	15–30,000/1	rare	gen, work, fem
Janet	24	B	sin.	Cath.	college	manager	—	rare	work
Pat	47	W	mar.	Jew.	ms	teacher	over 75,000/5	often	health
Lucy	47	W	div.	Cath.	some coll.	admin. asst.	—	often	gen
Cindy	34	W	mar.	Jew.	mfa	artist-sales	over 75,000/2	often	bio, fem
Melissa	30	W	sin.	Cath.	m	arch. cons.	15–30,000/1	mod.	gen, na
Bonnie	40	W	div.	Jew.	m	teacher	45–60,000/1	often	gen
Molly	28	W	div.	none	some coll.	arch. cons.	15–30,000/1	often	gen
Diane	47	W	div.	Jew.	college	manager	30–45,000/2	often	rel
Shelley	41	W	mar.	Jew.	phd	professor	over 75,000/6	mod.	gen, rel
Gloria	48	H	div.	Cath.	some coll.	p.prof. (nursing)	under 15,000/2	mod.	gen

TABLE 1. Totals

Age		*Employment*	
Mean:	37	Teaching:	6
Median:	36	Counseling:	5
		Secretarial:	5
Race		Sales:	3
Black:	5	Managerial:	3
White:	22	Administrative:	3
Hispanic:	2	Paraprofessional:	2
Mixed:	1	Architectural conservationist:	2
		Graduate student:	1
Marital Status			
Married:	11		
Single:	8	*Types Read**	
Divorced:	11	General:	25
		Religious:	5
Religion		New Age (inc. astrology)	5
Protestant:	6	Health:	1
Catholic:	11	Work-related:	2
Jewish:	11	Biography:	1
None:	2	Feminist:	4
Education		*Frequency of Reading*	
High school:	1	Often:	12
Some college:	8	Medium:	13
College graduate:	6	Rare:	5
postgraduate (any):	15		
Household Income (in *$1,000s*)		*Number of People Supported by Household Income:*	
Under 15:	3	One:	12
15–30:	10	Two:	11
30–45:	5	Three:	2
45–60:	4	Four:	1
60–75:	2	Five:	1
75 and up:	4	Six:	1
No info. given:	2	No info. given:	2

continued

Total does not add to 30, because many participants read more than one type.

Key:

Race: W = White; B = Black; H = Hispanic; AmIn = American Indian

Mar. (Marital Status): l.w.l. = living with lover

Ed. (Education): + = more than, but no advanced degree; m = master's

Emp. (Employment): arch. cons. = architectural conservationist; admin. asst. = administrative assistant; p.prof. = paraprofessional; tel. int'er = telephone interviewer

Inc./# supt'd. (Household income and number supported)

Types read: gen = general; na = New Age; rel = religious; bio = biography; fem = feminist; ast = astrology

TABLE 2. Bestselling Self-Help Books by Years on Bestseller Lists

1963	Friedan, *The Feminine Mystique*
1965–1968	Berne, *Games People Play*
1966	Masters & Johnson, *Human Sexual Response*
1966–1968	Maltz, *Psycho-Cybernetics*
1969	Goodman, *Linda Goodman's Sun Signs*
1969	Schutz, *Joy*
1970	Masters & Johnson, *Human Sexual Inadequacy*
1970–1971	Fast, *Body Language*
1970–1971	"J," *The Sensuous Woman*
1970–1971	Reuben, *Everything You Always Wanted To Know About Sex** but Were Afraid to Ask*
1971–1972	Greer, *The Female Eunuch*
1971–1972	"M," *The Sensuous Man*
1971–1972	Reuben, *Any Woman Can!*
1972–1973	O'Neill & O'Neill, *Open Marriage*
1972–1974	Harris, *I'm OK, You're OK*
1973	Berne, *What Do You Say after You Say Hello?*
1973–1975	Newman & Berkowitz, *How to Be Your Own Best Friend*
1973–1982	Comfort, *The Joy of Sex*
1974, 1977–1978	James and Jongewood, *Born To Win*
1974	Krantzler, *Creative Divorce*
1974	Lair, *I Ain't Much, Baby—but I'm All I've Got*
1974–1976	Comfort, *More Joy of Sex*
1974, 1976–1978	Boston Women's Health Collective, *Our Bodies, Ourselves*
1975	Denniston and McWilliams, *The Transcendental Meditation TM Book*
1975	Masters & Johnson, *The Pleasure Bond*
1975–1976	Benson, *The Relaxation Response*
1975–1976	Bloomfield, Cain, and Jaffe *TM*
1975–1976	Korda, *Power*
1975–1976	Morgan, *The Total Woman*
1975–1976	Ringer, *Winning through Intimidation*

continued

TABLE 2. *Continued*

1976–1977	Hite, *The Hite Report: A Nationwide Study of Female Sexuality*
1976–1978	Sheehy, *Passages*
1976–1979	Dyer, *Your Erroneous Zones*
1977	Newman and Berkowitz, *How to Take Charge of Your Life*
1977–1978	Ringer, *Looking Out for #1*
1978–1979	Dyer, *Pulling Your Own Strings*
1978–1979	Friday, *My Mother/ My Self*
1979	Brothers, *How to Get Whatever You Want Out of Life*
1979	Goodman, *Linda Goodman's Love Signs*
1979–1980	Landers, *The Ann Landers Encyclopedia, A to Z*
1979–1980	Winston, *Getting Organized*
1980	Scarf, *Unfinished Business*
1980	Shain, *When Lovers Are Friends*
1980–1981	Dyer, *The Sky's the Limit*
1981	Hite, *The Hite Report on Male Sexuality*
1981	Shahan, *Living Alone and Liking It*
1981–1982	Cohen, *You Can Negotiate Anything*
1981–1982	Dowling, *The Cinderella Complex*
1981–1982	Kassorla, *Nice Girls Do—*
1981–1982	Penney, *How to Make Love to a Man*
1981–1982	Sheehy, *Pathfinders*
1982	Brothers, *What Every Woman Should Know about Men*
1982	Morganstern, *How to Make Love to a Woman*
1982–1983	Brown, *Having It All*
1982–83, 1985–86	Buscaglia, *Love*
1982–1983	Buscaglia, *Personhood*
1982–1983	Kushner, *When Bad Things Happen to Good People*
1982–1985	Buscaglia, *Living, Learning, and Loving*
1983	Fisher and Ury, *Getting to Yes*
1983	Hayden, *How to Satisfy a Woman Every Time*
1983	Rubin, *One to One*
1983–1984	Kiley, *The Peter Pan Syndrome*
1983–1984	Schuller, *Tough Times Never Last, but Tough People Do*

continued

TABLE 2. *Continued*

1983–1991	Peck, *The Road Less Traveled*
1984	Kiley, *The Wendy Dilemma*
1984	Peck, *People of the Lie*
1984	Schuller, *Tough-Minded Faith for Tender-Hearted People*
1984–1985	Kassorla, *Go for It!*
1985	Friedman, *Smart Cookies Don't Crumble*
1985	Schuller, *The Be (Happy) Attitudes*
1985–1987	Cowan and Kinder, *Smart Women, Foolish Choices*
1985–1988	Norwood, *Women Who Love Too Much*
1986	Johnson, *One Minute for Myself*
1986	Robbins, *Unlimited Power*
1986	Schuller, *Be Happy You Are Loved*
1986	Wholey, *The Courage to Change*
1986–1987	Buscaglia, *Bus 9 to Paradise*
1986–1987	Forward, *Men Who Hate Women and the Women Who Love Them*
1986–1987	Woititz, *Adult Children of Alcoholics*
1986–1988	Hubbard, *Dianetics*
1986–1988	Kushner, *When All You've Ever Wanted Isn't Enough*
1986–1988	Viorst, *Necessary Losses*
1987	Carter & Sokol, *Men Who Can't Love*
1987	Kent, *How to Marry the Man of Your Choice*
1987	Pearsall, *Superimmunity*
1987	Peck, *The Different Drum*
1987–1988	Cowan & Kinder, *Women Men Love, Women Men Leave*
1987–1988	Scarf, *Intimate Partners*
1987–1991	Siegel, *Love, Medicine, and Miracles*
1988	Burns, *Feeling Good*
1988	Hay, *You Can Heal Your Life*
1988	Pearsall, *Super Marital Sex*
1988–1991	Beattie, *Codependent No More*
1989	Beattie, *Beyond Codependency*
1989	Lerner, *The Dance of Anger*
1989	Siegel, *Peace, Love, and Healing*
1989–1990	Forward & Buck, *Toxic Parents*

continued

TABLE 2. *Continued*

1989–1990	MacLaine, *Going Within*
1989, 1991	Kriedman, *Light His Fire*
1990	Bradshaw, *Healing the Shame that Binds You*
1990	Cousins, *Head First*
1990	De Angelis, *Secrets about Men Every Woman Should Know*
1990	Hendrix, *Getting the Love You Want*
1990	John-Roger and McWilliams, *Life 101*
1990	Kushner, *Who Needs God*
1990	Pearsall, *The Power of the Family*
1990–1991	Bly, *Iron John*
1990–1991	Tannen, *You Just Don't Understand*
1991	Bradshaw, *Homecoming*
1991	Covey, *The Seven Habits of Highly Effective People*
1991	John-Roger and McWilliams, *Do It: Let's Get Off Our Buts*
1991	Kriedman, *Light His Fire*

Notes

Introduction

1. Provocatively, Mannheim includes within his disparaging reading of then present-day sociology the statement: "There can no longer be any doubt that no real penetration into social reality is possible through this approach" (1936: 44).

Chapter 1

1. Several nearly synonymous areas were included: "love and relationships," "intimacy and sex," and "marriage and divorce." It seems likely that a respondent would choose the category "marriage and divorce" only if s/he were reading a book on *divorce,* or "intimacy and sex" if s/he were specifically reading a book about *sex;* but very few self-help books that *discuss* divorce are primarily about divorce, and very few that discuss intimacy are primarily about sex.

2. Belenky et al. have been criticized for replicating a hierarchical system of thinking, although, ironically, they claim it is this they are challenging in the first place, and for repeatedly comparing their work with other studies on men thinkers only, when they claim their aim is to focus on, and value, women's experience and ways of constructing knowledge (Crawford 1989).

3. *Men in Love* is a compilation of men's sexual fantasies, while *My Mother/ My Self* is a psychosocial analysis of mother-daughter relationships, and much more typical to the genre of self-help.

Chapter 2

1. A more detailed discussion of problems of identity and blame as they are seen by self-help authors will be provided in Chapter 6.

2. Scogin's own work continues to show the efficacy of bibliotherapy (see Scogin et al. 1989; Scogin 1990).

3. This notion of individual recovery from illnesslike psychological afflictions has become quite popular. "There are close to 300 recovery bookstores

in the United States—up by over 100% in the past year," Jacqueline Rivkin writes (1990: 26). It has been estimated that 85 percent of the buyers of recovery self-help books are women (Kaminer 1990: 26).

Chapter 3

1. Maybe it was an excerpt from *The Feminine Mystique* that Norwood read. We can only wonder.

2. Maternal malpractice thrives in self-help books addressed to women, and will be discussed in greater detail in Chapter 6.

3. In an interesting anomalous—and rather amusing—letter, an academically oriented reader criticized Friedan for taking the name Talcott Parsons in vain: "Your quotations from Talcott Parsons . . . are accurate, but are completely out of context. . . . The way in which you refer to the structural-functionalist point of view in your discussion, betrays either a lack of sophistication, or a lack of honesty. You take the writings of distinguished people, distort them, and transmute them into popular slop."

Chapter 4

1. Forty percent of the bestselling self-help books of the past twenty-five years advertise the advanced degrees of their authors on the covers.

2. In a rare confession, Robert Ringer acknowledges that he writes self-help to make money. He prefaces *Looking Out for #1* (1977) by remarking: "Anyone who is familiar with my philosophy would be disappointed if I didn't say that my sole reason for writing this book was to make as much money as possible" (7).

Chapter 5

1. Over the course of time, the bestseller lists varied: from 1963 to May 1965, there was no weekly paperback bestseller list. For the period July 1971 to December 1974, I consulted lists from the second week of each month because paperback lists were not always included in the first Sunday's listings. Beginning in January 1984, a separate listing of "advice, how-to, and miscellaneous" was added to both hardcover and paperback lists; prior to this, the paperback category was divided into "trade" and "mass-market" books. When the advice category was added, trade and mass-market books were lumped into one category, "nonfiction," on the paperback bestsellers lists.

In 1963, the *New York Times* bestseller lists were composed of "reports from more than 125 bookstores in 64 communities throughout the United States." Now (1991), their bestsellers listings "are based on computer-processed sales figures from 3,000 bookstores and from representative wholesalers with more than 38,000 other retail outlets, including various stores and supermarkets. The figures are statistically adjusted to represent sales in all such outlets across the United States." (This note is included with each week's listings.) Clearly, compilers' methodology has become more complex and more accurate.

2. Though these books would certainly be relevant to the themes developed by the more psychologically oriented self-help books that I have examined, I am primarily interested in books that center on emotional well-being, rather than its sheer physical manifestations. I see these others as how-to—rather than self-help—books, which are less philosophical and more concerned with issues of physical self-marketing than with ideas about self. The self-help books that will be discussed here also often provide advice on physical presentation also—advice which I felt would have been duplicated by how-to books on related topics.

3. In a content analysis of 232 paperback self-help books published between 1970 and 1983, Forest found 2,200 promises made; he writes, "The most frequent promises were related to fear and anxiety, self-awareness, successful life performance, happiness, and human potential" (1988: 599).

4. I am interpreting bestseller status to imply popularity resulting from actual reading, which is admittedly a flawed assumption, but not too flawed to abandon, I feel.

5. A resurgence of bestsellers that promise victory in the financial realm has occurred quite recently, not coincidentally along with the rise of recession and Republican capitalism. Bestselling titles include Harvey Mackay's *Swim with the Sharks without Being Eaten Alive* (1988) and *Beware the Naked Man Who Offers You His Shirt* (1990), Charles Givens's *Wealth without Risk* (1988) and *Financial Self-Defense* (1990) .

6. Peck informs readers in the introduction to *People of the Lie:* "After many years of vague identification with Buddhist and Islamic mysticism, I ultimately made a firm Christian commitment—signified by my non-denominational baptism on the ninth of March 1980, at the age of forty-three" (1983: 11).

7. It occurs to me that MacLaine could *really* get into the more relativist aspects of reader-response theory!.

8. An exception to this rule was *Open Marriage* (1972), in which the Nena O'Neill and George O'Neill propose that monogamy is unnatural and recommend that love and sex be practiced in a more diffuse, less selective manner. This book, despite its racy reputation, is not really a sex manual, but a deconstruction of traditional marriage.

9. Michael Morganstern (1982) renames successful G-spot stimulation "the peritoneal orgasm" in *How to Make Love to a Woman*. He describes its elusive but exceptional qualities and advises men on how they might attempt to produce one in a woman: "Less well known, somewhat controversial, but

more and more talked about is the fourth and final kind of female orgasm: the peritoneal orgasm. This orgasm can give a woman deep, ecstatic pleasure. It involves the sensitive lining of the abdominal cavity. . . . It can only be achieved by the deepest possible penetration. . . . To give a woman this kind of orgasm, avoid elaborate foreplay (especially stimulation of the clitoris)" (114–115). In *How to Make Love to Each Other* (1982), Alexandra Penney writes: "Exact location of the spot is unknown and indeed the G-spot itself is far from being universally acknowledged" (74). And in *Super Marital Sex* (1987), Paul Pearsall writes: "Publicity for a G spot far exceeds the actal 'product' performance" (166).

10. *How to Make Love to Each Other* was not a *New York Times* bestseller, but it was a *Publishers Weekly* bestseller. These two periodicals share most of the books on their lists, but because their methods are slightly different, these lists are not identical. It is also possible that my sampling method allowed a few books—such as Penney's second—to slip by. In any case, *How to Make Love to Each Other* remains of interest because it capped off the trilogy.

Chapter 6

1. Other parodies of self-help books addressed to women include: David A. Rudnitsky's *Men Who Hate Themselves* *and the Women Who Agree With Them* (1990), and Linda Sunshine's *Women Who Date Too Much (and Those Who Should Be So Lucky)* (1988). These books have their clever points (e.g., Sunshine provides a test readers can take to determine if they are "over-self-helped" "self-help-aholics" [36–37]), but as I read them, they wear thin after a while; in the same way that self-help books often do, they play out their gimmicks early on.

2. According to the articles from which this criticism emerged, Susan Reverby was director of women's studies at Wellesley College; Hannah Lerman was "a Los Angeles psychologist specializing in women's issues"; Paula Caplan was a "professor of applied psychology at the Ontario Institute for Studies in Education and author of *The Myth of Women's Masochism*" (1985); and Gerald Rosen was "a Seattle psychologist who is the chairman of the [American Psychological Association's] Task Force on Self-Help Therapies," as well as author of his own self-help volume, *Don't Be Afraid* (1976).

3. On occasion, authors may see psychological patterns as buttressed by biological imperatives. Carter and Sokol write, for example: "The most powerful force driving a woman to commit has to be her maternal instincts—her biological need to couple and reproduce. The survival of the species depends entirely on the continuation of the species, a task that Mother Nature has relegated primarily to women (a wise choice, no doubt). With few exceptions, all other fears and desires pale in the face of this most potent biological force" (1987: 78)

4. Judith Viorst (1986) provides an exception to the rule by addressing women readers as mothers. She encourages women to loosen their maternal grip:

> We sometimes may not be aware that it is hard for us to separate from our children, and that we are holding on to them too tightly. And this absence of awareness can sometimes make our separation problem their problem. . . . For believe it or not, there is a creature called the "too-good mother," the mother who insistently gives too much, the mother who stunts development by not allowing her child to feel any frustration. Furthermore such mothers may hasten to empathize so totally and immediately that their children can't tell if their feelings are really their own. (230–231).

5. Brown scoffs at ideas of discrimination against women in the workplace. Of sexual harassment on the job, she comments: "Of the millions of naughty suggestions made by millions of male employers to their 'defenseless' female employees yearly, I'd say half cheered the girls *up*, half brought the girls *down*, but probably nothing bad has come out of *most* of them" (1982: 34).

6. In her foreword, Woititz writes: "*Adult Children of Alcoholics* was originally written only with children of alcoholics in mind. Since its publication, we have learned that the material discussed here applies to other types of dysfunctional families as well. . . . It appears that much of what is true of children of alcoholics is also true for others, and that this understanding can help reduce the isolation of countless persons who also thought they were 'different' because of their life experience" (1983: ii).

7. Norwood, however, was not the first to link love and addictions. Stanton Peele's *Love and Addiction* (1975)—which never achieved bestseller status—laid out the basic ideas that Norwood would apply to women's relationship problems a decade later. Peele describes addiction as a manner of behavior that is encouraged by our culture: "Addiction is not an abnormality in our culture. It is not an aberration from the norm; it is itself the norm" (6). He sees obsessive behavior as resulting from a lack of moral direction and stability. He bemoans the complete transience and unreliability of modern life (as Alvin Toffler did), concluding that addictive behavior arises from a deeply felt lack of control and fears of impending momentous unpredictability. While Peele's focus on institutional weakness as a precursor to anomie can be seen as a sort of speculative and sketchy update of the philosophical views Emile Durkheim presented in *Suicide* (1897), Norwood's argument is firmly embedded in psychological theories of individualistic treatment.

8. Bradshaw (1988) provides several detailed visualization or meditation exercises for readers to try; here's an excerpt from what he calls "Magical Child Meditation":

Imagine that you are looking into the abyss of outer space . . . Look straight ahead and see a stairway of light beginning to form . . . When it is completely formed, look to the top of the stairs . . . Your Magical Child will appear there . . . the child will begin walking down the stairs toward you . . . Notice everything you can about this Magical Child. What does the child have on? . . . Look at the child's face as the child comes near . . . Notice the child's eyes . . . hair. When the child steps onto the porch embrace the child . . . Feel the connection with this powerful part of yourself . . . Talk things over. (224, ellipses in original)

Conclusion

1. The public reaction against "surrogate" mothers is a good example of how Americans expect certain aspects of life to be beyond the pale of the profit motive. Women who get paid to gestate are seen as suspect, in a way that adoptive parents are not.

2. A recent ad for Sprint nicely illustrates this point: Candice Bergen talks about how for every call one makes using Sprint, Sprint will donate money to help the environment (that cause of all causes). "Are the people at Sprint doing this because they want your money?" Bergen asks, and then, answering this cynicism with a cynical rejection of cynicism: "What difference does it make?" Within the self-help genre itself, an ad in the *New York Times Book Review* (September 1, 1991) for John-Roger and Peter McWilliam's *Do It!: Let's Get Off Our Buts* (1991) and *Life 101* (1990) boasts in bold print that these are "Self-Help Books for People Who Hate Self-Help Books"— acknowledging the disdain "out there" for the genre, as if this acknowledgment will act as the impetus that brings potential readers to finally trust *these* self-help authors (who are unlike all the others).

Bibliography

Adorno, T. W.; Else Frenkel-Brunswik; Daniel J. Levinson; and R. Nevitt Sanford. 1950. *The Authoritarian Personality.* New York: Norton.

Allen, Robert C. 1985. *Speaking of Soap Operas.* Chapel Hill, N.C.: University of North Carolina Press.

———. 1987. "Reader-Oriented Criticism and Television." In *Channels of Discourse: Television and Contemporary Criticism,* ed. Robert C. Allen, 74–112. Chapel Hill, N.C.: University of North Carolina Press.

Altman, Meryl. 1984. "Everything They Always Wanted You to Know: The Ideology of Popular Sex Literature." In *Pleasure and Danger: Exploring Female Sexuality,* ed. Carole S. Vance, 115–130. Boston: Routledge and Kegan Paul.

Ang, Ien. 1990. "Melodramatic Identifications: Television, Fiction, and Women's Fantasy." In *Television and Women's Culture: The Politics of the Popular,* ed. Mary Ellen Brown, 75–88. London: Sage.

Armstrong, Paul B. 1990. *Conflicting Readings: Variety and Validity in Interpretation.* Chapel Hill, N.C.: University of North Carolina Press.

Atwood, Margaret. 1985. *The Handmaid's Tale.* New York: Fawcett Crest.

Barthes, Roland. 1980. "Theory of the Text." In *Untying the Text: A Post-Structuralist Reader,* ed. Robert Young, 31–47. Boston: Routledge and Kegan Paul.

Baym, Nina. 1978. *Woman's Fiction: A Guide to Novels by and about Women in America, 1820–1870.* Ithaca, N.Y.: Cornell University Press.

Beattie, Melody. 1987. *Codependent No More: How to Stop Controlling Others and Start Caring for Yourself.* New York: Harper/Hazeldon.

———. 1989. *Beyond Codependency: And Getting Better All the Time.* San Francisco: Harper/Hazeldon.

Becker, Howard S. 1982. *Art Worlds.* Berkeley, Calif.: University of California Press.

Belenky, Mary Field; Blythe McVicker Clinchy; Nancy Rule Goldberger; and Jill Mattuck Tarule. 1986. *Women's Ways of Knowing: The Development of Self, Voice, and Mind.* New York: Basic Books.

Bellah, Robert N. 1976. "New Religious Consciousness and the Crisis in Modernity." In *The New Religious Consciousness,* ed. Charles Y. Glock and Robert N. Bellah, 333–352. Berkeley, Calif.: University of California Press.

Bellah, Robert N.; Richard Madsen; William M. Sullivan; Ann Swidler; and

Steven M. Tipton. 1985. *Habits of the Heart: Individualism and Commitment in American Life.* New York: Harper and Row.

Benson, Herbert. 1975. *The Relaxation Response.* New York: Avon.

Berelson, Bernard. 1949. *The Library's Public: A Report of the Public Library Inquiry.* New York: Columbia University Press.

Berger, Peter L., and Thomas Luckmann. 1966. *The Social Construction of Reality: A Treatise in the Sociology of Knowledge.* Garden City, N.Y.: Doubleday.

Bernard, Jessie. 1972. *The Future of Marriage.* New Haven: Yale University Press.

Berne, Eric. 1964. *Games People Play.* New York: Ballantine.

———. 1972. *What Do You Say after You Say Hello?: The Psychology of Human Destiny.* New York: Bantam.

Biggart, Nicole Woolsey. 1989. *Charismatic Capitalism: Direct Selling Organizations in America.* Chicago: University of Chicago Press.

Bloomfield, Harold H.; Michael Peter Cain; and Dennis T. Jaffe. 1975. *TM: Discovering Inner Energy and Overcoming Stress.* New York: Delacorte Press.

Bly, Robert. 1990. *Iron John: A Book about Men.* Reading, Mass.: Addison-Wesley.

Bolotin, Susan. 1987. "Women Who Read Too Much: Current Self-Help Books Trap Women in a Vicious Cycle of Man-Hating and Self-Hating." *Vogue* (February): 246, 254.

Bordewich, Fergus M. 1988. "Colorado's Thriving Cults." *New York Times Magazine* (May 1): 36–44.

Boston Women's Health Collective. 1971. *Our Bodies, Ourselves: A Book by and for Women.* 2nd ed. New York: Simon and Schuster.

Bourdieu, Pierre. 1984. *Distinction: A Social Critique of the Judgment of Taste.* Trans. R. Nice. Cambridge, Mass.: Harvard University Press.

Bradshaw, John. 1988. *Healing the Shame That Binds You.* Deerfield Beach, Fla.: Health Communications.

———. 1990. *Homecoming: Reclaiming and Championing Your Inner Child.* New York: Bantam.

Breathed, Berke. 1988. "Bloom County" (syndicated comic strip). February 26.

Brothers, Joyce. 1978. *How to Get Whatever You Want Out of Life.* New York: Ballantine.

———. 1981. *What Every Woman Should Know about Men.* New York: Ballantine.

Brown, Helen Gurley. 1982. *Having It All.* New York: Pocket Books.

Brown, Mary Ellen. 1990. "Motley Moments: Soap Opera, Carnival, Gossip, and the Power of the Utterance." In *Television and Women's Culture: The Politics of the Popular,* ed. Mary Ellen Brown, 183–198. London: Sage.

Burns, David D. 1980. *Feeling Good: The New Mood Therapy.* New York: Signet.

Buscaglia, Leo F. *Love.* 1972. New York: Fawcett Crest.

————. 1978. *Personhood: The Art of Being Fully Human.* New York: Fawcett Columbine.

————. 1982. *Living, Loving, and Learning.* Thorofare, N.J.: Slack.

————. 1984. *Loving Each Other: The Challenge of Human Relationships.* Thorofare, N.J.: Slack.

————. 1986. *Bus 9 to Paradise: A Loving Voyage.* Thorofare, N.J.: Slack.

Cancian, Francesca. 1987. *Love in America: Gender and Self-Development.* Cambridge, Mass.: Cambridge University Press.

Caplan, Paula. 1985. *The Myth of Women's Masochism.* New York: Dutton.

Carnegie, Dale. 1936. *How to Win Friends and Influence People.* New York: Pocket.

Carter, Steven, and Julia Sokol. 1987. *Men Who Can't Love: When a Man's Fear Makes Him Run from Commitment (and What a Smart Woman Can Do about It).* New York: Berkley.

Cohen, Herb. 1980. *You Can Negotiate Anything.* New York: Bantam.

Collins, Patricia Hill. 1990. *Black Feminist Thought: Knowledge, Consciousness, and the Politics of Empowerment.* Boston, Mass.: Unwin Hyman.

Comfort, Alex. 1972. *The Joy of Sex: A Gourmet Guide to Love Making.* New York: Simon and Schuster.

————. 1973. *More Joy of Sex: A Lovemaking Companion to The Joy of Sex.* New York: Pocket.

Conner, Steven. 1989. *Postmodernist Culture: An Introduction to Theories of the Contemporary.* London: Basil Blackwell.

Conway, Flo, and Jim Siegelman. 1978. *Snapping: America's Epidemic of Sudden Personality Change.* New York: Delta.

Coser, Lewis A.; Charles Kadushin; and Walter W. Powell. 1982. *Books: The Culture and Commerce of Publishing.* New York: Basic Books.

Cott, Nancy F. 1977. *The Bonds of Womanhood: "Woman's Sphere" in New England, 1780–1835.* New Haven, Conn.: Yale University Press.

Cousins, Norman. 1989. *Head First: The Biology of Hope.* New York: Dutton.

Covey, Stephen R. 1989. *The Seven Habits of Highly Effective People.* New York: Simon and Schuster.

Cowan, Connell, and Melvyn Kinder. 1985. *Smart Women, Foolish Choices: Finding the Right Men, Avoiding the Wrong Ones.* New York: Signet.

————. 1987. *Women Men Love, Women Men Leave.* New York: Signet.

Crawford, Mary. 1989. "Agreeing to Differ: Feminist Epistemologies and Women's Ways of Knowing." In *Gender and Thought: Psychological Perspectives,* ed. Mary Crawford and Margaret Gentry, 128–145.

Crichton, Jean. 1989. "On the Road to Recovery With Prentice Hall, Ballantine, et al." *Publishers Weekly,* 236 (November 3): 52–53.

Crosman, Robert. 1980. "Do Readers Make Meaning?" In *The Reader in the Text: Essays on Audience and Interpretation,* ed. Susan R. Suleiman and Inge Crosman, 149–164. Princeton, N.J.: Princeton University Press.

Davis, Kenneth C. 1984. *Two-Bit Culture: The Paperbacking of America.* Boston: Houghton Mifflin.

De Angelis, Barbara. 1990. *Secrets about Men Every Woman Should Know*. New York: Delacorte.

Denniston, Denise, and Peter McWilliams. 1975. *The Transcendental Meditation TM Book: How to Enjoy the Rest of Your Life*. New York: Warner.

Dessauer, John P. 1981. *Book Publishing: What It Is, What It Does*. 2nd ed. New York: Bowker.

Douglas, Ann. 1977. *The Feminization of American Culture*. New York: Avon.

Douglas, Mary. 1982. "The Effects of Modernization on Religious Change." In *Religion and America: Spirituality in a Secular Age*, ed. Mary Douglas and Steven M. Tipton, 25–43. Boston: Beacon.

Dowling, Colette. 1981. *The Cinderella Complex*. New York: Pocket Books.

Durkheim, Émile. 1893 (1933 rpt.). *The Division of Labor in Society*. Trans. George Simpson. New York: Free Press.

———. 1897 (1951 rpt.). *Suicide: A Study in Sociology*. Trans. John A. Spaulding and George Simpson. New York: Free Press.

Dyer, Wayne. 1976. *Your Erroneous Zones*. New York: Funk and Wagnalls.

———. 1978. *Pulling Your Own Strings*. New York: Avon.

———. 1980. *The Sky's the Limit*. New York: Pocket Books.

Eagleton, Terry. 1983. *Literary Theory: An Introduction*. Minneapolis, Minn.: University of Minnesota Press.

Echols, Alice. 1989. *Daring to Be Bad: Radical Feminism in America, 1967–1975*. Minneapolis, Minn.: University of Minnesota Press.

Ehrenreich, Barbara. 1983. *The Hearts of Men: American Dreams and the Flight from Commitment*. Garden City, N.Y.: Anchor Press/Doubleday.

———. 1987. "The New Right Attack on Social Welfare. In *The Mean Season*, ed. Fred Block, 161–195. New York: Pantheon.

Ehrenreich, Barbara, and Deirdre English. 1978. *For Her Own Good: 150 Years of the Experts' Advice to Women*. Garden City, N.Y.: Anchor Press/Doubleday.

Ehrenreich, Barbara; Elizabeth Hess; and Gloria Jacobs. 1986. *Re-Making Love: The Feminization of Sex*. Garden City, N.Y.: Anchor Press/Doubleday.

Faludi, Susan. 1991. "Blame It on Feminism." *Mother Jones* (September/October): 24–29.

Fast, Julius. 1970. *Body Language*. New York: Pocket Books.

Ferguson, Moira. 1985. *First Feminists: British Women Writers, 1578–1799*. Bloomington, Ind.: Indiana University Press.

Fetterley, Judith. 1978. *The Resisting Reader: A Feminist Approach to American Fiction*. Bloomington, Ind.: Indiana University Press.

Fish, Stanley. 1980. *Is There a Text in This Class?: The Authority of Interpretive Communities*. Cambridge, Mass.: Harvard University Press.

Fisher, Roger, and William Ury. 1981. *Getting to Yes: Negotiating Agreement without Giving In*. New York: Houghton Mifflin.

Fiske, John. 1989. *Understanding Popular Culture*. Boston: Unwin Hyman.

———. 1990. "Women and Quiz Shows: Consumerism, Patriarchy, and

Resisting Pleasures." In *Television and Women's Culture: The Politics of the Popular,* ed. Mary Ellen Brown, 134–43. London: Sage.

Forest, James J. 1988. "Self-Help Books." *American Psychologist* (July): 599.

Forster, E. M. 1921. *Howards End.* New York: Vintage.

Forward, Susan, with Craig Buck. 1989. *Toxic Parents: Overcoming Their Hurtful Legacy and Reclaiming Your Life.* New York: Bantam.

Forward, Susan, and Joan Torres. 1986. *Men Who Hate Women and the Women Who Love Them: When Loving Hurts and You Don't Know Why.* New York: Bantam.

Friday, Nancy. 1977. *My Mother/ My Self: The Daughter's Search for Identity.* New York: Dell.

Friedan, Betty. 1963. *The Feminine Mystique.* New York: Norton.

Friedman, Sonya. 1985. *Smart Cookies Don't Crumble: A Modern Woman's Guide to Living and Loving Her Own Life.* New York: Pocket Books.

Gilbert, Sandra M., and Susan Gubar. 1979. *The Madwoman in the Attic: The Woman Writer and the Nineteenth-Century Literary Imagination.* New Haven, Conn.: Yale University Press.

Gilligan, Carol. 1982. *In a Different Voice: Psychological Theory and Women's Development.* Cambridge, Mass.: Harvard University Press.

Gitlin, Todd. 1983. *Inside Prime Time.* New York: Pantheon.

———, ed. 1986. *Watching Television: A Pantheon Guide to Popular Culture.* New York: Pantheon.

———. 1987. *The Sixties: Years of Hope, Days of Rage.* New York: Bantam.

Givens, Charles J. 1988. *Wealth without Risk: How to Develop a Personal Fortune without Going Out on a Limb.* New York: Simon and Schuster.

———. 1990. *Financial Self-Defense: How to Win the Fight for Financial Freedom.* New York: Simon and Schuster.

Glock, Charles Y. 1976. "Consciousness among Contemporary Youth: An Interpretation." In *The New Religious Consciousness,* ed. Charles Y. Glock and Robert N. Bellah, 353–366. Berkeley, Calif.: University of California Press.

Goleman, Daniel. 1989. "Feeling Gloomy? A Good Self-Help Book May Actually Help." *New York Times* (July 6): B6.

Goodman, Linda. 1968. *Linda Goodman's Sun Signs.* New York: Avon.

———. 1978. *Linda Goodman's Love Signs: A New Approach to the Human Heart.* New York: Harper and Row.

Graubard, Stephen, ed. 1983. *Reading in the 1980s.* New York: Bowker.

Greer, Germaine. 1970. *The Female Eunuch.* New York: Bantam.

Griffin, Susan. 1981. *Pornography and Silence: Culture's Revenge against Nature.* New York: Harper and Row.

Griswold, Wendy. 1986. *Renaissance Revivals: City Comedy and Revenge Tragedy in the London Theatre, 1576–1980.* Chicago, Ill.: University of Chicago Press.

———. 1987. "A Methodological Framework for the Sociology of Culture." In *Sociological Methodology,* vol. 17, 1–35.

Guisewite, Cathy. 1987. "Cathy" (syndicated comic strip). June 28.

Harding, Sandra, and Merrill B. Hintikka, eds. 1983. *Dis-covering Reality: Feminist Perspectives on Epistempology, Methodology, and Philosophy of Science.* Boston: Reidel.

Harris, Thomas A. 1969. *I'm OK, You're OK.* New York: Avon.

Hay, Louise L. 1987. Rev. ed. *You Can Heal Your Life.* Santa Monica, Calif.: Hay House.

Hayden, Naura. 1983. *How to Satisfy a Woman Every Time and Have Her Beg for More.* New York: Dutton.

Hendrix, Harville. 1988. *Getting the Love You Want: A Guide for Couples.* New York: Henry Holt.

Henkin, Josh. 1989. "Individualism Unbound: Reconsidering Modern-Day Romance." *Utne Reader* (March/April): 64–66, 68–69.

Hinds, Michael deCourcy. 1988. "Coping with Self-Help Books." *New York Times* (January 16): 33.

Hite, Shere. 1976. *The Hite Report: A Nationwide Study of Female Sexuality.* New York: Dell.

———. 1981. *The Hite Report on Male Sexuality.* New York: Knopf.

Hobson, Dorothy. 1990. "Women Audiences and the Workplace." In *Television and Women's Culture: The Politics of the Popular,* ed. Mary Ellen Brown, 61–74. London: Sage.

Hochschild, Arlie Russell. 1983. *The Managed Heart: Commercialization of Human Feeling.* Berkeley, Calif.: University of California Press.

Holland, Norman N. 1975. *5 Readers Reading.* New Haven, Conn.: Yale University Press.

Hubbard, L. Ron. 1985. *Dianetics: The Modern Science of Mental Health.* Los Angeles, Calif.: Bridge Publications.

Iser, Wolfgang. 1978. *The Act of Reading.* Baltimore, Md.: Johns Hopkins University Press.

"J." 1969. *The Sensuous Woman.* New York: Dell.

James, Muriel, and Dorothy Jongewood. 1971. *Born to Win: Transactional Analysis with Gestalt Experiments.* Reading, Mass.: Addison-Wesley.

Jauss, Hans Robert. 1982. *Toward an Aesthetic of Reception.* Vol. 2 of *Theory and History of Literature.* Trans. Timothy Bahti. Minneapolis, Minn.: University of Minnesota Press.

John-Roger, and Peter McWilliams. 1990. *Life 101: Everything We Wish We Had Learned about Life in School—but Didn't.* Los Angeles, Calif.: Prelude.

———. 1991. *Do It! Let's Get Off Our Buts.* Los Angeles, Calif.: Prelude.

Johnson, Benton. 1981. "A Sociological Perspective on the New Religions." In *In Gods We Trust: New Patterns of Religious Pluralism in America,* ed. Thomas Robbins and Dick Anthony, 51–66. New Brunswick, N.J.: Transaction.

Johnson, Spencer. 1985. *One Minute for Myself: A Small Investment, a Big Reward.* New York: William Morrow.

Jones, Jacqueline. 1985. *Labor of Love, Labor of Sorrow: Black Women, Work, and the Family, From Slavery to the Present.* New York: Vintage.

Jones, Margaret. 1989a. "Convergence at the Bookstore." *Publishers Weekly,* 236 (November 3): 32–34.

———. 1989b. "New Age on the Brink." *Publishers Weekly,* 236 (November 3):14–16, 18.

———. 1989c. "Sorting Out the Strata." *Publishers Weekly,* 236 (November 3): 20, 22, 28, 30–31.

———. 1990. "The Rage for Recovery." *Publishers Weekly,* 237 (November 23): 16–18, 20, 22, 24.

Kaminer, Wendy. 1990. "Chances Are You're Codependent Too." *New York Times Book Review* (February 11): 1, 26–27.

Kassorla, Irene. 1980. *Nice Girls Do—.* Los Angeles, Calif.: Stratford.

———. 1984. *Go for It!: How to Win at Love, Work, and Play.* New York: Delacorte.

Kent, Margaret. 1984. *How to Marry the Man of Your Choice.* New York: Warner.

Kiley, Dan. 1983. *The Peter Pan Syndrome: Men Who Have Never Grown Up.* New York: Dodd, Mead.

———. 1984. *The Wendy Dilemma: When Women Stop Mothering Their Men.* New York: Avon.

Kimmel, Michael S., ed. 1990. *Men Confront Pornography.* New York: Crown.

Kinsey, A. C., et al. 1948. *Sexual Behavior in the Human Male.* Philadelphia, Pa.: Saunders.

———. 1953. *Sexual Behavior in the Human Female.* Philadelphia, Pa.: Saunders.

Korda, Michael. 1975. *Power!: How to Get It, How to Use It.* New York: Ballantine.

Kowinski, William Severini. 1985. *The Malling of America: An Inside Look at the Great Consumer Paradise.* New York: William Morrow.

Krantzler, Mel. 1973. *Creative Divorce.* New York: Signet.

Kriedman, Ellen. 1989. *Light His Fire: How to Keep Your Man Passionately and Hopelesssly in Love With You.* New York: Dell.

———. 1991. *Light Her Fire: How to Ignite Passion and Excitement in the Woman You Love.* New York: Villard.

Kushner, Harold. 1981. *When Bad Things Happen to Good People.* New York: Avon.

———. 1986. *When All You've Ever Wanted Isn't Enough.* New York: Pocket.

———. 1989. *Who Needs God.* New York: Summit.

Lacy, Dan. 1983. "Reading in an Audiovisual and Electronic Era." in *Reading in the 1980s,* ed. Stephen Granbard, 117–127. New York: Bowker.

Ladas, Alice Kahn; Beverly Whipple; and John D. Perry. 1982. *The G Spot and Other Recent Discoveries about Human Sexuality.* New York: Dell.

Lair, Jess. 1969. *I Ain't Much, Baby—But I'm All I've Got.* New York: Fawcett Crest.

Landers, Ann. 1978. *The Ann Landers Encyclopedia, A to Z.* Garden City, N.Y.: Doubleday.

Landi, Ann. 1987. "Smart Women, Foolish Books." *Mademoiselle,* 93 (October):180–181, 245–247.

Lasch, Christopher. 1979. *The Culture of Narcissism: American Life in an Age of Diminishing Expectations*. New York: Warner.

————. 1984. *The Minimal Self: Psychic Survival in Troubled Times*. New York: Norton.

Lawson, Carol. 1986. "Women, Success, and Romantic Advice." *New York Times* (August 25).

Lerner, Harriet Goldhor. 1985. *The Dance of Anger*. New York: Harper and Row.

Lewis, Lisa A. "Consumer Girl Culture: How Music Video Appeals to Girls." In *Television and Women's Culture: The Politics of the Popular*, ed. Mary Ellen Brown, 89–101. London: Sage.

Long, Elizabeth. 1985. *The American Dream and the Popular Novel*. Boston: Routledge and Kegan Paul.

————. 1986. "Women, Reading, and Cultural Authority: Some Implications of the Audience Perspective in Cultural Studies." *American Quarterly* (Fall): 591–611.

"M." 1971. *The Sensuous Man*. New York: Dell.

Mackay, Harvey. 1988. *Swim with the Sharks without Being Eaten Alive*. New York: Ivy.

————. 1990. *Beware the Naked Man Who Offers You His Shirt: Do What You Love, Love What You Do, and Deliver More Than You Promise*. New York: Ivy.

MacLaine, Shirley. 1989. *Going Within: A Guide for Inner Transformation*. New York: Bantam.

Mahoney, Michael J. 1988. "Beyond the Self-Help Polemics." *American Psychologist* (July): 598–599.

Maltz, Maxwell. 1960. *Psycho-Cybernetics*. New York: Simon and Schuster.

Mannheim, Karl. 1936. *Ideology and Utopia: An Introduction to the Sociology of Knowledge*. Trans. Louis Wirth and Edward Shils. New York: Harcourt, Brace and World.

————. 1956. *Essays on the Sociology of Culture*. Ed. Ernest Mannheim. New York: Oxford University Press.

Marsoli, Lisa Ann, and Mel Green. 1987. *Smart Women, Stupid Books: Stop Reading and Learn to Love Losers*. Los Angeles, Calif.: Price Stern Sloan.

Marx, Karl. 1844 (1963 rpt.). "Contribution to the Critique of Hegel's Philosophy of Right: Introduction." In *Early Writings*. ed. and trans. T. B. Bottomore, 41–59. New York: McGraw-Hill.

Masters, William H., and Virginia E. Johnson. 1966. *Human Sexual Response*. New York: Bantam.

————. 1970. *Human Sexual Inadequacy*. New York: Bantam.

————. 1975. *The Pleasure Bond: A New Look at Sexuality and Commitment*. New York: Bantam.

Maynard, Joyce. 1987. "Addicted to Love." *Mademoiselle*, 93 (August): 91–92, 98, 276.

Miller, Mark Crispin. 1986. "Prime Time: Deride and Conquer." In *Watching*

Television: A Pantheon Guide to Popular Culture, ed. Todd Gitlin, 183–228. New York: Pantheon.

Miller, Nancy K. 1986. "Changing the Subject: Authorship, Writing, and the Reader." In *Feminist Studies: Critical Studies*, ed. Teresa de Lauretis, 102–120. Bloomington, Ind.: Indiana University Press.

Miller, Patricia Y., and Martha R. Fowlkes. 1980. "Social and Behavioral Constructions of Female Sexuality." In *Women: Sex and Sexuality*, ed. Catharine R. Stimpson and Ethel Spector Person, 256–273. Chicago, Ill.: University of Chicago Press.

Miner, Madonne M. 1984. *Insatiable Appetites: Twentieth-Century American Women's Bestsellers*. Westport, Conn.: Greenwood.

Mishler, Elliot G. 1986. *Research Interviewing: Context and Narrative*. Cambridge, Mass.: Harvard University Press.

Modleski, Tania. 1982. *Loving with a Vengeance: Mass-Produced Fantasies for Women*. New York: Methuen.

Morgan, Marabel. 1973. *The Total Woman*. New York: Pocket Books.

Morganstern, Michael. 1982. *How to Make Love to a Woman*. New York: Ballantine.

Newman, Mildred, and Bernard Berkowitz. 1971. *How to Be Your Own Best Friend*. New York: Ballantine.

———. 1977. *How to Take Charge of Your Life*. New York: Bantam.

Norwood, Robin. 1985. *Women Who Love Too Much: When You Keep Wishing and Hoping He'll Change*. New York: Pocket.

———. 1988. *Letters from Women Who Love Too Much*. New York: Pocket.

O'Neill, Nena, and George O'Neill. 1972. *Open Marriage: A New Life Style for Couples*. New York: Avon.

Oakley, Ann. 1981. "Interviewing Women: A Contradiction in Terms." In *Doing Feminist Research*, ed. Helen Roberts, 30–61. London: Routledge and Kegan Paul.

———. 1984. *Taking It Like a Woman: A Personal History*. New York: Random House.

Peale, Norman Vincent. 1952. *The Power of Positive Thinking*. New York: Fawcett Crest.

Pearsall, Paul. 1987. *Superimmunity: Master Your Emotions & Improve Your Health*. New York: Fawcett Crest.

———. 1987. *Super Marital Sex: Loving for Life*. New York: Doubleday.

———. 1990. *The Power of the Family: Strength, Comfort, and Healing*. New York: Doubleday.

Peck, M. Scott. 1978. *The Road Less Traveled: A New Psychology of Love, Traditional Values, and Spiritual Growth*. New York: Simon and Schuster.

———. 1983. *People of the Lie: The Hope for Healing Human Evil*. New York: Simon and Schuster.

Peele, Stanton, with Archie Brodsky. 1975. *Love and Addiction*. New York: New American Library.

Penney, Alexandra. 1981. *How to Make Love to a Man*. New York: Dell.

———. 1982. *How to Make Love to Each Other.* New York: Putnam's.

Polan, Dana. 1988. "Postmodernism and Cultural Analysis Today." In *Postmodernism and Its Discontents,* ed. E. Ann Kaplan, 45–58. London: Verso.

Powell, Walter W. 1983. "Whither the Local Bookstore?" In *Reading in the 1980s,* ed. Stephen Graubard, 51–64. New York: Bowker.

———. 1985. *Getting into Print.* Chicago, Ill.: University of Chicago Press.

Press, Andrea L. 1990. "Class, Gender, and the Female Viewer: Women's Responses to Dynasty." In *Television and Women's Culture: The Politics of the Popular,* ed. Mary Ellen Brown, 158–183. London: Sage.

———. 1991. *Women Watching Television: Gender, Class, and Generation in the American Television Experience.* Philadelphia, Pa.: University of Pennsylvania Press.

Rabinowitz, Peter J. 1987. *Before Reading: Narrative Conventions and the Politics of Interpretation.* Ithaca, N.Y.: Cornell University Press.

Radway, Janice A. 1984. *Reading the Romance: Women, Patriarchy, and Popular Literature.* Chapel Hill, N.C.: University of North Carolina Press.

Reuben, David. 1969. *Everything You Always Wanted to Know about Sex* *but Were Afraid to Ask.* New York: Bantam.

———. 1971. *Any Woman Can!* *Love and Sexual Fulfillment for the Single, Widowed, Divorced . . . and Married.* New York: Bantam.

Rieff, David. 1991. "Victims All?: Recovery, Co-dependency, and the Art of Blaming Somebody Else." *Harper's* (October): 49–56.

Rieff, Philip. 1966. *The Triumph of the Therapeutic: Uses of Faith after Freud.* New York: Harper and Row.

Riesman, David. 1950. *The Lonely Crowd: A Study of the Changing American Character.* New Haven, Conn.: Yale University Press.

Riessman, Catherine Kohler. 1990. *Divorce Talk: Women and Men Make Sense of Personal Relationships.* New Brunswick, N.J.: Rutgers University Press.

Ringer, Robert J. 1974. *Winning through Intimidation.* New York: Fawcett Crest.

———. 1977. *Looking Out for #1.* New York: Fawcett Crest.

Rivkin, Jacqueline. 1990. "Recovery Stores: A Sense of Mission." *Publishers Weekly* (November 23): 26, 28.

Robbins, Anthony. 1986. *Unlimited Power: The New Science of Personal Achievement.* New York: Simon and Schuster.

Robbins, Thomas, and Dick Anthony, eds. 1981. *In Gods We Trust: New Patterns of Religious Pluralism in America.* New Brunswick, N.J.: Transaction.

Roberts, Helen, ed. 1981. *Doing Feminist Research.* London: Routledge and Kegan Paul.

Roiphe, Anne. 1986. "Gunfight at the I'm O. K. Corral: M. Scott Peck Duels with the Devil." *New York Times Book Review* (January 19): 22.

Roof, Wade Clark. 1981. "Alienation and Apostasy." In *In Gods We Trust: New Patterns of Religious Pluralism in America,* ed. Thomas Robbins and Dick Anthony, 87–99. New Brunswick, N.J.: Transaction.

————. 1982. "America's Voluntary Establishment: Mainline Religion in Transition." In *Religions and America: Spirituality in a Secular Age,* ed. Mary Douglas and Steven M. Tipton, 130–149. Boston: Beacon.

Rosen, Gerald. 1976. *Don't Be Afraid: A Program for Overcoming Your Fears and Phobias.* New York: Prentice-Hall.

Rosen, Richard Dean. 1975. *Psychobabble: Fast Talk and Quick Cure in the Era of Feeling.* New York: Atheneum.

Rosen, Ruth. 1986. "Search for Yesterday." In *Watching Television: A Pantheom Guide to Popular Culture,* ed. Todd Gitlin, 42–67. New York: Pantheon.

Rothman, Barbara Katz. 1989. *Recreating Motherhood: Ideology and Technology in a Patriarchal Society.* New York: Norton.

Rubin, Lillian Breslow. 1976. *Worlds of Pain: Life in the Working-Class Family.* New York: Basic Books.

Rubin, Theodore Isaac. 1983. *One to One: Understanding Personal Relationships.* New York: Pinnacle.

Rudnitsky, David A. 1990. *Men Who Hate Themselves* *and the Women Who Agree with Them* New York: Plume.

Russ, Joanna. 1983. *How to Suppress Women's Writing.* Austin, Tex.: University of Texas Press.

Scarf, Maggie. 1980. *Unfinished Business: Pressure Points in the Lives of Women.* New York: Ballantine.

————. 1987. *Intimate Partners: Patterns in Love and Marriage.* New York: Ballantine.

Schuller, Robert H. 1982. *Tough Times Never Last, But Tough People Do!* Nashville, Tenn.: Thomas Nelson.

————. 1983. *Tough-Minded Faith for Tender-Hearted People.* New York: Bantam.

————. 1985. *The Be(Happy)Attitudes.* New York: Bantam.

————. 1986. *Be Happy You Are Loved.* Nashville, Tenn.: Thomas Nelson.

Schutz, William C. 1967. *Joy: Expanding Human Awareness.* New York: Grove.

Scogin, Forrest; Christine Jamison; and Kimberly Gochneaur. 1989. "Comparative Efficacy of Cognitive and Behavioral Bibliotherapy for Mildly and Moderately Depressed Older Adults." *Journal of Consulting and Clinical Psychology,* 57 (June): 403–407.

————. 1990. "Two Year Follow-Up of Bibliotherapy for Depression in Older Adults." *Journal of Consulting and Clinical Psychology,* 58 (October): 665–657.

Shahan, Lynn. 1981. *Living Alone and Liking It.* New York: Warner.

Shain, Merle. 1978. *When Lovers Are Friends.* New York: Bantam.

Shapiro, Laura. 1987. "Advice Givers Strike Gold." *Newsweek,* 109 (June 1): 64–65.

Shatzkin, Leonard. 1982. *In Cold Type: Overcoming the Book Crisis.* Boston: Houghton Mifflin.

Sheehy, Gail. 1974. *Passages: Predictable Crises of Adult Life.* New York: Dutton.

————. 1981. *Pathfinders: Overcoming the Crises of Adult Life and Finding Your Own Path to Well-Being.* New York: William Morrow.

Siegel, Bernie S. 1988. *Love, Medicine, & Miracles: Lessons Learned about*

Self-Healing from a Surgeon's Experience with Exceptional Patients. New York: Harper and Row.

——. 1989. *Peace, Love, and Healing: Bodymind Communication and the Path to Self-Healing: An Exploration.* New York: Harper and Row.

Simonds, Wendy, and Barbara Katz Rothman. 1992. *Centuries of Solace: Expressions of Maternal Grief in Popular Literature.* Philadelphia, Pa.: Temple University Press.

Smith, Barbara Herrnstein. 1983. "Contingencies of Value." *Critical Inquiry,* 10: 1–35.

Smith, Dorothy E. 1987. *The Everyday World as Problematic: A Feminist Sociology.* Boston, Mass.: Northeastern University Press.

Smith-Rosenberg, Carroll. 1985. *Disorderly Conduct: Visions of Gender in Victorian America.* New York: Oxford University Press.

Spacks, Patricia Meyer. 1972. *The Female Imagination.* New York: Avon.

Starker, Steven. 1989. *Oracle at the Supermarket: The American Preoccupation with Self-Help Books.* New Brunswick, N.J.: Transaction.

Stone, Donald. 1981. "Social Consciousness in the Human Potential Movement." In *In Gods We Trust: New Patterns of Religious Pluralism in America,* ed. Thomas Robbins and Dick Anthony, 215–227. New Brunswick, N.J.: Transaction.

Suleiman, Susan R., and Inge Crosman, eds. 1980. *The Reader in the Text: Essays on Audience and Interpretation.* Princeton, N.J.: Princeton University Press.

Sunshine, Linda. 1988. *Women Who Date Too Much (and Those Who Should Be So Lucky.)* New York: Plume.

Tannen, Deborah. 1990. *You Just Don't Understand: Women and Men in Conversation.* New York: Ballantine.

Tebbel, John. 1987. *Between Covers: The Rise and Transformation of American Book Publishing.* New York: Oxford University Press.

Thurber, James. 1931. *The Thurber Carnival.* New York: Dell.

Tipton, Steven M. 1982a. *Getting Saved from the Sixties: Moral Meaning in Conversion and Cultural Change.* Berkeley, Calif.: University of California Press.

——. 1982b. "The Moral Logic of Alternative Religions." In *Religion and America: Spirituality in a Secular Age,* ed. Mary Douglas and Steven M. Tipton, 79–107. Boston: Beacon.

Tocqueville, Alexis de. 1848 (1969 rpt.). *Democracy in America.* Trans. George Lawrence, ed. J. P. Meyer. Garden City, N.Y.: Doubleday.

Todd, Alexandra Dumas, and Sue Fisher. 1988. *Gender and Discourse: The Power of Talk.* Norwood, N.J.: Ablex.

Todorov, Tzvetan. 1980. "Reading as Construction." In *The Reader in the Text: Essays on Audience and Interpretation,* ed. Susan R. Suleiman and Inge Crosman, 67–82. Princeton, N.J.: Princeton University Press.

Toffler, Alvin. 1970. *Future Shock.* New York: Bantam.

Tompkins, Jane P., ed. 1980. *Reader-Response Criticism: From Formalism to Post Structuralism.* Baltimore: Johns Hopkins University Press.

———. 1985. *Sensational Designs: The Cultural Work of American Fiction, 1790–1860.* New York: Oxford University Press.

Vaughan, Samuel S. 1983. "The Community of the Book." In *Reading in the 1980s*, ed. Stephen Graubard, 85–115. New York: Bowker.

Viorst, Judith. 1986. *Necessary Losses: The Loves, Illusions, Dependencies, and Impossible Expectations that All of Us Have to Give Up in Order to Grow.* New York: Fawcett Gold Medal.

Warner, Susan. 1892 (1987 rpt.). *The Wide, Wide World.* New York: Feminist Press.

Weber, Max. 1905 (1958 rpt.). *The Protestant Ethic and the Spirit of Capitalism.* Trans. Talcott Parsons. New York: Charles Scribner's Sons.

———. 1915 (1946 rpt.). "Religious Rejections of the World and Their Directon." In *From Max Weber*, ed. and trans. H. H. Gerth and C. Wright Mills, 323–359. New York: Oxford University Press.

———. 1922 (1963 rpt.). *The Sociology of Religion.* Trans. Ephram Fischoff. Boston: Beacon.

West, Candace, and Don H. Zimmerman. 1987. "Doing Gender." *Gender and Society*, 1, no. 2 (June): 125–151.

Whiteside, Thomas. 1980. *The Blockbuster Complex: Conglomerates, Show Business and Book Publishing.* Middletown, Conn.: Wesleyan University Press.

Wholey, Dennis. 1984. *The Courage to Change: Hope and Help for Alcoholics and Their Families.* New York: Houghton Mifflin.

Williams, Raymond. 1958. *Culture and Society, 1780–1950.* Garden City, N.Y.: Doubleday.

Winston, Stephanie. 1978. *Getting Organized: The Easy Way to Put Your Life in Order.* New York: Norton.

Woititz, Janet Geringer. 1983. *Adult Children of Alcoholics.* Deerfield Beach, Fla.: Health Communications.

Wolff, Janet. 1981. *The Social Production of Art.* New York: St. Martin's Press.

Wood, Leonard. 1988. "The Gallup Survey: Self-Help Buying Trends." *Publishers Weekly*, 234 (October 14): 33.

Wuthnow, Robert. 1981. "Political Aspects of the Quietistic Revival." In *In Gods We Trust: New Patterns of Religious Pluralism in America*, ed. Thomas Robbins and Dick Anthony, 229–243. New Brunswick, N.J.: Transaction.

Yankelovich, Daniel. 1981. *New Rules: Searching for Self-Fulfillment in a World Turned Upside Down.* New York: Random House.

Yankelovich, Skelly, and White, Inc. 1978. *Consumer Research Study on Reading and Book Purchasing.* Book Industry Study Group, Inc. Report no. 6.

Index